D0442697

ALSO BY BARBARA W. TUCHMAN

Bible and Sword (1956)

The Zimmermann Telegram (1958)

The Guns of August (1962)

The Proud Tower (1966)

Stilwell and the American Experience in China (1971)

Notes from China (1972)

A Distant Mirror: The Calamitous 14th Century (1978)

PRACTICING HISTORY

PRACTICING HISTORY

Selected Essays by
Barbara W. Tuchman

ALFRED A. KNOPF
New York   1981

THIS IS A BORZOI BOOK
PUBLISHED BY ALFRED A. KNOPF, INC.

Copyright 1936, 1937, © 1959, 1962, 1964, 1965, 1966, 1967, 1968, 1971, 1972, 1973, 1974, 1976, 1977, 1979, 1980, 1981 by Alma Tuchman, Lucy T. Eisenberg, and Jessica Tuchman Matthews. Introduction copyright © 1981 by Barbara Tuchman.

All but two of the essays in this book have been previously published.

Library of Congress Cataloging in Publication Data
Tuchman, Barbara Wertheim.   Practicing history.
    1. Historiography—Addresses, essays,
lectures. 2. History, Modern—20th century—
Addresses, essays, lectures. I. Title.
D13.T83   1981   907'.2   81-47509
ISBN 0-394-52086-6   AACR2

Manufactured in the United States of America

Published September 1981
Second Printing Published Before Publication

Contents

PRACTICING HISTORY

Preface

It is surprising to find, on reviewing one's past work, which are the pieces that seem to stand up and which are those that have wilted. The only rule I can discover as a determinant—and it is a rule riddled with exceptions—is that, on the whole, articles or reports which have a "hard," that is to say factual, subject matter or a personally observed story to tell are more readable today than "think" pieces intended as satire or advocacy, or written from the political passions of the moment. These tend to sound embarrassing after the passage of time, and have not, with one or two exceptions been revived.

Exceptions pursued every principle of inclusion or exclusion I tried to formulate. Two eyewitness accounts of historic episodes which I would have thought would read well in this collection failed, on rereading, to have the quality worthy of revival. One was an account of President Kennedy's funeral, written for the *St. Louis Post-Dispatch*, and the other an account of the reuniting of Jerusalem in June 1967 after the Six-Day War, written for the *Washington Post*. In the first case, presumably because of the opening paragraphs on the funeral of Edward VII in *The Guns of August*, I was asked to cover the Kennedy ceremony, and accepted more out of curiosity than commitment. Equipped with press card, I observed the lying-in-state in the Capitol rotunda, circulated among the crowds in Lafayette Square next morning, watched the rather haphazard procession of the visiting heads of state, with De Gaulle towering over the rest, attended the services at Arlington, and retired afterward to a hotel room to turn out my commentary by midnight for next morning's paper. But what could one write when the entire country had been watching every moment of the proceedings on TV for the last thirty-six hours? One could not simply describe what everyone had already seen; one had to offer some extra significance. For me it was too soon: I did not share the mystique of Camelot; I had no sense at that moment of Kennedy's place or significance in history, if any, and besides I was unnerved by the midnight deadline. My piece, which took a rather cool view, was a disappointment to readers who wanted the grand tone.

On the occasion in Jerusalem, when against all advice Mayor Kollek ordered the barbed wire and no-man's-land barriers removed, I was present and accompanied an Israeli family on a visit to Arab friends whom they had not seen in nineteen years, and watched Arab street vendors with their goats warily enter the New City, gaping at the sights and already choosing street corners where they could sell soft drinks and pencils. It was a day of tension and drama and immense interest, yet the report I wrote, like the Kennedy piece, lacked punch. These two examples, though not here for the reader to judge, illustrate the difficulty of establishing a principle of selection: I shared the emotion of the moment in one case but not in the other, and both results were flat.

Oddly enough, a report on Israel written for the *Saturday Evening Post* (page 123) in the previous year, on my first visit, turned out and still reads well, I think. Perhaps it was the freshness of the experience, perhaps the fact that I was writing for readers who, as I conceived them, probably knew little or nothing about the country and had no emotional tie to it. I wanted to convey the feeling, the facts, and the historical nature and meaning of the new nation all in one article. One does not always achieve one's purpose in a given attempt, but this one, I believe, succeeded. Subsequently Fodor used it as the Introduction to their *Guide to Israel* for several years.

Some of the essays in the following pages, like the little Japanese piece at the opening of Part II, require explanation of the circumstances that gave them rise. After graduating from college in 1933—the fateful year that saw the advent both of Franklin Roosevelt as President and Adolf Hitler as Chancellor—I went to work (as a volunteer—paying jobs did not hang from the trees in 1933) for the American Council of the Institute of Pacific Relations, an international organization of member countries bordering on the Pacific—Britain, France, Holland, the U.S., Canada, as well as China and Japan. The directors felt at the time that the Japanese Council of the IPR, representing the hard-pressed liberals of the country, needed whatever encouragement and prestige the main body could give them, and to this end it was decided to make Tokyo the headquarters for the compilation of the IPR's major project of the time, *The Economic Handbook of the Pacific*. Accordingly, the international secretary of the IPR, William L. Holland, was assigned to the Japanese Council in Tokyo to supervise work on the *Handbook*, and in October 1934 I followed as his assistant. I remained in Tokyo for a year and, after a month's sojourn in Peking, returned home late in 1935 via the Trans-Siberian Railway, Moscow, and Paris.

During the year in Japan I had written a number of pieces for the IPR publications *Far Eastern Survey* and *Pacific Affairs*, generally on matters of not very avid public interest like the Russo-Japanese Fisheries controversy. However, on reviewing a book on Japan by a French historian, I was thrilled to receive from the author a letter addressed *"Chère consoeur"* (the feminine of *confrère*, or as we would say, "colleague"). I felt admitted into an international circle of professionals. This, and the $40 paid for my first piece in *Pacific Affairs*, with which I bought a gramophone and a record of *"Un bel di"* from *Madame Butterfly*, made me feel I had begun a career.

On returning to America, I tried to express something of what I had learned and thought about the Japanese in the little piece reprinted here. I do not remember when or how it was submitted to so august a journal as *Foreign Affairs*, but suddenly there I was in print, a novice of twenty-four, among the foreign ministers and opinion-makers and, more important, making the acquaintance of a wise and fine man, the editor, Hamilton Fish Armstrong.

Meantime, in 1936, I went to work for the *Nation*, which my father, Maurice Wertheim, a banker of rather eclectic interests, had bought from Oswald Garrison Villard to save it from bankruptcy. Freda Kirchwey, Villard's successor as editor and a friend of my parents, was left in control, along with a new colleague, Max Lerner. My job at first was to clip and file a far-flung variety of newspapers and periodicals, and gradually to write some of the two hundred-word paragraphs on current events which appeared each week on the *Nation's* opening pages. Writing on assigned subjects one knew nothing about—recidivism, migrant labor, the death of Georges Chicherin, TVA, AAA, the Nye Munitions Committee, the Montreux Straits Convention, the Nazi Party Congress—one had to collect the relevant facts, condense the subject in two hundred words incorporating the *Nation's* point of view, and have it ready on time. The experience was invaluable, even if the pieces were ephemeral.

Accredited by the *Nation*, I went to Valencia and Madrid during the Spanish Civil War in 1937, and afterward stayed on in Europe, caught up in the frenzy of activities against Non-Intervention and appeasement and what was called by the other side "premature anti-fascism." It was a somber, exciting, believing, betraying time, with heroes, hopes, and illusions. I have always felt that the year and decade of reaching one's majority, rather than of one's birth, is the stamp one bears. I think of myself as a child of the '30s. I was a believer then, as I suppose people in their twenties must be (or were, in my generation). I believed that the right and the rational would win in the end. In London I put together a little book entitled *The Lost British Policy*, designed to show how it had always been a cardinal principal of British foreign policy to keep Spain (and the gates to the Mediterranean) free of control by the dominant power on the continent (currently Hitler). It was a respectable piece of research but, as a reviewer said, "tendentious." I worked also for a weekly information bulletin called the *War in Spain*, subsidized by the Spanish government, but I have kept no files of my contributions.

About the time of Munich I came home and continued to engage in Spanish affairs and in compiling a chronological record of the origins of the war in collaboration with Jay Allen, the most knowledgeable of American correspondents on Spain. With the defeat of the Republic in 1939 I met the event that cracked my heart, politically speaking, and replaced my illusions with recognition of *realpolitik*; it was the beginning of adulthood. I wrote a threnody on the role of the Western nations in the Spanish outcome, called "We Saw Democracy Fail," for the *New Republic*, but as one of the pieces that embarrass me thirty-odd years later, it has not been included.

On June 18, 1940, the day Hitler entered Paris, I was married to Dr. Lester R. Tuchman, a physician of New York, who not unreasonably felt at that time that the world was too unpromising to bring children into. Sensible for once, I argued that if we waited for the outlook to improve, we might wait forever, and that if we wanted a child at all we should have it now, regardless of Hitler. The tyranny of men not being quite as total as today's feminists would have us believe, our first daughter was born nine months later. After Pearl Harbor and my husband's joining the Medical Corps, the baby and I followed him to Camp Rucker in Alabama, and when he went overseas with his hospital early in 1943, we came home and I went to work for the Office of War Information (OWI) in New York.

While the OWI in San Francisco broadcast America's news to the Far East, our operations from New York were beamed to Europe. Because of my first-hand experience of Japan, such as it was, I was assigned to the Far East desk, whose task was to explain the Pacific war and the extent of the American effort in Asia to our European listeners. In the course of this duty I covered at second hand General Stilwell's campaign in Burma, which remained in the back of my mind over the next twenty-odd years until it emerged as a book with Stilwell as the focus of the American experience in China.

Otherwise, I cannot remember writing anything of any great interest while at OWI except two "backgrounders," as they were called, in anticipation of expected events. One was on the history and geography of the China coast in preparation for an American landing, and one was on the Soviet Far East for use when and if Russia entered the war against Japan. The desk editor, a newspaperman by training, grew very impatient with my work on these pieces. "Don't look up so much material," he said. "You can turn out the job much faster if you don't know too much." While this was doubtless true for a journalist working against a deadline, it was not advice that suited my temperament. In any event, at that point the war suddenly ended, and I do not know what became of my "backgrounders." I would like to read them again, but any papers I may have retained from OWI days seem to have vanished.

Nothing appears in this collection from the 1940s nor until the last year of the '50s, for the reason that after the war, when my husband came home, we had two more children, and domesticity for a while prevailed, combined with beginning the work I had always wanted to do, which was writing a book. In 1948 I started work on my first book, *Bible and Sword*, which took six or seven years of very interrupted effort and quite a while longer to find a publisher. It was followed by *The Zimmermann Telegram* and then by "Perdicaris," which, proving too slight for a book, was reduced to the short-story length that appears here.

From the 1960s on, the selections speak more or less for themselves. "The Citizen Versus the Military" represents something of an aberration as my only commencement address (except for one in 1967 at my daughter's graduation from Radcliffe, which is not included). For general use, I have a firm rule against commencement speeches, because I have no idea what to tell the young people and no desire merely to fill a required occasion with generalities. In 1972, however, on receiving the invitation to speak at Williams, I felt I did have something specific that I wanted to say about what seemed to me the foolish and mindless squawking of the young against ROTC and military service. I believed the war in Vietnam to be unjustifiable, wicked, and unsuccessful besides, but for the civilian citizen to leave the dirty work to the military while holding himself distinct from and above them seemed to me irresponsible and not the best way for the coming generation to gain control of our military policies. If they wanted to control the officer corps, I suggested, they should join the ROTC and then strike. Distributed by a newspaper syndicate, this speech was widely reprinted, besides, as I later learned, causing an irate alumnus of Williams to file a complaint about me with the FBI.

Following the publication of *Stilwell* in 1971, I wrote a number of pieces on the American relationship to China and its echoes in Vietnam, but when the main theme has already been expressed in the book, reviving the ephemera serves no purpose. The exception is the Mao article (p. 188) which, as the first uncovering and report of this incident, is a piece of primary historical research of which I am rather proud. It was gratifyingly publicized by *Foreign Affairs* to mark their fiftieth-anniversary issue—and mark privately for me the awesome passage of thirty-six years since my first mousy penetration of their pages.

Two absences which I rather regret are "The Book," given as the Sillcox Lecture at the Library of Congress in 1979, and an essay of the same year entitled "An Inquiry into the Persistence of Unwisdom in Government." The first seemed not to qualify as history for this collection. The second, which is now serving as the nucleus of a future book, is in retirement for the time being, until it emerges from the chrysalis.

The texts that appear below are reprinted as originally published (or spoken), with one or two corrections of fact (Jacob, not, as originally appeared, Joseph, wrestled with the angel, an error no one caught until time for this publication), a few cuts and eliminations of repeated phrases, a few changes of awkward language, though none of ideas, and some changes of the published title in cases where editors had substituted their choices (invariably regrettable, of course) for mine. These have now had my original titles restored.

Whether these selections when gathered together offer any philosophy of history is a question I hesitate to answer because I am rather afraid of philosophies. They contain a risk for the historian of being tempted to manipulate his facts in the interest of his system, which results in histories stronger in ideology than in "how it really was." Yet I do not suppose one can practice the writing of history over a long period without arriving at certain principles and guidelines. From these essays emerges, I think, a sense of history as accidental and perhaps cyclical, of human conduct as a steady stream running through endless fields of changing circumstances, of good and bad always co-existing and inextricably mixed in periods as in people, of cross-currents and counter-currents usually present to contradict too-easy generalizations. As to treatment, I believe that the material must precede the thesis, that chronological narrative is the spine and the blood stream that bring history closer to "how it really was" and to a proper understanding of cause and effect; that, whatever the subject, it must be written in terms of what was known and believed at the time, not from the perspective of hindsight, for otherwise the result will be invalid. While laying no claim to originality, these are principles I discovered for myself in the course of learning the craft and following the practice of my profession.

I
THE
CRAFT

In Search of History

History began to exert its fascination upon me when I was about six, through the medium of the Twins series by Lucy Fitch Perkins. I became absorbed in the fortunes of the Dutch Twins; the Twins of the American Revolution, who daringly painted the name *Modeerf*, or "freedom" spelled backward, on their row boat; and especially the Belgian Twins, who suffered under the German occupation of Brussels in 1914.

After the Twins, I went through a G. A. Henty period and bled with Wolfe in Canada. Then came a prolonged Dumas period, during which I became so intimate with the Valois kings, queens, royal mistresses, and various Ducs de Guise that when we visited the French *châteaux* I was able to point out to my family just who had stabbed whom in which room. Conan Doyle's *The White Company* and, above all, Jane Porter's *The Scottish Chiefs* were the definitive influence. As the noble Wallace, in tartan and velvet tam, I went to my first masquerade party, stalking in silent tragedy among the twelve-year-old Florence Nightingales and Juliets. In the book the treachery of the Countess of Mar, who betrayed Wallace, carried a footnote that left its mark on me. "The crimes of this wicked woman," it said darkly, "are verified by history."

By the time I reached Radcliffe, I had no difficulty in choosing a field of concentration, although it turned out to be History and Lit rather than pure history. I experienced at college no moment of revelation that determined me to write historical narrative. When that precise moment occurred I cannot say; it just developed and there

Phi Beta Kappa Address, Radcliffe College, April 1963. *Radcliffe Quarterly*, May 1963.

was a considerable time lag. What Radcliffe *did* give me, however, was an *impetus* (not to mention an education, but I suppose that goes without saying). Part of the impetus came from great courses and great professors. Of the three to which I owe most, two, curiously enough, were in literature rather than history. They were Irving Babbitt's Comp Lit 11 and John Livingston Lowes's English 72, which included his spectacular tour de force on the origins of "The Ancient Mariner" and "Kubla Khan." He waved at Wordsworth, bowed briefly to Keats and Shelley, and really let himself go through twelve weeks of lectures, tracing the sources of Coleridge's imagery, and spending at least a week on the fatal apparition of the person from Porlock. What kept us, at least me, on the edge of my seat throughout this exploit was Lowes's enthusiasm for his subject.

This quality was the essence, too, of Professor C. H. McIlwain's Constitutional History of England, which came up as far as Magna Carta. It did not matter to McIlwain, a renowned scholar and historian, that only four of us were taking his course, or that he had already given it at Harvard and had to come over to repeat it to us (yes, that was the quaint custom of the time). It did not matter because McIlwain was conducting a passionate love affair with the laws of the Angles and the articles of the Charter, especially, as I remember, Article 39. Like any person in love, he wanted to let everyone know how beautiful was the object of his affections. He had white hair and pink cheeks and the brightest blue eyes I ever saw, and though I cannot remember a word of Article 39, I do remember how his blue eyes blazed as he discussed it and how I sat on the edge of my seat then too, and how, to show my appreciation, I would have given anything to write a brilliant exam paper, only to find that half the exam questions were in Anglo-Saxon, about which he had neglected to forewarn us. That did not matter either, because he gave all four of us A's anyway, perhaps out of gratitude for our affording him another opportunity to talk about his beloved Charter.

Professor Babbitt, on the other hand, being a classicist and antiromantic, frowned on enthusiasm. But his contempt for zeal was so zealous, so vigorous and learned, pouring out in a great organ fugue of erudition, that it amounted to enthusiasm in the end and held not only me, but all his listeners, rapt.

Although I did not know it or formulate it consciously at the time, it is this quality of being in love with your subject that is indispensable for writing good history—or good anything, for that matter. A few months ago when giving a talk at another college, I was invited to meet the faculty and other guests at dinner. One young member of the History Department who said he envied my subject in *The Guns of August* confessed to being bogged down and brought to a dead stop halfway through his doctoral thesis. It dealt, he told me, with an early missionary in the Congo who had never been "done" before. I asked what was the difficulty. With a dreary wave of his cocktail he said, "I just don't like him." I felt really distressed and depressed—both for him and for the conditions of scholarship. I do not know how many of you are going, or will go, to graduate school, but when you come to write that thesis on, let us say, "The Underwater Imagery Derived from the Battle of Lepanto in the Later Poetic Dramas of Lope de Vega," I hope it will be because you care passionately about this imagery rather than because your department has suggested it as an original subject.

In the process of doing my own thesis—not for a Ph.D., because I never took a graduate degree, but just my undergraduate honors thesis—the single most formative experience in my career took place. It was not a tutor or a teacher or a fellow student or a great book or the shining example of some famous visiting lecturer—like Sir Charles Webster, for instance, brilliant as he was. It was the stacks at Widener. They were *my* Archimedes' bathtub, my burning bush, my dish of mold where I found my personal penicillin. I was allowed to have as my own one of those little cubicles with a table under a window, queerly called, as I have since learned, carrels, a word I never knew when I sat in one. Mine was deep in among the 942s (British History, that is) and I could roam at liberty through the rich stacks, taking whatever I wanted. The experience was marvelous, a word I use in its exact sense meaning full of marvels. The happiest days of my intellectual life, until I began writing history again some fifteen years later, were spent in the stacks at Widener. My daughter Lucy, class of '61, once said to me that she could not enter the labyrinth of Widener's stacks without feeling that she ought to carry a compass, a sandwich, and a whistle. I too was never altogether sure I could find the way out, but I was blissful as a cow put to graze in a field of fresh clover and would not have cared if I had been locked in for the night.

Once I stayed so late that I came out after dark, long after the dinner hour at the dorm, and found to my horror that I had only a nickel in my purse. The weather was freezing and I was very hungry. I could not decide whether to spend the nickel on a chocolate bar and walk home in the cold or take the Mass Avenue trolley and go home hungry. This story ends like "The Lady or the Tiger," because although I remember the agony of having to choose, I cannot remember how it came out.

My thesis, the fruit of those hours in the stacks, was my first sustained attempt at writing history. It was called "The Moral Justification for the British Empire," an unattractive title and, besides, inaccurate, because what I meant was the moral *justifying* of empire by the imperialists. It was for me a wonderful and terrible experience. Wonderful because finding the material, and following where it led, was constantly exciting and because I was fascinated by the subject, which I had thought up for myself—much to the disapproval of my tutor, who was in English Lit, not History, and interested only in Walter Pater—or was it Walter Savage Landor? Anyway, it was *not* the British Empire, and since our meetings were consequently rather painfully uncommunicative, I think he was relieved when I took to skipping them.

The experience was terrible because I could not make the piece sound, or rather read, the way I wanted it to. The writing fell so far short of the ideas. The characters, who were so vivid inside my head, seemed so stilted when I got them on paper. I finished it, dissatisfied. So was the department: "Style undistinguished," it noted. A few years ago, when I unearthed the thesis to look up a reference, that impression was confirmed. It reminded me of *The Importance of Being Earnest*, when Cecily says that the letters she wrote to herself from her imaginary fiancé when she broke off their imaginary engagement were so beautiful and so badly spelled she could not reread them without crying. I felt the same way about my thesis: so beautiful—in intent—and so badly written. Enthusiasm had not been enough; one must also know how to use the language.

One learns to write, I have since discovered, in the practice thereof. After seven years' apprenticeship in journalism I discovered that an essential element for good writing is a good ear. One must *listen* to the sound of one's own prose. This, I think, is one of the failings of much American writing. Too many writers do not listen to the sound of their own words. For example, listen to this sentence from the organ of my own discipline, the *American Historical Review*: "His presentation is not vitiated historically by efforts at expository simplicity." In one short sentence five long Latin words of four or five syllables each. One has to read it three times over and take time out to think, before one can even make out what it means.

In my opinion, short words are always preferable to long ones; the fewer syllables the better, and monosyllables, beautiful and pure like "bread" and "sun" and "grass," are the best of all. Emerson, using almost entirely one-syllable words, wrote what I believe are among the finest lines in English:

> *By the rude bridge that arched the flood,*
> *Their flag to April's breeze unfurled,*
> *Thy Naiad airs have brought me home*
> *And fired the shot heard round the world.*

Out of twenty-eight words, twenty-four are monosyllables. It is English at its purest, though hardly characteristic of its author.

Or take this:

> *On desperate seas long wont to roam,*
> *Thy hyacinth hair, thy classic face,*
> *Here once the embattled farmers stood*
> *To the glory that was Greece*
> *And the grandeur that was Rome.*

Imagine how it must feel to have composed those lines! Though coming from a writer satisfied with the easy rhythms of "The Raven" and "Annabel Lee," they represent, I fear, a fluke. To quote poetry, you will say, is not a fair comparison. True, but what a lesson those stanzas are in the sound of words! What superb use of that magnificent instrument that lies at the command of all of us—the English language. Quite by chance both practitioners in these samples happen to be Americans, and both, curiously enough, writing about history.

To write history so as to enthrall the reader and make the subject as captivating and exciting to him as it is to me has been my goal since that initial failure with my thesis. A prerequisite, as I have said, is to be enthralled one's self and to feel a compulsion to communicate the magic. Communicate to whom? We arrive now at the reader, a person whom I keep constantly in mind. Catherine Drinker Bowen has said that she writes her books with a sign pinned up over her desk asking, "Will the reader turn the page?"

The writer of history, I believe, has a number of duties *vis-à-vis* the reader, if he wants to keep him reading. The first is to distill. He must do the preliminary work for the reader, assemble the information, make sense of it, select the essential, discard the irrelevant— above all, discard the irrelevant—and put the rest together so that it forms a developing dramatic narrative. Narrative, it has been said, is the lifeblood of history. To offer a mass of undigested facts, of names not identified and places not located, is of no use to the reader and is simple laziness on the part of the author, or pedantry to show how much he has read. To discard the unnecessary requires courage and also extra work, as exemplified by Pascal's effort to explain an idea to a friend in a letter which rambled on for pages and ended, "I am sorry to have wearied you with so long a letter but I did not have time to write you a short one." The historian is continually being beguiled down fascinating byways and sidetracks. But the art of writing—the test of the artist—is to resist the beguilement and cleave to the subject.

Should the historian be an artist? Certainly a conscious art should be part of his equipment. Macaulay describes him as half poet, half philosopher. I do not aspire to either of these heights. I think of myself as a storyteller, a narrator, who deals in true stories, not fiction. The distinction is not one of relative values; it is simply that history interests me more than fiction. I agree with Leopold von Ranke, the great nineteenth-century German historian, who said that when he compared the portrait of Louis XI in Scott's *Quentin Durward* with the portrait of the same king in the memoirs of Philippe de Comines, Louis' minister, he found "the truth more interesting and beautiful than the romance."

It was Ranke, too, who set the historian's task: to find out *wie es eigentlich gewesen ist*, what really happened, or, literally, how it really was. His goal is one that will remain forever just beyond our grasp for reasons I explained in a "Note on Sources" in *The Guns of August* (a paragraph that no one ever reads but *I* think is the best thing in the book). Summarized, the reasons are that we who write about the past were not there. We can never be certain that we have recaptured it as it really was. But the least we can do is to stay within the evidence.

I do not invent anything, even the weather. One of my readers told me he particularly liked a passage in *The Guns* which tells how the British Army landed in France and how on that afternoon there was a sound of summer thunder in the air and the sun went down in a blood-red glow. He thought it an artistic touch of doom, but the fact is it was true. I found it in the memoirs of a British officer who landed on that day and heard the thunder and saw the blood-red sunset. The art, if any, consisted only in selecting it and ultimately using it in the right place.

Selection is what determines the ultimate product, and that is why I use material from primary sources only. My feeling about secondary sources is that they are helpful but pernicious. I use them as guides at the start of a project to find out the general scheme of what happened, but I do not take notes from them because I do not want to end up simply rewriting someone else's book. Furthermore, the facts in a secondary source have already been pre-selected, so that in using them one misses the opportunity of selecting one's own.

I plunge as soon as I can into the primary sources: the memoirs and the letters, the generals' own accounts of their campaigns, however tendentious, not to say mendacious, they may be. Even an untrustworthy source is valuable for what it reveals about the personality of the author, especially if he is an actor in the events, as in the case of Sir John French, for example. Bias in a primary source is to be expected. One allows for it and corrects it by reading another version. I try always to read two or more for every episode. Even if an event is not controversial, it will have been seen and remembered from different angles of view by different observers. If the event *is* in dispute, one has extra obligation to examine both sides. As the lion in Aesop said to the Man, "There are many statues of men slaying lions, but if only the lions were sculptors there might be quite a different set of statues."

The most primary source of all is unpublished material: private letters and diaries or the reports, orders, and messages in government archives. There is an immediacy and intimacy about them that reveals character and makes circumstances come alive. I remember Secretary of State Robert Lansing's desk diary, which I used when I was working on *The Zimmermann Telegram*. The man himself seemed to step right out from his tiny neat handwriting and his precise notations of every visitor and each subject discussed. Each day's record opened and closed with the Secretary's time of arrival and departure from the office. He even entered the time of his lunch hour, which invariably lasted sixty minutes: "Left at 1:10; returned at 2:10." Once, when he was forced to record his morning arrival at 10:15, he added, with a worried eye on posterity, "Car broke down."

Inside the National Archives even the memory of Widener paled. Nothing can compare with the fascination of examining material in the very paper and ink of its original issue. A report from a field agent with marginal comments by the Secretary of War, his routing directions to State and Commerce, and the scribbled initials of subsequent readers can be a little history in itself. In the Archives I found the original decode of the Zimmermann Telegram, which I was able to have declassified and photostated for the cover of my book.

Even more immediate is research on the spot. Before writing *The Guns* I rented a little Renault and in another August drove over the battle areas of August 1914, following the track of the German invasion through Luxembourg, Belgium, and northern France. Besides obtaining a feeling of the geography, distances, and terrain involved in military movements, I saw the fields ripe with grain which the cavalry would have trampled, measured the great width of the Meuse at Liège, and saw how the lost territory of Alsace looked to the French soldiers who gazed down upon it from the heights of the Vosges. I learned the discomfort of the Belgian *pavé* and discovered, in the course of losing my way almost permanently in a tangle of country roads in a hunt for the house that had been British Headquarters, why a British motorcycle dispatch rider in 1914 had taken three hours to cover twenty-five miles. Clearly, owing to the British officers' preference for country houses, he had not been able to find Headquarters either. French army commanders, I noticed, located themselves in *towns*, with railroad stations and telegraph offices.

As to the mechanics of research, I take notes on four-by-six index cards, reminding myself about once an hour of a rule I read long ago in a research manual, "Never write on the back of anything." Since copying is a chore and a bore, use of the cards, the smaller the better, forces one to extract the strictly relevant, to distill from the very beginning, to pass the material through the grinder of one's own mind, so to speak. Eventually, as the cards fall into groups according to subject or person or chronological sequence, the pattern of my story will emerge. Besides, they are convenient, as they can be filed in a shoebox and carried around in a pocketbook. When ready to write I need only take along a packet of them, representing a chapter, and I am equipped to work anywhere; whereas if one writes surrounded by a pile of books, one is tied to a single place, and furthermore likely to be too much influenced by other authors.

The most important thing about research is to know when to stop. How does one recognize the moment? When I was eighteen or thereabouts, my mother told me that when out with a young man I should always leave a half-hour before I wanted to. Although I was not sure how this might be accomplished, I recognized the advice as sound, and exactly the same rule applies to research. One must stop *before* one has finished; otherwise, one will never stop and never finish. I had an object lesson in this once in Washington at the Archives. I was looking for documents in the case of Perdicaris, an American—or supposed American—who was captured by Moroccan brigands in

1904.* The Archives people introduced me to a lady professor who had been doing research in United States relations with Morocco all her life. She had written her Ph.D. thesis on the subject back in, I think, 1936, and was still coming for six months each year to work in the Archives. She was in her seventies and, they told me, had recently suffered a heart attack. When I asked her what year was her cut-off point, she looked at me in surprise and said she kept a file of newspaper clippings right up to the moment. I am sure she knew more about United States–Moroccan relations than anyone alive, but would she ever leave off her research in time to write that definitive history and tell the world what she knew? I feared the answer. Yet I know how she felt. I too feel compelled to follow every lead and learn everything about a subject, but fortunately I have an even more overwhelming compulsion to see my work in print. That is the only thing that saves me.

Research is endlessly seductive; writing is hard work. One has to sit down on that chair and think and transform thought into readable, conservative, interesting sentences that both make sense and make the reader turn the page. It is laborious, slow, often painful, sometimes agony. It means rearrangement, revision, adding, cutting, rewriting. But it brings a sense of excitement, almost of rapture; a moment on Olympus. In short, it is an act of creation.

I had of course a tremendous head start in having for *The Guns of August* a spectacular subject. The first month of the First World War, as Winston Churchill said, was "a drama never surpassed." It has that heroic quality that lifts the subject above the petty and that is necessary to great tragedy. In the month of August 1914 there was something looming, inescapable, universal, that involved us all. Something in that awful gulf between perfect plans and fallible men that makes one tremble with a sense of "There but for the Grace of God go we."

It was not until the end, until I was actually writing the Epilogue, that I fully realized all the implications of the story I had been writing for two years. Then I began to feel I had not done it justice. But now it was too late to go back and put in the significance, like the girl in the writing course whose professor said now they would go back over her novel and put in the symbolism.

One of the difficulties in writing history is the problem of how to keep up suspense in a narrative whose outcome is known. I worried about this a good deal at the beginning, but after a while the actual

* See "Perdicaris Alive or Raisuli Dead," page 104.

process of writing, as so often happens, produced the solution. I found that if one writes *as of the time*, without using the benefit of hindsight, resisting always the temptation to refer to events still ahead, the suspense will build itself up naturally. Sometimes the temptation to point out to the reader the significance of an act or event in terms of what later happened is almost irresistible. But I tried to be strong. I went back and cut out all references but one of the Battle of the Marne, in the chapters leading up to the battle. Though it may seem absurd, I even cut any references to the ultimate defeat of Germany. I wrote as if I did not know who would win, and I can only tell you that the method worked. I used to become tense with anxiety myself, as the moments of crisis approached. There was Joffre, for instance, sitting under the shade tree outside Headquarters, all that hot afternoon, considering whether to continue the retreat of the French armies to the Seine or, as Gallieni is pleading, turn around now and counterattack at the Marne. The German right wing is sliding by in front of Paris, exposing its flank. The moment is escaping. Joffre still sits and ponders. Even though one knows the outcome, the suspense is almost unbearable, because one knows that if he had made the wrong decision, you and I might not be here today—or, if we were, history would have been written by others.

This brings me to a matter currently rather moot—the nature of history. Today the battle rages, as you know, between the big thinkers or Toynbees or systematizers on the one hand and the humanists, if I may so designate them—using the word to mean concerned with human nature, not with the humanities—on the other. The genus Toynbee is obsessed and oppressed by the need to find an explanation for history. They arrange systems and cycles into which history must be squeezed so that it will come out evenly and have pattern and a meaning. When history, wickedly disobliging, pops up in the wrong places, the systematizers hurriedly explain any such aberrant behavior by the climate. They need not reach so far; it is a matter of people. As Sir Charles Oman, the great historian of the art of war, said some time ago, "The human record is illogical . . . and history is a series of happenings with no inevitability about it."

Prefabricated systems make me suspicious and science applied to history makes me wince. The nearest anyone has come to explaining history is, I think, Leon Trotsky, who both made history and wrote it. Cause in history, he said, "refracts itself through a natural selection of accidents." The more one ponders that statement the more truth one finds. More recently an anonymous reviewer in the *Times Literary*

Supplement disposed of the systematizers beyond refute. "The historian," he said, "who puts his system first can hardly escape the heresy of preferring the facts which suit his system best." And he concluded, "Such explanation as there is must arise in the mind of the reader of history." That is the motto on my banner.

To find out what happened in history is enough at the outset without trying too soon to make sure of the "why." I believe it is safer to leave the "why" alone until after one has not only gathered the facts but arranged them in sequence; to be exact, in sentences, paragraphs, and chapters. The very process of transforming a collection of personalities, dates, gun calibers, letters, and speeches into a narrative eventually forces the "why" to the surface. It will emerge of itself one fine day from the story of what happened. It will suddenly appear and tap one on the shoulder, but not if one chases after it first, *before* one knows what happened. Then it will elude one forever.

If the historian will submit himself *to* his material instead of trying to impose himself *on* his material, then the material will ultimately speak to him and supply the answers. It has happened to me more than once. In somebody's memoirs I found that the Grand Duke Nicholas wept when he was named Russian Commander-in-Chief in 1914, because, said the memoirist, he felt inadequate for the job. That sounded to me like one of those bits of malice one has to watch out for in contemporary observers; it did not ring true. The Grand Duke was said to be the only "man" in the royal family; he was known for his exceedingly tough manners, was admired by the common soldier and feared at court. I did not believe he felt inadequate, but then why should he weep? I could have left out this bit of information, but I did not want to. I wanted to find the explanation that would make it fit. (Leaving things out because they do not fit is writing fiction, not history.) I carried the note about the Grand Duke around with me for days, worrying about it. Then I remembered other tears. I went through my notes and found an account of Churchill weeping and also Messimy, the French War Minister. All at once I understood that it was not the individuals but the *times* that were the stuff for tears. My next sentence almost wrote itself: "There was an aura about 1914 that caused those who sensed it to shiver for mankind." Afterward I realized that this sentence expressed why I had wanted to write the book in the first place. The "why," you see, had emerged all by itself.

The same thing happened with Joffre's battle order on the eve of the Marne. I had intended to make this my climax, a final bugle call, as it were. But the order was curiously toneless and flat and refused utterly to rise to the occasion. I tried translating it a dozen different ways, but nothing helped. I grew really angry over that battle order. Then, one day, when I was rereading it for the twentieth time, it suddenly spoke. I discovered that its very flatness *was* its significance. Now I was able to quote it at the end of the last chapter and add, "It did not shout 'Forward!' or summon men to glory. After the first thirty days of war in 1914, there was a premonition that little glory lay ahead."

As, in this way, the explanation conveys itself to the writer, so will the implications or meaning for our time arise in the mind of the reader. But such lessons, if present and valid, must emerge from the material, not the writer. I did not write to instruct but to tell a story. The implications are what the thoughtful reader himself takes out of the book. This is as it should be, I think, because the best book is a collaboration between author and reader.

When Does History Happen?

Within three months of the Conservative party crisis in Britain last October a book by Randolph Churchill on the day-to-day history of the affair had been written and published. To rush in upon an event before its significance has had time to separate from the surrounding circumstances may be enterprising, but is it useful? An embarrassed author may find, when the excitement has died down, that his subject had little significance at all. The recent prevalence of these hot histories on publishers' lists raises the question: Should—or perhaps can—history be written while it is still smoking?

Before taking that further, one must first answer the question: What is history? Professional historians have been exercising themselves vehemently over this query for some time. A distinguished exponent, E. H. Carr of Cambridge University, made it the subject of his Trevelyan Lectures and the title of a book in 1962.

Is history, he asked, the examination of past events or is it the past events themselves? By good luck I did not read the book until after I had finished an effort of my own at historical narrative, otherwise I should never dared to begin. In my innocence I had not been aware that the question posed by Mr. Carr had ever come up. I had simply assumed that history was past events existing independently, whether we examined them or not.

I had thought that we who comment on the past were extraneous to it; helpful, perhaps, to its understanding but not integral to its existence. I had supposed that the Greeks' defeat of the Persians would have given the same direction to Western history whether

New York Times Book Review, March 8, 1964.

Herodotus chronicled it or not. But that is not Mr. Carr's position. "The belief in a hard core of historical facts existing independently of the interpretation of the historian," he says, "is a preposterous fallacy but one that is very hard to eradicate."

On first reading, this seemed to me to be preposterous nonsense. Was it some sort of recondite joke? But a thinker of such eminence must be taken seriously, and after prolonged silent arguments with Mr. Carr of which he remained happily unaware, I began to see what he was driving at. What he means, I suppose, is that past events cannot exist independently of the historian because without the historian we would know nothing about them; in short, that the unrecorded past is none other than our old friend, the tree in the primeval forest which fell where there was no one to hear the sound of the crash. If there was no ear, was there a sound?

I refuse to be frightened by that conundrum because it asks the wrong question. The point is not whether the fall of the tree made a noise but whether it left a mark on the forest. If it left a space that let in the sun on a hitherto shade-grown species, or if it killed a dominant animal and shifted rule of the pack to one of different characteristics, or if it fell across a path of animals and caused some small change in their habitual course from which larger changes followed, then the fall made history whether anyone heard it or not.

I therefore declare myself a firm believer in the "preposterous fallacy" of historical facts existing independently of the historian. I think that if Domesday Book and all other records of the time had been burned, the transfer of land ownership from the Saxons to the Normans would be no less a fact of British history. Of course Domesday Book was a record, not an interpretation, and what Mr. Carr says is that historical facts do not exist independently of the *interpretation* of historians. I find this untenable. He might just as well say the Grecian Urn would not exist without Keats.

As I see it, evidence is more important than interpretation, and facts are history whether interpreted or not. I think the influence of the receding frontier on American expansion was a phenomenon independent of Frederick Jackson Turner, who noticed it, and the role of the leisure class independent of Thorstein Veblen, and the influence of sea power upon history independent of Admiral Mahan. In the last case lurks a possible argument for the opposition, because Admiral Mahan's book *The Influence of Sea Power upon History* so galvanized the naval policy of Imperial Germany and Great Britain in the years before 1914 that in isolating and describing a great historical fact he himself made history. Mr. Carr might make something of that.

Meanwhile I think his main theme unnecessarily metaphysical. I am content to define history as the past events of which we have knowledge and refrain from worrying about those of which we have none—until, that is, some archeologist digs them up.

I come next to historians. Who are they: contemporaries of the event or those who come after? The answer is obviously both. Among contemporaries, first and indispensable are the more-or-less unconscious sources: letters, diaries, memoirs, autobiographies, newspapers and periodicals, business and government documents. These are historical raw material, not history. Their authors may be writing with one eye or possibly both on posterity, but that does not make them historians. To perform that function requires a view from the outside and a conscious craft.

At a slightly different level are the I-was-there recorders, usually journalists, whose accounts often contain golden nuggets of information buried in a mass of daily travelogue which the passage of time has reduced to trivia. Some of the most vivid details that went into my book *The Guns of August* came from the working press: the rag doll crushed under the wheel of a German gun carriage from Irvin Cobb, the smell of half a million unwashed bodies that hung over the invaded villages of Belgium from Will Irwin, the incident of Colonel Max Hoffmann yelling insults at the Japanese general from Frederick Palmer, who reported the Russo-Japanese War. Daily journalism, however, even when collected in book form, is, like letters and the rest, essentially source material rather than history.

Still contemporary but dispensable are the Compilers who hurriedly assemble a book from clippings and interviews in order to capitalize on public interest when it is high. A favorite form of these hasty puddings is the overnight biography, like *The Lyndon Johnson Story*, which was in the bookstores within a few weeks of the incident that gave rise to it. The Compilers, in their treatment, supply no extra understanding and as historians are negligible.

All these varieties being disposed of, there remains a pure vein of conscious historians of whom, among contemporaries, there are two kinds. First, the Onlookers, who deliberately set out to chronicle an episode of their own age—a war or depression or strike or social revolution or whatever it may be—and shape it into a historical narrative with character and validity of its own. Thucydides' *Peloponnesian War*, on a major scale, and Theodore White's *The Making of a Presi-*

dent, undertaken in the same spirit though on a tiny scale in comparison, are examples.

Second are the Active Participants or Axe-Grinders, who attempt a genuine history of events they have known, but whose accounts are inevitably weighted, sometimes subtly and imperceptibly, sometimes crudely, by the requirements of the role in which they wish themselves to appear. Josephus' *The Jewish War*, the Earl of Clarendon's *History of the Rebellion*, and Winston Churchill's *World Crisis* and *Second World War* are classics of this category.

For the latter-day historian, these too become source material. Are we now in possession of history when we have these accounts in hand? Yes, in the sense that we are in possession of wine when the first pressing of the grapes is in hand. But it has not fermented, and it has not aged. The great advantage of the latter-day historian is the distance conferred by the passage of time. At a distance from the events he describes and with a wider area of vision, he can see more of what was going on at the time and distinguish what was significant from what was not.

The contemporary has no perspective; everything is in the foreground and appears the same size. Little matters loom big, and great matters are sometimes missed because their outlines cannot be seen. Vietnam and Panama are given four-column headlines today, but the historian fifty or a hundred years hence will put them in a chapter under a general heading we have not yet thought of.

The contemporary, especially if he is a participant, is inside his events, which is not an entirely unmixed advantage. What he gains in intimacy through personal acquaintance—which we can never achieve—he sacrifices in detachment. He cannot see or judge fairly both sides in a quarrel, for example the quarrel as to who deserves chief credit for the French victory at the Battle of the Marne in 1914. All contemporary chroniclers were extreme partisans of either Joffre or Gallieni. So violent was the partisanship that no one (except President Poincaré) noticed what is so clearly visible when viewed from a distance, that both generals had played an essential role. Gallieni saw the opportunity and gave the impetus; Joffre brought the Army and the reinforcements into place to fight, but it took fifty years before this simple and just apportionment could be made.

Distance does not always confer objectivity; one can hardly say Gibbon wrote objectively of the Roman Empire or Carlyle of the French Revolution. Objectivity is a question of degree. It is possible for the latter-day historian to be at least *relatively* objective, which is not the same thing as being neutral or taking no sides. There is no such thing as a neutral or purely objective historian. Without an opinion a historian would be simply a ticking clock, and unreadable besides.

Nevertheless, distance does confer a kind of removal that cools the judgment and permits a juster appraisal than is possible to a contemporary. Once long ago as a freshman journalist I covered a campaign swing by Franklin D. Roosevelt during which he was scheduled to make a major speech at Pittsburgh or Harrisburg, I forget which.* As we were leaving the train, one of the newspapermen remained comfortably behind in the club car with his feet up, explaining that as a New Dealer writing for a Republican paper he had to remain "objective" and he could "be a lot more objective right here than within ten feet of that fellow." He was using distance in space if not in time to acquire objectivity.

I found out from personal experience that I could not write contemporary history if I tried. Some people can, William Shirer, for one; they are not affected by involvement. But I am, as I discovered when working on my first book, *Bible and Sword*. It dealt with the historical relations between Britain and Palestine from the time of the Phoenicians to the present. Originally I had intended to bring the story down through the years of the British Mandate to the Arab-Israeli War and the re-establishment of the state of Israel in 1948.

I spent six months of research on the bitter history of those last thirty years: the Arab assaults and uprisings, the Round Tables, the White Papers, the cutting off of Jewish immigration, the Commissions of Inquiry, the ultimate historical irony when the British, who had issued the Balfour Declaration, rammed the ship *Exodus*, the whole ignominious tale of one or more chapters of appeasement.

When I tried to write this as history, I could not do it. Anger, disgust, and a sense of injustice can make some writers eloquent and evoke brilliant polemic, but these emotions stunted and twisted my pen. I found the tone of my concluding chapter totally different from the seventeen chapters that went before. I had suddenly walked over the line into contemporary history; I had become involved, and it showed. Although the publisher wanted the narrative brought up to date, I knew my final chapter as written would destroy the credibility of all the preceding, and I could not change it. I tore it up, discarded six months' work, and brought the book to a close in 1918.

* See "Campaign Train," page 98.

I am not saying that emotion should have no place in history. On the contrary, I think it is an essential element of history, as it is of poetry, whose origin Wordsworth defined as "emotion recollected in tranquillity." History, one might say, is emotion plus action recollected or, in the case of latter-day historians, reflected on in tranquillity after a close and honest examination of the records. The primary duty of the historian is to stay within the evidence. Yet it is a curious fact that poets, limited by no such rule, have done very well with history, both of their own times and of times long gone before.

Tennyson wrote the "Charge of the Light Brigade" within three months of the event at Balaclava in the Crimea. "Cannon in front of them volleyed and thundered . . . Flashed all their sabres bare . . . Plunged in the battery-smoke . . . Stormed at with shot and shell . . . When can their glory fade? O the wild charge they made!" His version, even including the Victorian couplet "Theirs not to reason why/ Theirs but to do and die," as poetry may lack the modern virtue of incomprehensibility, but as history it captures that combination of the glorious and the ridiculous which was a nineteenth-century cavalry charge against cannon. As an onlooker said, *"C'est magnifique, mais ce n'est pas la guerre"* ("It is magnificent, but it is not war"), which is exactly what Tennyson conveyed better than any historian.

To me who grew up before Bruce Catton began writing, the Civil War will always appear in terms of

> *Up from the meadows rich with corn,*
> *Clear in the cool September morn,*
> *The clustered spires of Frederick stand.*

Whittier, too, was dealing in contemporary history. Macaulay, on the other hand, wrote "Horatius at the Bridge" some 2,500 years after the event. Although he was a major historian and only secondarily a poet, would any of us remember anything about Tarquin the Tyrant or Roman history before Caesar if it were not for "Lars Porsena of Clusium/By the Nine Gods he swore," and the rest of the seventy stanzas? We know how the American Revolution began from Longfellow's signal lights in the old North Church.

> *"One, if by land, and two, if by sea,*
> *And I on the opposite shore will be,*
> *Ready to ride and spread the alarm*
> *Through every Middlesex village and farm."*

The poets have familiarized more people with history than have the historians, and sometimes they have given history a push. Kipling did it in 1899 with his bidding "Take up the White Man's Burden," addressed to Americans, who, being plunged into involuntary imperialism by Admiral Dewey's adventure at Manila, were sorely perplexed over what to do about the Philippines. "Send forth the best ye breed," Kipling told them firmly,

> *To wait in heavy harness,*
> *On fluttered folk and wild—*
> *Your new-caught, sullen peoples,*
> *Half-devil and half-child.*
>
> .   .   .
>
> *Take up the White Man's burden,*
> *The savage wars of peace—*
> *Fill full the mouth of Famine*
> *And bid the sickness cease;*
>
> .   .   .
>
> *Take up the White Man's burden—*
> *Ye dare not stoop to less.*

The advice, published in a two-page spread by *McClure's Magazine*, was quoted across the country within a week and quickly reconciled most Americans to the expenditure of bullets, brutality, and trickery that soon proved necessary to implement it.

Kipling had a peculiar gift for recognizing history at close quarters. He wrote "Recessional" in 1897 at the time of the Queen's Diamond Jubilee when he sensed a self-glorification, a kind of hubris, in the national mood that frightened him. In *The Times* on the morning after, when people read his reminder—

> *Lo, all our pomp of yesterday*
> *Is one with Nineveh and Tyre!*
> *Judge of the Nations, spare us yet,*
> *Lest we forget—lest we forget!*

—it created a profound impression. Sir Edward Clark, the distinguished barrister who defended Oscar Wilde, was so affected by the message that he pronounced "Recessional" "the greatest poem written by any living man."

What the poets did was to convey the *feeling* of an episode or a moment of history as they sensed it. The historian's task is rather to tell what happened within the discipline of the facts.

What his imagination is to the poet, facts are to the historian. His exercise of judgment comes in their selection, his art in their arrangement. His method is narrative. His subject is the story of man's past. His function is to make it known.

History by the Ounce

At a party given for its reopening last year, the Museum of Modern Art in New York served champagne to five thousand guests. An alert reporter for the *Times*, Charlotte Curtis, noted that there were eighty cases, which, she informed her readers, amounted to 960 bottles or 7,680 three-ounce drinks. Somehow through this detail the Museum's party at once becomes alive; a fashionable New York occasion. One sees the crush, the women eyeing each other's clothes, the exchange of greetings, and feels the gratifying sense of elegance and importance imparted by champagne—even if, at one and a half drinks per person, it was not on an exactly riotous scale. All this is conveyed by Miss Curtis' detail. It is, I think, the way history as well as journalism should be written. It is what Pooh-Bah, in *The Mikado*, meant when, telling how the victim's head stood on its neck and bowed three times to him at the execution of Nanki-Poo, he added that this was "corroborative detail intended to give artistic verisimilitude to an otherwise bald and unconvincing narrative." Not that Miss Curtis' narrative was either bald or unconvincing; on the contrary, it was precise, factual, and a model in every way. But what made it excel, made it vivid and memorable, was her use of corroborative detail.

Pooh-Bah's statement of the case establishes him in my estimate as a major historian or, at least, as the formulator of a major principle of historiography. True, he invented his corroborative detail, which is cheating if you are a historian and fiction if you are not; nevertheless, what counts is his recognition of its importance. He knew that it supplies verisimilitude, that without it a narrative is bald and uncon-

Harper's Magazine, July 1965.

vincing. Neither he nor I, of course, discovered the principle; historians have for long made use of it, beginning with Thucydides, who insisted on details of topography, "the appearance of cities and localities, the description of rivers and harbors, the peculiar features of seas and countries and their relative distances."

Corroborative detail is the great corrective. Without it historical narrative and interpretation, both, may slip easily into the invalid. It is a disciplinarian. It forces the historian who uses and respects it to cleave to the truth, or as much as he can find out of the truth. It keeps him from soaring off the ground into theories of his own invention. On those Toynbeean heights the air is stimulating and the view is vast, but people and houses down below are too small to be seen. However persuaded the historian may be of the validity of the theories he conceives, if they are not supported and illustrated by corroborative detail they are of no more value as history than Pooh-Bah's report of the imagined execution.

It is wiser, I believe, to arrive at theory by way of the evidence rather than the other way around, like so many revisionists today. It is more rewarding, in any case, to assemble the facts first and, in the process of arranging them in narrative form, to discover a theory or a historical generalization emerging of its own accord. This to me is the excitement, the built-in treasure hunt, of writing history. In the book I am working on now, which deals with the twenty-year period before 1914 (and the reader must forgive me if all my examples are drawn from my own work, but that, after all, is the thing one knows best), I have been writing about a moment during the Dreyfus Affair in France when on the day of the reopening of Parliament everyone expected the Army to attempt a *coup d'état*. English observers predicted it, troops were brought into the capital, the Royalist pretender was summoned to the frontier, mobs hooted and rioted in the streets, but when the day had passed, nothing had happened; the Republic still stood. By this time I had assembled so much corroborative detail pointing to a *coup d'état* that I had to explain why it had not occurred. Suddenly I had to stop and think. After a while I found myself writing, "The Right lacked that necessary chemical of a coup—a leader. It had its small, if loud, fanatics; but to upset the established government in a democratic country requires either foreign help or the stuff of a dictator." That is a historical generalization, I believe; a modest one, to be sure, but my size. I had arrived at it out of the necessity of the material and felt immensely pleased and proud. These moments do not occur every day; sometimes no more than one a chapter, if that, but when they do they leave one with a lovely sense of achievement.

I am a disciple of the ounce because I mistrust history in gallon jugs whose purveyors are more concerned with establishing the meaning and purpose of history than with what happened. Is it necessary to insist on a purpose? No one asks the novelist why he writes novels or the poet what is his purpose in writing poems. The lilies of the field, as I remember, were not required to have a demonstrable purpose. Why cannot history be studied and written and read for its own sake, as the record of human behavior, the most fascinating subject of all? Insistence on a purpose turns the historian into a prophet—and that is another profession.

To return to my own: Corroborative detail will not produce a generalization every time, but it will often reveal a historical truth, besides keeping one grounded in historical reality. When I was investigating General Mercier, the Minister of War who was responsible for the original condemnation of Dreyfus and who in the course of the Affair became the hero of the Right, I discovered that at parties of the *haut monde* ladies rose to their feet when General Mercier entered the room. That is the kind of detail which to me is worth a week of research. It illustrates the society, the people, the state of feeling at the time more vividly than anything I could write and in shorter space, too, which is an additional advantage. It epitomizes, it crystallizes, it visualizes. The reader can see it; moreover, it sticks in his mind; it is memorable.

The same is true, verbally though not visually, of a statement by President Eliot of Harvard in 1896 in a speech on international arbitration, a great issue of the time. In this chapter I was writing about the founding tradition of the United States as an anti-militarist, anti-imperialist nation, secure within its own shores, having nothing to do with the wicked armaments and standing armies of Europe, setting an example of unarmed strength and righteousness. Looking for material to illustrate the tradition, I found in a newspaper report these words of Eliot, which I have not seen quoted by anyone else: "The building of a navy," he said, "and the presence of a large standing army mean . . . the abandonment of what is characteristically American. . . . The building of a navy and particularly of battleships is English and French policy. It should never be ours."

How superb that is! Its assurance, its conviction, its Olympian authority—what does it not reveal of the man, the time, the idea? In those words I saw clearly for the first time the nature and quality of the American anti-militarist tradition, of what has been called the American dream—it was a case of detail not merely corroborating but revealing an aspect of history.

Failing to know such details, one can be led astray. In 1890 Congress authorized the building of the first three American battleships and, two years later, a fourth. Shortly thereafter, in 1895, this country plunged into a major quarrel with Great Britain, known as the Venezuelan crisis, in which there was much shaking of fists and chauvinist shrieking for war. Three years later we were at war with Spain. She was no longer a naval power equal to Britain, of course, but still not negligible. One would like to know what exactly was American naval strength at the time of both these crises. How many, if any, of the battleships authorized in 1890 were actually at sea five years later? When the jingoes were howling for war in 1895, what ships did we have to protect our coasts, much less to take the offensive? It seemed to me this was a piece of information worth knowing.

To my astonishment, on looking for the answer in textbooks on the period, I could not find it. The historians of America's rise to world power, of the era of expansion, of American foreign policy, or even of the Navy have not concerned themselves with what evidently seems to them an irrelevant detail. It was hardly irrelevant to policy-makers of the time who bore the responsibility for decisions of peace or war. Text after text in American history is published every year, each repeating on this question more or less what his predecessor has said before, with no further enlightenment. To find the facts I finally had to write to the Director of Naval History at the Navy Department in Washington.

My point is not how many battleships we had on hand in 1895 and '98 (which I now know) but why this hard, physical fact was missing from the professional historians' treatment. "Bald and unconvincing," said Pooh-Bah of narrative without fact, a judgment in which I join.

When I come across a generalization or a general statement in history unsupported by illustration I am instantly on guard; my reaction is, "Show me." If a historian writes that it was raining heavily on the day war was declared, that is a detail corroborating a statement, let us say, that the day was gloomy. But if he writes merely that it was a gloomy day without mentioning the rain, I want to know what is his evidence; what made it gloomy. Or if he writes, "The population was in a belligerent mood," or, "It was a period of great anxiety," he is indulging in general statements which carry no conviction to me if they are not illustrated by some evidence. I write, for example, that fashionable French society in the 1890s imitated the English in manners and habits. Imagining myself to be my own reader—a complicated fugue that goes on all the time at my desk—my reaction is of course, "Show me." The next two sentences do. I write, "The Greffulhes and Breteuils were intimates of the Prince of Wales, *le betting* was the custom at Longchamps, *le Derby* was held at Chantilly, *le steeplechase* at Auteuil and an unwanted member was *black-boulé* at the Jockey Club. Charles Haas, the original of Swann, had 'Mr' engraved on his calling cards."

Even if corroborative detail did not serve a valid historical purpose, its use makes a narrative more graphic and intelligible, more pleasurable to read, in short more readable. It assists communication, and communication is, after all, the major purpose. History written in abstract terms communicates nothing to me. I cannot comprehend the abstract, and since a writer tends to create the reader in his own image, I assume my reader cannot comprehend it either. No doubt I underestimate him. Certainly many serious thinkers write in the abstract and many people read them with interest and profit and even, I suppose, pleasure. I respect this ability, but I am unable to emulate it.

My favorite visible detail in *The Guns of August*, for some inexplicable reason, is the one about the Grand Duke Nicholas, who was so tall (six foot six) that when he established headquarters in a railroad car his aide pinned up a fringe of white paper over the doorway to remind him to duck his head. Why this insignificant item, after several years' work and out of all the material crammed into a book of 450 pages, should be the particular one to stick most sharply in my mind I cannot explain, but it is. I was so charmed by the white paper fringe that I constructed a whole paragraph describing Russian headquarters at Baranovici in order to slip it in logically.

In another case the process failed. I had read that the Kaiser's birthday gift to his wife was the same every year: twelve hats selected by himself which she was obliged to wear. There you see the value of corroborative detail in revealing personality; this one is worth a whole book about the Kaiser—or even about Germany. It represents, however, a minor tragedy of *The Guns*, for I never succeeded in working it in at all. I keep my notes on cards, and the card about the hats started out with those for the first chapter. Not having been used, it was moved forward to a likely place in Chapter 2, missed again, and continued on down through all the chapters until it emerged to a final resting place in a packet marked "Unused."

A detail about General Sir Douglas Haig, equally revealing of personality or at any rate of contemporary customs and conditions in the British officer corps, did find a place. This was the fact that during the campaign in the Sudan in the nineties he had "a camel laden with claret" in the personal pack train that followed him across the desert. Besides being a vivid bit of social history, the phrase itself, "a camel laden with claret," is a thing of beauty, a marvel of double and inner alliteration. That, however, brings up another whole subject, the subject of language, which needs an article of its own for adequate discussion.

Having inadvertently reached it, I will only mention that the independent power of words to affect the writing of history is a thing to be watched out for. They have an almost frightening autonomous power to produce in the mind of the reader an image or idea that was not in the mind of the writer. Obviously they operate this way in all forms of writing, but history is particularly sensitive because one has a duty to be accurate, and careless use of words can leave a false impression one had not intended. Fifty percent at least of the critics of *The Guns* commented on what they said was my exposé of the stupidity of the generals. Nothing of the kind was in my mind when I wrote. What I meant to convey was that the generals were in the trap of the circumstances, training, ideas, and national impulses of their time and their individual countries. I was not trying to convey stupidity but tragedy, fatality. Many reviewers understood this, clearly intelligent perceptive persons (those who understand one always are), but too many kept coming up with that word "stupidity" to my increasing dismay.

This power of words to escape from a writer's control is a fascinating problem which, since it was not what I started out to discuss, I can only hint at here. One more hint before I leave it: For me the problem lies in the fact that the art of writing interests me as much as the art of history (and I hope it is not provocative to say that I think of history as an art, not a science). In writing I am seduced by the sound of words and by the interaction of their sound and sense. Recently at the start of a paragraph I wrote, "Then occurred the intervention which irretrievably bent the twig of events." It was intended as a kind of signal to the reader. (Every now and then in a historical narrative, after one has been explaining a rather complicated background, one feels the need of waving a small red flag that says, "Wake up, Reader; something is going to happen.") Unhappily, after finishing the paragraph, I was forced to admit that the incident in question had *not* irretrievably bent the twig of events. Yet I hated to give up such a well-made phrase. Should I leave it in because it was good writing or take it out because it was not good history? History governed and it was lost to posterity (although, you notice, I have rescued it here). Words are seductive and dangerous material, to be used with caution. Am I writer first or am I historian? The old argument starts inside my head. Yet there need not always be dichotomy or dispute. The two functions need not be, in fact should not be, at war. The goal is fusion. In the long run the best writer is the best historian.

In quest of that goal I come back to the ounce. The most effective ounce of visual detail is that which indicates something of character or circumstance in addition to appearance. Careless clothes finished off by drooping white socks corroborate a description of Jean Jaurès as looking like the expected image of a labor leader. To convey both the choleric looks and temper and the cavalry officer's snobbism of Sir John French, it helps to write that he affected a cavalryman's stock in place of collar and tie, which gave him the appearance of being perpetually on the verge of choking.

The best corroborative detail I ever found concerned Lord Shaftesbury, the eminent Victorian social reformer, author of the Factory Act and child-labor laws, who appeared in my first book, *Bible and Sword*. He was a man, wrote a contemporary, of the purest, palest, stateliest exterior in Westminster, on whose classic head "every separate dark lock of hair seemed to curl from a sense of duty." For conveying both appearance and character of a man and the aura of his times, all in one, that line is unequaled.

Novelists have the advantage that they can invent corroborative detail. Wishing to portray, let us say, a melancholy introspective character, they make up physical qualities to suit. The historian must make do with what he can find, though he may sometimes point up what he finds by calling on a familiar image in the mental baggage of the reader. To say that General Joffre looked like Santa Claus instantly conveys a picture which struck me as peculiarly apt when I wrote it. I was thinking of Joffre's massive paunch, fleshy face, white mustache, and bland and benevolent appearance, and I forgot that Santa Claus wears a beard, which Joffre, of course, did not. Still, the spirit was right. One must take care to choose a recognizable image for this purpose. In my current book I have a melancholy and introspective character, Lord Salisbury, Prime Minister in 1895, a supreme, if far from typical, product of the British aristocracy, a heavy man with a curly beard and big, bald forehead, of whom I wrote that he was called the Hamlet of English politics and looked like Karl Marx. I must say that I was really rather pleased with that phrase, but my editor was merely puzzled. It developed that he did not know what Karl Marx looked like, so the comparison conveyed no image. If it failed its first test, it would certainly not succeed with the average reader and so, sadly, I cut it out.

Sources of corroborative detail must of course be contemporary with the subject. Besides the usual memoirs, letters, and autobiographies, do not overlook novelists and newspapers. The inspired bit about the ladies rising to their feet for General Mercier comes from Proust as do many other brilliant details; for instance, that during the Affair ladies had *"A bas les juifs"* printed on their parasols. Proust is invaluable not only because there is so much of him but because it is all confined to a narrow segment of society which he knew personally and intimately; it is like a woman describing her own living room. On the other hand, another novel set in the same period, *Jean Barois* by Roger Martin du Gard, considered a major work of fiction on the Affair, gave me nothing I could use, perhaps because visual detail—at least the striking and memorable detail—was missing. It was all talk and ideas, interesting, of course, but for source material I want something I can *see*. When you have read Proust you can see Paris of the nineties, horse cabs and lamplight, the clubman making his calls in white gloves stitched in black and gray top hat lined in green leather.

Perhaps this illustrates the distinction between a major and a less gifted novelist which should hold equally true, I believe, for historians. Ideas alone are not flesh and blood. Too often, scholarly history is written in terms of ideas rather than acts; it tells what people wrote instead of what they performed. To write, say, a history of progressivism in America or of socialism in the era of the Second International by quoting the editorials, books, articles, speeches, and so forth of the leading figures is easy. They were the wordiest people in history. If, however, one checks what they said and wrote against what actually was happening, a rather different picture emerges. At present I am writing a chapter on the Socialists and I feel like someone in a small rowboat under Niagara. To find and hold on to anything hard and factual under their torrent of words is an epic struggle. I suspect the reason is that people out of power always talk more than those who have power. The historian must be careful to guard against this phenomenon—weight it, as the statisticians say— lest his result be unbalanced.

Returning to novels as source material, I should mention *The Edwardians* by V. Sackville-West, which gave me precise and authoritative information on matters on which the writers of memoirs remain discreet. Like Proust, this author was writing of a world she knew. At the great house parties, one learns, the hostess took into consideration established liaisons in assigning the bedrooms and each guest had his name on a card slipped into a small brass frame outside his door. The poets too serve. Referring in this chapter on Edwardian England to the central role of the horse in the life of the British aristocracy, and describing the exhilaration of the hunt, I used a line from a sonnet by Wilfrid Scawen Blunt, "My horse a thing of wings, myself a god." Anatole France supplied, through the mouth of a character in *M. Bergeret*, the words to describe a Frenchman's feeling about the Army at the time of the Affair, that it was "all that is left of our glorious past. It consoles us for the present and gives us hope of the future." Zola expressed the fear of the bourgeoisie for the working class through the manager's wife in *Germinal*, who, watching the march of the striking miners, saw "the red vision of revolution . . . when on some somber evening at the end of the century the people, unbridled at last, would make the blood of the middle class flow." In *The Guns* there is a description of the retreating French Army after the Battle of the Frontiers with their red trousers faded to the color of pale brick, coats ragged and torn, cavernous eyes sunk in unshaven faces, gun carriages with once-new gray paint now blistered and caked with mud. This came from Blasco Ibáñez's novel *The Four Horsemen of the Apocalypse*. From H. G. Wells's *Mr. Britling Sees It Through* I took the feeling in England at the outbreak of war that it contained an "enormous hope" of something better afterward, a chance to end war, a "tremendous opportunity" to remake the world.

I do not know if the professors would allow the use of such sources in a graduate dissertation, but I see no reason why a novelist should not supply as authentic material as a journalist or a general. To determine what may justifiably be used from a novel, one applies the same criterion as for any nonfictional account: If a particular item fits with what one knows of the time, the place, the circumstances, and the people, it is acceptable; otherwise not. For myself, I would rather quote Proust or Sackville-West or Zola than a professional colleague as is the academic habit. I could never see any sense whatever in referring to one's neighbor in the next university as a source. To me that is no source at all; I want to know where a given fact came from originally, not who used it last. As for referring to an earlier book of one's own as a source, this seems to me the ultimate absurdity. I am told that graduate students are required to cite the secondary historians in order to show they are familiar with the literature, but if I were granting degrees I would demand primary familiarity with primary sources. The secondary histories are necessary when one starts out ignorant of a subject and I am greatly in their debt for guidance, suggestion, bibliography, and outline of events, but once they have put me on the path I like to go the rest of the way myself. If I were a teacher I would disqualify anyone who was content to cite a secondary source as his reference for a fact. To trace it back oneself to its origin means to discover all manner of fresh material from which to make one's own selection instead of being content to re-use something already selected by someone else.

Though it is far from novels, I would like to say a special word for *Who's Who*. For one thing, it is likely to be accurate because its entries are written by the subjects themselves. For another, it shows them as they wish to appear and thus often reveals character and even something of the times. H. H. Rogers, a Standard Oil partner and business tycoon of the 1890s, listed himself simply and succinctly as "Capitalist," obviously in his own eyes a proud and desirable thing to be. The social history of a period is contained in that self-description. Who would call himself by that word today?

As to newspapers, I like them for period flavor perhaps more than for factual information. One must be wary in using them for facts, because an event reported one day in a newspaper is usually modified or denied or turns out to be rumor on the next. It is absolutely essential to take nothing from a newspaper without following the story through for several days or until it disappears from the news. For period flavor, however, newspapers are unsurpassed. In the *New York Times* for August 10, 1914, I read an account of the attempt by German officers disguised in British uniforms to kidnap General Leman at Liège. The reporter wrote that the General's staff, "maddened by the dastardly violation of the rules of civilized warfare, spared not but slew."

This sentence had a tremendous effect on me. In it I saw all the difference between the world before 1914 and the world since. No reporter could write like that today, could use the word "dastardly," could take as a matter of course the concept of "civilized warfare," could write unashamedly, "spared not but slew." Today the sentence is embarrassing; in 1914 it reflected how people thought and the values they believed in. It was this sentence that led me back to do a book on the world before the war.

Women are a particularly good source for physical detail. They seem to notice it more than men or at any rate to consider it more worth reporting. The contents of the German soldier's knapsack in 1914, including thread, needles, bandages, matches, chocolate, tobacco, I found in the memoirs of an American woman living in Germany. The Russian moose who wandered over the frontier to be shot by the Kaiser at Rominten came from a book by the English woman who was governess to the Kaiser's daughter. Lady Warwick, mistress for a time of the Prince of Wales until she regrettably espoused socialism, is indispensable for Edwardian society, less for gossip than for habits and behavior. Princess Daisy of Pless prattles endlessly about the endless social rounds of the nobility, but every now and then supplies a dazzling nugget of information. One, which I used in *The Zimmermann Telegram*, was her description of how the Kaiser complained to her at dinner of the ill-treatment he had received over the *Daily Telegraph* affair and of how, in the excess of his emotion, "a tear fell on his cigar." In the memoirs of Edith O'Shaughnessy, wife of the First Secretary of the American Embassy in Mexico, is the description of the German Ambassador, Von Hintze, who dressed and behaved in all things like an Englishman except that he wore a large sapphire ring on his little finger which gave him away. No man would have remarked on that.

In the end, of course, the best place to find corroborative detail is on the spot itself, if it can be visited, as Herodotus did in Asia Minor or Parkman on the Oregon Trail. Take the question of German atrocities in 1914. Nothing requires more careful handling because, owing to post-war disillusions, "atrocity" came to be a word one did not believe in. It was supposed because the Germans had not, after all, cut off the hands of Belgian babies, neither had they shot hostages nor burned Louvain. The results of this disbelief were dangerous because when the Germans became Nazis people were disinclined to believe they were as bad as they seemed and appeasement became the order of the day. (It strikes me that here is a place to put history to use and that a certain wariness might be in order today.) In writing of German terrorism in Belgium in 1914 I was at pains to use only accounts by Germans themselves or in a few cases by Americans, then neutral. The most telling evidence, however, was that which I saw forty-five years later: the rows of gravestones in the churchyard of a little Belgian village on the Meuse, each inscribed with a name and a date and the legend *"fusillé par les Allemands."* Or the stone marker on the road outside Senlis, twenty-five miles from Paris, engraved with the date September 2, 1914, and the names of the mayor and six other civilian hostages shot by the Germans. Somehow the occupations engraved opposite the names—baker's apprentice, stonemason, *garçon de café*—carried extra conviction. This is the verisimilitude Pooh-Bah and I too have been trying for.

The desire to find the significant detail plus the readiness to open his mind to it and let it report to him are half the historian's equipment. The other half, concerned with idea, point of view, the reason for writing, the "Why" of history, has been left out of this discussion although I am not unconscious that it looms in the background. The art of writing is the third half. If that list does not add up, it is because history is human behavior, not arithmetic.

The Historian as Artist

I would like to share some good news with you. I recently came back from skiing at Aspen, where on one occasion I shared the double-chair ski-lift with an advertising man from Chicago. He told me he was in charge of all copy for his firm in all media: TV, radio, *and* the printed word. On the strength of this he assured me—and I quote— that "Writing is coming back. *Books* are coming back." I cannot tell you how pleased I was, and I knew you would be too.

Now that we know that the future is safe for writing, I want to talk about a particular kind of writer—the Historian—not just as historian but as artist; that is, as a creative writer on the same level as the poet or novelist. What follows will sound less immodest if you will take the word "artist" in the way I think of it, not as a form of praise but as a category, like clerk or laborer or actor.

Why is it generally assumed that in writing, the creative process is the exclusive property of poets and novelists? I would like to suggest that the thought applied by the historian to his subject matter can be no less creative than the imagination applied by the novelist to his. And when it comes to writing as an art, is Gibbon necessarily less of an artist in words than, let us say, Dickens? Or Winston Churchill less so than William Faulkner or Sinclair Lewis?

George Macaulay Trevelyan, the late professor of modern history at Cambridge and the great champion of literary as opposed to scien-

New York Herald Tribune Book Week, March 6, 1966.

tific history, said in a famous essay on his muse that ideally history should be the exposition of facts about the past, "in their full emotional and intellectual value to a wide public by the difficult art of literature." Notice "wide public." Trevelyan always stressed writing for the general reader as opposed to writing just for fellow scholars because he knew that when you write for the public you have to be *clear* and you have to be *interesting* and these are the two criteria which make for good writing. He had no patience with the idea that only imaginative writing is literature. Novels, he pointed out, if they are bad enough, are *not* literature, while even pamphlets, if they are good enough, and he cites those of Milton, Swift, and Burke, are.

The "difficult art of literature" is well said. Trevelyan was a dirt farmer in that field and he knew. I may as well admit now that I have always *felt* like an artist when I work on a book but I did not think I ought to say so until someone else said it first (it's like waiting to be proposed to). Now that an occasional reviewer here and there has made the observation, I feel I can talk about it. I see no reason why the word should always be confined to writers of fiction and poetry while the rest of us are lumped together under that despicable term "Nonfiction"—as if we were some sort of remainder. I do not feel like a Non-something; I feel quite specific. I wish I could think of a name in place of "Nonfiction." In the hope of finding an antonym I looked up "Fiction" in Webster and found it defined as opposed to "Fact, Truth and Reality." I thought for a while of adopting FTR, standing for Fact, Truth, and Reality, as my new term, but it is awkward to use. "Writers of Reality" is the nearest I can come to what I want, but I cannot very well call us "Realtors" because that has been pre-empted —although as a matter of fact I would like to. "Real Estate," when you come to think of it, is a very fine phrase and it is exactly the sphere that writers of nonfiction deal in: the real estate of man, of human conduct. I wish we could get it back from the dealers in land. Then the categories could be poets, novelists, and realtors.

I should add that I do not entirely go along with Webster's statement that fiction is what is distinct from fact, truth, and reality because good fiction (as opposed to junk), even if it has nothing to do with fact, is usually *founded* on reality and *perceives* truth—often more truly than some historians. It is exactly this quality of perceiving truth, extracting it from irrelevant surroundings and conveying it to the reader or the viewer of a picture, which distinguishes the artist. What the artist has is an *extra* vision and an *inner* vision plus the ability to express it. He supplies a view or an understanding that the viewer or reader would not have gained without the aid of the artist's creative vision. This is what Monet does in one of those shimmering rivers reflecting poplars, or El Greco in the stormy sky over Toledo, or Jane Austen compressing a whole society into Mr. and Mrs. Bennet, Lady Catherine, and Mr. Darcy. We realtors, at least those of us who aspire to write literature, do the same thing. Lytton Strachey perceived a truth about Queen Victoria and the Eminent Victorians, and the style and form which he created to portray what he saw have changed the whole approach to biography since his time. Rachel Carson perceived truth about the seashore or the silent spring, Thoreau about Walden Pond, De Tocqueville and James Bryce about America, Gibbon about Rome, Karl Marx about Capital, Carlyle about the French Revolution. Their work is based on study, observation, and accumulation of fact, but does anyone suppose that these realtors did not make use of their imagination? Certainly they did; that is what gave them their extra vision.

Trevelyan wrote that the best historian was he who combined knowledge of the evidence with "the largest intellect, the warmest human sympathy and the highest imaginative powers." The last two qualities are no different than those necessary to a great novelist. They are a necessary part of the historian's equipment because they are what enable him to *understand* the evidence he has accumulated. Imagination stretches the available facts—extrapolates from them, so to speak, thus often supplying an otherwise missing answer to the "Why" of what happened. Sympathy is essential to the understanding of motive. Without sympathy and imagination the historian can copy figures from a tax roll forever—or count them by computer as they do nowadays—but he will never know or be able to portray the people who paid the taxes.

When I say that I felt like an artist, I mean that I constantly found myself perceiving a historical truth (at least, what *I* believe to be truth) by seizing upon a suggestion; then, after careful gathering of the evidence, conveying it in turn to the reader, not by piling up a list of all the facts I have collected, which is the way of the Ph.D., but by exercising the artist's privilege of selection.

Actually the idea for *The Proud Tower* evolved in that way from a number of such perceptions. The initial impulse was a line I quoted in *The Guns of August* from Belgian Socialist poet Emile Verhaeren. After a lifetime as a pacifist dedicated to the social and humanitarian ideas which were then believed to erase national lines, he found himself filled with hatred of the German invader and disillusioned in all he had formerly believed in. And yet, as he wrote, "Since it seems to me that in this state of hatred my conscience becomes diminished, I dedicate these pages, with emotion, to the man I used to be."

I was deeply moved by this. His confession seemed to me so poignant, so evocative of a time and mood, that it decided me to try to retrieve that vanished era. It led to the last chapter in *The Proud Tower* on the Socialists, to Jaurès as the authentic Socialist, to his prophetic lines, "I summon the living, I mourn the dead," and to his assassination as the perfect and dramatically right ending for the book, both chronologically and symbolically.

Then there was Lord Ribblesdale. I owe this to *American Heritage*, which back in October 1961 published a piece on Sargent and Whistler with a handsome reproduction of the Ribblesdale portrait. In Sargent's painting Ribblesdale stared out upon the world, as I later wrote in *The Proud Tower*, "in an attitude of such natural arrogance, elegance and self-confidence as no man of a later day would ever achieve." Here too was a vanished era which came together in my mind with Verhaeren's line, "the man I used to be"—like two globules of mercury making a single mass. From that came the idea for the book. Ribblesdale, of course, was the suggestion that ultimately became the opening chapter on the Patricians. This is the reward of the artist's eye: It always leads you to the right thing.

As I see it, there are three parts to the creative process: first, the extra vision with which the artist perceives a truth and conveys it by suggestion. Second, medium of expression: language for writers, paint for painters, clay or stone for sculptors, sound expressed in musical notes for composers. Third, design or structure.

When it comes to language, nothing is more satisfying than to write a good sentence. It is no fun to write lumpishly, dully, in prose the reader must plod through like wet sand. But it is a pleasure to achieve, if one can, a clear running prose that is simple yet full of surprises. This does not just happen. It requires skill, hard work, a good ear, and continued practice, as much as it takes Heifetz to play the violin. The goals, as I have said, are clarity, interest, and aesthetic pleasure. On the first of these I would like to quote Macaulay, a great historian and great writer, who once wrote to a friend, "How little the all important art of making meaning pellucid is studied now! Hardly any popular writer except myself thinks of it."

As to structure, my own form is narrative, which is not every historian's, I may say—indeed, it is rather looked down on now by the advanced academics, but I don't mind because no one could possibly persuade me that telling a story is not the most desirable thing a writer can do. Narrative history is neither as simple nor as straightforward as it might seem. It requires arrangement, composition, planning just like a painting—Rembrandt's "Night Watch," for example. He did not fit in all those figures with certain ones in the foreground and others in back and the light falling on them just so, without much trial and error and innumerable preliminary sketches. It is the same with writing history. Although the finished result may look to the reader natural and inevitable, as if the author had only to follow the sequence of events, it is not that easy. Sometimes, to catch attention, the crucial event and the causative circumstance have to be reversed in order—the event first and the cause afterwards, as in *The Zimmermann Telegram*. One must juggle with time.

In *The Proud Tower*, for instance, the two English chapters were originally conceived as one. I divided them and placed them well apart in order to give a feeling of progression, of forward chronological movement to the book. The story of the Anarchists with their ideas and deeds set in counterpoint to each other was a problem in arrangement. The middle section of the Hague chapter on the Paris Exposition of 1900 was originally planned as a separate short centerpiece, marking the turn of the century, until I saw it as a bridge linking the two Hague Conferences, where it now seems to belong.

Structure is chiefly a problem of selection, an agonizing business because there is always more material than one can use or fit into a story. The problem is how and what to select out of all that happened without, by the very process of selection, giving an over- or underemphasis which violates truth. One cannot put in everything: The result would be a shapeless mass. The job is to achieve a narrative line without straying from the essential facts or leaving out any essential facts and without twisting the material to suit one's convenience. To do so is a temptation, but if you do it with history you invariably get tripped up by later events. I have been tempted once or twice and I know.

The most difficult task of selection I had was in the Dreyfus chapter. To try to skip over the facts about the *bordereau* and the handwriting and the forgeries—all the elements of the Case as distinct from the Affair—in order to focus instead on what happened to France and yet at the same time give the reader enough background information to enable him to understand what was going on, nearly drove me to despair. My writing slowed down to a trickle until one dreadful day when I went to my study at nine and stayed there all day in a blank coma until five, when I emerged without having written a single word. Anyone who is a writer will know how frightening that was. You feel you have come to the end of your powers; you will not finish the book; you may never write again.

There are other problems of structure peculiar to writing history: how to explain background and yet keep the story moving; how to create suspense and sustain interest in a narrative of which the outcome (like who won the war) is, to put it mildly, known. If anyone thinks this does not take creative writing, I can only say, try it.

Mr. Capote's *In Cold Blood*, for example, which deals with real life as does mine, is notable for conscious design. One can see him planning, arranging, composing his material until he achieves his perfectly balanced structure. That is art, although the hand is too obtrusive and the design too contrived to qualify as history. His method of investigation, moreover, is hardly so new as he thinks. He is merely applying to contemporary material what historians have been doing for years. Herodotus started it more than two thousand years ago, walking all over Asia Minor asking questions. Francis Parkman went to live among the Indians: hunted, traveled, and ate with them so that his pages would be steeped in understanding; E. A. Freeman, before he wrote *The Norman Conquest*, visited every spot the Conqueror had set foot on. New to these techniques, Mr. Capote is perhaps naïvely impressed by them. He uses them in a deliberate effort to raise what might be called "creative" journalism to the level of literature. A great company from Herodotus to Trevelyan have been doing the same with history for quite some time.

The Historian's Opportunity

Given the current decline of the novel and the parallel decline of poetry and the drama, public interest has turned toward the literature of actuality. It may be that in a time of widening uncertainty and chronic stress the historian's voice is the most needed, the more so as others seem inadequate, often absurd. While the reasons may be argued, the opportunity, I think, is plain for the historian to become the major interpreter in literary experience of man's role in society. The task is his to provide both the matter to satisfy the public interest and those insights into the human condition without which any reading matter is vapid.

Historians have performed this role before. Although we have no figures on readership in classical Greece and Rome, it is evident from their continuers and imitators and from later references that Herodotus, Thucydides and Xenophon, Tacitus, Polybius, Josephus, Plutarch, Livy, and the others were significant voices to their contemporaries. Since the outbreak of World War II the statistics of the book trade reflect the growing appetite of the public for biography, autobiography, science, sociology, and history—especially contemporary history.

The last category, as we have lately been made rather tiresomely aware, has its special problems, although in the long tradition of

Address, American Historical Association, December 1966. *Saturday Review*, February 25, 1967.

authorized biography a subject's family has usually found quieter means than legal recourse for retaining control over personal matters. The simple way to keep private affairs private is not to talk about them—to the authorized, or even the "hired," writer.

I do not cite as evidence of the public interest in the literature of actuality the fact that since 1964 nonfiction, so called, has outsold fiction by two to one, because that merely reflects the mass buying of cookbooks and peace-of-mind books (the two front runners), plus voyeur books—that is, the sex life of everybody else—cartoon books, and how-to books on baby care, home decorating, curing arthritis, counting calories, golf, etiquette, and that recent sleeper, avoiding probate. Non-books aside, by whatever criterion you use—number of titles published and book-club choices, hardcovers and paperbacks, new titles and reprints—the categories concerned with reality all show greater increases than fiction.

People are turning to the books of reality for a truer image of man and society than is offered by contemporary novels. To look for the reason why fictional truth has gone askew is part of the historian's task. The novelists' failure is a consequence, I believe, of the historical experience of the twentieth century, which since the First World War has been one of man's cumulative disillusionment in himself. The idea of progress was the greatest casualty of that war, and its aftermath was cynicism, confirmed by a second round of world conflict and by the implications of the Nazis' gas chambers. Then the advent into man's hands of unlimited lethal power has been topped by the frightening pressure of overpopulation, so that now we live under the weight of a weird paradox which threatens us simultaneously with too many people in the world and too much power to destroy them. Finally, we are faced with mounting evidence—in pollution of air and water, in destruction of the balance of nature, in the coming ear-shattering boom of supersonic flight—that we cannot refrain from despoiling our environment.

The experience has been enough to destroy in many of our generation their inherited belief in human goodness. Gilbert Murray found the same despair of the world overtaking the Greeks after their own period of prolonged internecine warfare and ascribed it to a sense of "the pressure of forces that man could not control or understand."

Man in the twentieth century is not a creature to be envied. Formerly he believed himself created by the divine spark. Now, bereft of that proud confidence, and contemplating his recent record and present problems, he can no longer, like the Psalmist, respect himself as "a little lower than the angels." He cannot picture himself today, as Michelangelo did on the Sistine ceiling, in the calm and noble image of Adam receiving the spark from the finger of God. Overtaken by doubt of human purpose and divine purpose, he doubts his capacity to be good or even to survive. He has lost certainty, including moral and ethical certainty, and is left with a sense of footloose purposelessness and self-disgust which literature naturally reflects. The result is what the *Times Literary Supplement* has named the "Ugh" school of fiction.

Writers who dislike their fellow men have taken over the literary world. The mainstream of their work is epitomized by the recent novel advertised as an "engrossing" treatment of "more or less random adventures touching on thievery, homosexuality, pimping, sadism, voyeurism, a gang bang." Unaccountably, drug addiction was missing. As we all know, this is not exceptional, but run-of-the-mill, and the drama, in the dreary examples that reach the stage today, does its best to keep pace. The preferred characters of current fiction are the drifters and derelicts of life in whose affairs or ultimate fate it is impossible to sustain interest. They do not excite the question that is the heart of narrative—"What happens next?"—because one cannot care what happens to them.

Perhaps the fault is not in the novelists but in the times that their characters are underlings; anti-heroes who reflect a general sense of man as victim. Perhaps the novelist today cannot honestly create a protagonist who is master of his fate and captain of his soul because man in the image of Henley seems obsolete. That man belonged to the self-confident nineteenth century, whereas the twentieth finds its exponent in losers, "beautiful losers" according to the title of a recent novel, although few seem to deserve the adjective. Oedipus was a loser and so was King Lear, but their losing was universal and profound, not pointless.

Since fiction and drama no longer present a true balance of human activity and motive, it is not to be wondered that they are losing their audience. According to a recent report from the capital, "Official Washington does not read contemporary novels" for the reason given by a sub-Cabinet officer in these words: "I try to read them and give up. Why should I spend my time on [books] . . . where the central character spends 350 pages quivering about whether to cross the street or go to the toilet?"

He has a point. Reading, which is to say writing, is the greatest gift with which man has endowed himself, by whose means we may soar on unlimited voyages. Are we to spend it picking through the garbage of humanity? Certainly the squalid and worthless, the mean and depraved are part of the human story just as dregs are part of wine, but the wine is what counts. Sexual perversion and hallucinatory drugs, as Eliot Fremont-Smith said of a recent novel, "are not what drive us, not what human history is about."

The task then devolves upon historians to tell what human history *is* about and what are the forces that *do* drive us. That is not to say that history excludes the squalid and depraved, but, being concerned as it is with reality and subject as it is to certain disciplines, it deals with these in proportion to the whole.

Historians start with a great advantage over fiction in that our characters, being public, are invested with power to affect destiny. They are the captains and kings, saints and fanatics, traitors, rogues and villains, pathfinders and explorers, thinkers and creators, even, occasionally, heroes. They are significant—if not necessarily admirable. They may be evil or corrupt or mad or stupid or even stuffed shirts, but at least, by virtue of circumstance or chance or office or character, they *matter*. They are the actors, not the acted upon, and are consequently that much more interesting.

Readers want to see man shaping his destiny or, at least, struggling with it, and this is the stuff of history. They want to know how things happened, why they happened, and particularly what they themselves have lived through, just as after a record heat or heavy snow the first thing one turns to in the morning paper is the account of yesterday's weather. And now more than ever, when man's place in the world has never been so subject to question, when "alienation" is the prevailing word, the public also hopes to find some guidelines to destiny, some pattern or meaning to our presence on this whirling globe. Whether or not, as individuals, historians believe in one pattern or another, or some of us in none, the evidence we have to present provides reassurance in showing that man has gone through his dark ages before.

When I was a young parent a series of books appeared on child behavior by Dr. Arnold Gesell and his associates of the Yale Clinic in which one discovered that the most aberrant, disturbing, or apparently psychotic behavior of one's own child turned out to be the common age pattern of the group innocently disporting itself behind Dr. Gesell's one-way observation screen. Nothing was ever so comforting. Historians provide a one-way screen on the past through which one can see man, at one time or another, committing every horror, indecency, or idiocy that he is capable of today. It is all already on his record, in kind if not in degree. I do not suggest that history can be as comforting as Gesell because the difference in degree that we face today is so great—in the speed and impact of the mechanisms we have created—that problems and dangers multiply faster than we can devise solutions. Henry Adams' law of acceleration is proving perilously true. Nevertheless, Adams' law is one of those guidelines historians have to offer. The story and study of the past, both recent and distant, will not reveal the future, but it flashes beacon lights along the way and it is a useful nostrum against despair.

Historians cannot expect to take over the leading role in literature without competition. Last summer Albert Rosenfeld, science editor of *Life*, wrote in an editorial that creative writers must turn to science to revive literature because "That is where the action is." There is a great and challenging truth in his statement. Science is formidably relevant and dynamic. "Great writing in any age," Rosenfeld continued, "casts some illumination on the major contemporary dilemmas." That is equally cogent. If science can evoke great creative writers who will do for space aeronautics or genetics or nuclear energy what Rachel Carson, for example, did for the sea around us, they will certainly win a large share of the public interest. The chief obstacle is language. Great writing in science must come from inside the discipline, and everything will depend on the rare talent which can break through the meshes of a technical vocabulary and express itself in words of common usage.

Here, too, we have a head start. Historians can—though not all do—make themselves understood in everyday English, the language in use from Chaucer to Churchill. Let us beware of the plight of our colleagues, the behavioral scientists, who by use of a proliferating jargon have painted themselves into a corner—or isolation ward—of unintelligibility. *They* know what they mean, but no one else does. Psychologists and sociologists are the farthest gone in the disease and probably incurable. Their condition might be pitied if one did not suspect it was deliberate. Their retreat into the arcane is meant to set them apart from the great unlearned, to mark their possession of some unshared, unsharable expertise. No matter how illuminating their discoveries, if the behavioral scientists write only to be understood by one another, they must come to the end of the Mandarins.

Communication, after all, is what language was invented for. If history is to share its insights with a public in need of them, it must practice communication as an art, as Gibbon did, or Parkman. History has, of course, other parts; like that other famous property, it is divisible into three: the investigative or research, the didactic or theory, and the narrated or communication. The elements that enter into communication are what I want to discuss, because history, it seems to me, is nothing if not communicated. Research provides the material, and theory a pattern of thought, but it is through communication that history is heard and understood.

At the risk of stating the obvious, it is worth remarking that success of communication depends upon the charm (I use the word in its most serious sense) of the narrative. "Writings are useless," declared Theodore Roosevelt, speaking as president of the American Historical Association in 1912, "unless they are read, and they cannot be read unless they are readable."

The history most successfully communicated, as far as the public is concerned, can in one sense be determined by the annual lists of the top ten best-sellers. Up to 1960 the all-time best-seller in history was H. G. Wells's *Outline of History*, first published in 1921, which stayed among the top ten for three years in a row and reappeared on the list in a cheaper edition in 1930. It is the only book of history up to 1960 to have sold more than two million copies—more, oddly enough, than *The Kinsey Report*. Since then the leading work in history has been William L. Shirer's *Rise and Fall of the Third Reich*, which had sold, at last report, close to three million copies in the United States alone.

These names suggest what the evidence confirms: During the 1920s and 1930s, when serious books had a better chance of reaching the top ten, the best-sellers in historical biography and straight history (as distinct from personal history and current events) included four academics, James Harvey Robinson, Charles Beard, Carl Van Doren, and James Truslow Adams three times over; and twelve non-academics, Emil Ludwig with four books, Hendrik van Loon with three, Lytton Strachey, Claude Bowers, Van Wyck Brooks, André Maurois, Francis Hackett, Stefan Zweig with two each, Will Durant, Frederick Lewis Allen, Margaret Leech, and Douglas Southall Freeman with one each. During the 1940s, when the war books took over, one academic, Arnold Toynbee (with his one-volume condensation) and one non-academic, Catherine Drinker Bowen, made the top ten. After that, except for Shirer and Frederic Morton's *The Rothschilds*, the swamping effect of the non-books begins and one has to look just beneath the top ten to the books which have been best-sellers during the course of the year without making the final list. Taking only the 1960s, these included three academics, Garrett Mattingly,

Samuel Eliot Morison, Arthur Schlesinger, Jr., and nine independent writers, Winston Churchill, Bruce Catton, Alan Moorehead, Thomas Costain, Walter Lord, Cecil Woodham-Smith, and myself with two or more books each, Stewart Holbrook and George Kennan each with one.

To be a best-seller is not necessarily a measure of quality, but it *is* a measure of communication. That the independent writers have done better is hardly surprising, since communicating is their business; they know how. To capture and hold the interest of an audience is their object, as it has been that of every storyteller since Homer. Perhaps the academic historian suffers from having a captive audience, first in the supervisor of his dissertation, then in the lecture hall. Keeping the reader turning the page has not been his primary concern.

My intention is not to exacerbate the distinction between the professional historian and the so-called amateur but to clarify its terms. "Professional"—meaning someone who has had graduate training leading to a professional degree and who practices within a university—is a valid term, but "amateur"—used to mean someone outside the university without a graduate degree—is a misnomer. Graduate training certainly establishes a difference of which I, who did not have it, am deeply aware, sometimes regretfully, sometimes thankfully. But I would prefer to recognize the difference by distinguishing between academics and independents, or between scholars and writers, rather than between professionals and amateurs, because the question is not one of degree of professionalism but which profession. The faculty people are professional historians, we outside are professional writers. Insofar as they borrow our function and we borrow their subject, each of us has a great deal to learn from the other.

An objection often made to the independents is that they are insufficiently acquainted or careless with the facts. An extreme case is the Cortez of Keats, staring at the Pacific with a wild surmise, silent upon a peak in Darien. Keats, of course, got the name wrong but the idea right. Through the power of marvelous phrasing and the exercise of a poet's imagination he immortalized a historic moment. It is possible that his vision of the man on the peak is more important, for conveying history, than the name of the man. Poets aside, historians of course should offer both. There is no need to choose between accuracy and beauty; one should be clothed in the other.

In pockets of survival there may be some historians who still retain the old notion imposed by scientific history that, as another president of the American Historical Association, Walter Prescott Webb, put it, "There is something historically naughty about good writing," that "a great gulf exists between truth and beauty and the scholar who attempts to bridge it deserves to fall in and drown," and that "the real scholar must choose truth and somehow it is better if it is made so ugly that nobody could doubt its virginity." If some still believe this, communication is not for them.

For the first element in communication, Webb gave the perfect triple criterion: a writer's belief that he has something to say, that it is worth saying, and that he can say it better than anyone else—and, he added, "not for the few but for the many." For coupled with compulsion to write must go desire to be read. No writing comes alive unless the writer sees across his desk a reader, and searches constantly for the word or phrase which will carry the image he wants the reader to see and arouse the emotion he wants him to feel. Without consciousness of a live reader, what a man writes will die on his page. Macaulay was a master of this contact with the reader. His sister Hannah cried when he read the *History of England* aloud to her. What writer could ask for more?

When it comes to content, inspiration, what Webb calls the moment of synthesis—the revealing flash of a synthesizing idea—is obviously a help. Webb describes his own moment of insight when the idea came to him that the emergence of Americans from the life of the forests to the life of the plains was of dramatic significance. Admiral Mahan had his moment when, from the study of Hannibal's failure to control sea communication with Carthage, the idea flashed on him of the influence of sea power on history. The moment is exciting but not, I think, essential. A theme may do as well to begin with as a thesis and does not involve, like the overriding theory, a creeping temptation to adjust the facts. The integrating idea or insight then evolves from the internal logic of the material, in the course of putting it together. From the gathering of the particulars one arrives at the general, at that shining grail we are all in search of, the historical generalization. To state it in advance does not seem necessary to me. The process is more persuasive and the integrating idea more convincing if the reader discovers it for himself out of the evidence laid before him.

All theses run the risk of obsolescence. The pathways of history, said the great historian of the frontier, Frederick Jackson Turner, are "strewn with the wrecks" of once known and acknowledged truths, discarded by a later generation. Revision and counter-revision roll against the shores of history as rhythmically as waves. Even so, a true inspiration or integrating idea such as Mahan's or Turner's will be valid and enlightening for its time, regardless of subsequent fortune.

Though some will debate it, intuition, too, is an aid. The intuitive historian can reach an understanding of long-past circumstance in much the same way as Democritus, the predecessor of Aristotle, arrived at the idea of the atom. His mind, mulling over observed phenomena, worked out a theory of matter as composed of an infinite number of mobile particles. The process may have been cerebral, but its impetus was intuitive. Strict disciples of history as a science may scorn the intuitive process, but that attitude comes from being more Catholic than the Pope. True scientists know its value. It is an arrow shot into the air, which will often pierce the same target that the scientific historian with his nose on the ground will take months to reach on foot.

Of all the historian's instruments, belief in the grandeur of his theme is the most compelling. Parkman, in his preface to *Montcalm and Wolfe*, describes his subject, the Seven Years' War in the American theater, as "the most momentous and far-reaching question ever brought to issue on this continent." Its outcome determined that there would be an American Revolution. "With it began a new chapter in the annals of the world." That is the way an author should feel about his subject. It ensures that no reader can put the book down.

Enthusiasm, which is not quite the same thing, has a no less leavening effect. It was recognized by Admiral Mahan, who, in the course of studying Britain's contest with Napoleon, developed a particular admiration for Pitt. "His steadfast nature," Mahan wrote, "aroused in me an enthusiasm which I did not seek to check; for I believe enthusiasm no bad spirit in which to realize history to yourself and to others."

Mahan's prescription disposes of the myth of "pure objectivity" when used to mean "without bias." As John Gunther once said of journalism, "A reporter with no bias at all would be a vegetable." If such a thing as a "purely objective" historian could exist, his work would be unreadable—like eating sawdust. Bias is only misleading when it is concealed. After reading *The Proud Tower*, a onetime member of the Asquith government scolded me in a letter for misrepresenting, as he thought, his party. "Your bias against the Liberals sticks out," he wrote. I replied that it was better to have it stick out than be hidden. It can then be taken into account. I cannot deny that I acquired a distaste for Mr. Asquith as, for other reasons, I did for

Henry Adams. There are some people in history one simply dislikes, and as long as they are not around to have their feelings hurt, I see no reason to conceal it. To take no sides in history would be as false as to take no sides in life.

A historian tries to be objective in the sense of learning as much as possible, and presenting as sympathetically as possible the motives and conditions of both sides, because to do so makes the drama more intense—and more believable. But let us not pretend that this is being without bias—as if historians were mere recorders who have given up the exercise of judgment. Bias means a *leaning* which *is* the exercise of judgment as well as a source of insight. Admittedly, it is usually helped by emotional conditioning, but that is what makes for commitment. The great historians more often than not have been passionately committed to a cause or a protagonist, as Mommsen was to Julius Caesar or Michelet to the glorious power of the people.

How commitment can generate insight and heighten communication is nowhere better shown than in G. M. Trevelyan's *Garibaldi and the Thousand*, one of the finest works of history, I think, both for investigation and narrative, produced in this century. Trevelyan's commitment to his hero is explicit. Describing the foot track from the Villa Spinola down to the embarkation point in Genoa, he writes in a footnote, "I had the honor of going down it" with a veteran of the Thousand. There is no doubt where he stands. His feeling of personal involvement led Trevelyan to visit every place connected with the Garibaldini, to walk in their footsteps, to interview those still living, until he knew the persons, terrain, view, sounds, smells, sights, distances, weather—in short, the feel—of every scene of action he was to write about.

As the Thousand marched to the Battle of Calatafimi, Trevelyan writes, "Their hearts were light with the sense that they were enviable above all Italians, that their unique campaign was poetry made real." The quality of emotion here is not, as so often, created out of the historian's feelings and foisted onto his characters, but drawn from the evidence. A footnote gives the original from a letter of one of the Garibaldini to his mother, telling her, "*Questa spedizione è così poetica.*" ("This expedition is a poetical thing.") Approaching the battle, they pass through a green valley at early morning. "In the bloom of the early Sicilian summer," Trevelyan writes, "the vale fresh from last night's rain, and sung over by the nightingale at dawn, lay ready to exhale its odors to the rising sun. Nature seemed in tune with the hearts of Garibaldi and his men." Here, too, he worked from evidence in diaries and letters that it had rained the night before and that the nightingale had sung. In these two passages he has conveyed the sense of miraculous freshness and noble enterprise which the Garibaldi expedition signalized for the liberal spirit of the nineteenth century. He could accomplish this, first, because of his quick sensitivity to source material, and, second, because he himself was in tune with the hearts of Garibaldi and his men.

Again, when Garibaldi's bugler blew reveille, "the unexpected music rang through the noonday stillness like a summons to the soul of Italy." In the verb of sound, "rang," the reader hears the bugle and in the phrase "like a summons to the soul of Italy" feels the emotion of the listener. Without knowing that he is being told, he has learned the meaning to history of the expedition.

To visit the scene before writing, even the scene of long-dead adventures, is, as it were, to start business with money in the bank. It was said of Arthur Waley, the great Orientalist who died a few months ago, that he had never visited Asia, explaining that he was content with the ideal image of the East in his imagination. For a historian that would be a risky position. On the terrain motives become clear, reasons and explanations and origins of things emerge that might otherwise have remained obscure. As a source of understanding, not to mention as a corrective for fixed ideas and mistaken notions, nothing is more valuable than knowing the scene in person, and, even more so, living the life that belongs to it. Without that intimacy Francis Parkman would not have been the master he was.

Parkman's hero was really the forest. Through experience he learned passion for it, and fear, and understood both its savagery and beauty. In those long days of intermittent blindness when he was not allowed to write, his mind must have worked over remembered visions of the forest so that they come through on the page with extra clarity. As a scout paddles across the lake in autumn, "the mossed rocks double in the watery mirror" and sumachs on the shore glow like rubies against the dark green spruce. Or the frontier settler, returning at evening, sees "a column of blue smoke rising quietly in the still evening air" and runs to find the smoldering logs of his cabin and the scalped bodies of his murdered wife and children.

Vision, knowledge, experience will not make a great writer without that extra command of language which becomes their voice. This, too, was Parkman's. When the English are about to descend the rapids of the upper St. Lawrence, they look on the river whose "reckless surges dashed and bounded in the sun, beautiful and terrible as young tigers at play." In choice of verbs and nouns and images that is a masterpiece. It is only physical description, to be sure, not a great thought, but it takes perfect command of words to express great thoughts in the event one has them.

Steeped in the documents he spent his life collecting, as he was steeped in the forest, Parkman understood the hardship and endurance, grim energy, and implacable combat that underlay the founding of the American nation. He knew the different groups of combatants as if he had lived with each, and could write with equal sympathy of French or Indians, English or colonials. Consider his seventeenth-century French courtiers, "the butterflies of Versailles . . . facing death with careless gallantry, in their small three-cornered hats, powdered perukes, embroidered coats, and lace ruffles. Their valets served them with ices in the trenches, under the cannon of besieged towns." In this case the ices in the trenches is a specimen of the historian's selective insight at work. He has chosen a vivid item to represent a larger whole. It distills an era and a culture in a detail.

Distillation is selection, and selection, as I am hardly the first to affirm, is the essence of writing history. It is the cardinal process of composition, the most difficult, the most delicate, the most fraught with error as well as art. Ability to distinguish what is significant from what is insignificant is *sine qua non*. Failure to do so means that the point of the story, not to mention the reader's interest, becomes lost in a morass of undifferentiated matter. What it requires is simply the courage and self-confidence to make choices and, above all, to leave things out.

In history as in painting, wrote the great stylist Macaulay, to put in everything achieves a less, rather than a more, truthful result. The best picture and the best history, he said, are those "which exhibit such parts of the truth as most nearly produce the effect of the whole." This is such an obvious rule that it is puzzling why so many historians today seem to practice a reverse trend toward total inclusion. Perhaps the reason is timidity: fear of being criticized for having left something out, or, by injudicious selection, of not conforming to the dominant thesis of the moment. Here the independent writer has an advantage over the professional historian: He need not be afraid of the outstuck neck.

Finally, the historian cannot do without imagination. Parkman, intense as always in his effort to make the reader "feel the situation," chose to picture the land between the Hudson and Montreal as it would look to a wild goose flying northward in spring. He sees the blue line of the river, the dark mass of forests and shimmer of lakes, the geometric lines and mounds of man-made forts, "with the flag of the Bourbons like a flickering white speck" marking Ticonderoga, and the "mountain wilderness of the Adirondacks like a stormy sea congealed." On reading that passage I feel the excitement of the Count of Monte Cristo when he opened the treasure chest. It would not be remarkable for one of us who has traveled in airplanes to think of the device of the bird's-eye view, but Parkman had never been off the ground. It was a pure effort of imagination to put himself behind the eye of the goose, to see the flag as a flickering white speck and the mountains, in that perfect phrase, as "a stormy sea congealed."

Great as this is, the more necessary use of imagination is in application to human behavior and to the action of circumstance on motive. It becomes a deliberate effort at empathy, essential if one is to understand and interpret the actions of historical figures. With antipathetic characters it is all the more necessary. The historian must put himself inside them, as Parkman put himself inside the wild goose, or as I tried to do inside Sir John French in an effort to understand the draining away of his will to fight. As soon as the effort was made, the explanation offered itself. I could feel the oppression, the weight of responsibility, the consciousness of the absence of any trained reserves to take the place of the BEF if it were lost. The effort to get *in*side is, obviously enough, a path to insight. It is the *Einfühlung* that Herder demanded of historians: the effort to "feel oneself into everything." The interpreter of the Hebrew scriptures, as he put it, must be "a shepherd with shepherds, a peasant in the midst of an agricultural people, an oriental with the primitive dwellers of the East."

To describe the historian's task today in terms of narrative history and two romantic practitioners, Parkman and Trevelyan, will seem old-fashioned at a time when interdisciplinary techniques, and horizontal subjects such as demography, and the computerized mechanics of quantification are the areas of fresh endeavor. These are methods of research, not of communication, for one reason because the people who use them tend to lose contact with ordinary language; they have caught the jargon disease. Their efforts are directed, I take it, toward uncovering underlying patterns in history and human behavior which presumably might help in understanding the past and managing the future, or even the present. Whether quantification will reveal anything which could not have been discerned by deduction is not yet clear. What seems to be missing in the studies that I have seen is a certain element of common sense.

The new techniques will, I am sure, turn up suggestive material and open avenues of thought, but they will not, I think, transform history into a science, and they can never make it literature. Events happen; but to become history they must be communicated and understood. For that, history needs writers—preferably great writers —a Trevelyan who can find and understand the *cosi poetica* in a soldier's letter and make the right use of it, a Parkman who can see and feel, and report with Shakespeare's gift of words; both, I need not add, assemblers of their own primary material. To be a really great historian, Macaulay said, "is the rarest of intellectual distinctions." For all who try, the opportunity is now and the audience awaits.

Problems in Writing the Biography of General Stilwell

I have to begin with a disclaimer. My book on Stilwell is not really a military biography even though the protagonist is a soldier. The book is really two-in-one, like an egg with two yolks: Stilwell *and* the American Experience in China, with the man chosen to represent the experience—to serve, as I stated in the Foreword, as vehicle of the theme, which is not military. The larger theme is the Sino-American experience. For purposes of making it comprehensible to the reader and writing a narrative, it needed a human vehicle. I chose Stilwell for that function, and the more I investigated, the more valid the choice appeared. He was, I think, exactly right, but the fact that he happened to be a soldier was, for my purposes, more or less incidental. It was not of the essence; it was merely the form his career took.

With regard to sources for the military aspect, I met only two problems: For the period of World War II there is too much, a problem I will return to later. The second was minor: What happened during the maneuvers of 1940–1? This was when Stilwell earned the great reputation as tactician and field commander that led to his being rated number-one corps commander in the U.S. Army and to his

Address, National Archives Conference on Research in the Second World War, June 1971. *Maryland Historian*, Fall 1971.

being selected after Pearl Harbor for the first overseas command of the war. Maneuvers do not seem to be a very well-documented subject; in fact, for public affairs of the time they have the unique distinction of being *under*-documented. Yet as Stilwell's biographer I obviously had to find out what the maneuvers demonstrated. It is not enough to know the result; one wants to show it happening.

This is a frequent problem in military history: One always knows the result of a battle; the difficulty is in reconstructing the course of events *during* it. It is only when the time comes to write the narrative that you discover that you really don't know what went on. I had that problem with the loss of Alsace in August 1914. In that case I never did find out enough to make it clear in my own mind. I faked it, but nobody noticed.

This time I spent endless hours searching. I read all the critiques in the *Infantry Journal*. OCMH (Office of the Chief of Military History) came up with a history of the Third Army, in which Stilwell commanded a division during the first maneuvers, but it didn't tell me anything. The best source, oddly enough, proved to be the press, which can hardly be said of it later on when the war was for real in China and Burma.

At that stage the American public was reading fairy tales, largely based on Chinese communiqués—which could teach Munchausen a thing or two. For a while, presumably on the theory that you would come nearer to the truth if you got out of Asia altogether, the *New York Times* covered the Burma campaign from London! The whole fairy tale of the Chinese war effort became in itself a factor of history because the attitudes and myths it created influenced our policy—but that is another story.

It has led me, however, to the proposition that the press might do well never to publish anything its reporters have not personally witnessed. It would eschew all communiqués, press releases, canned speeches. Just imagine! The news without press releases! We would be reading what happened, not what someone wants us to think happened—it might even be, on some delightful day, nothing at all. I proposed this once to Turner Catledge when the *Times* published a report about an alleged Israeli air raid which Cairo said killed fifty civilians while Tel Aviv said no planes had left the ground. Why not send a reporter to the spot, I asked Mr. Catledge; why bother to print the communiqué and the denial at all? He said something about being a paper of record, but I don't see much point in putting into the record something that may never have taken place, just because some propaganda office has put it into a communiqué. That is simply being a sucker. Communiqués have about as much relation to what actually happens as astrology has to the real science of the stars.

To get back to the maneuvers, the best account of all I found in a press-clipping book kept by the Stilwell family, which was a mine of wonderful things you never would find in a paper of record, but suffered from the disability that neither date nor name of newspaper was supplied for any of the clippings. Needless to say, the scrapbook was, to put it gently, a nightmare to the researcher.

From the point of view of World War II historians, my research was characterized by two unorthodoxies: no clearance and no tape-recorder. As regards the first, I may say that when I first opened relations with the Pentagon I dutifully applied for clearance as I was told to do, had myself fingerprinted, and filled out a questionnaire as long as a Chinese scroll painting—two, in fact: one for the Department of Defense and one for the State Department, though I can't say I was happy with the thought that I would have to submit notes on classified material, *and* the finished manuscript, for official sanction. The more I thought about it, the less the prospect pleased. In the meantime, while the bureaucratic mills were grinding, I was working on the Stilwell papers in the family home at Carmel and in the Hoover Library, where Stilwell's World War II papers were deposited. At some point *after* Hoover acquired them, the Army got to thinking about it, and had gone through the deposit and removed the more "sensitive" (if that's the word) of the classified reports, helpfully leaving a blank sheet of white paper in each place as mute token of its passage. This was not as frustrating as might be supposed, since I discovered that duplicates of the removed material remained in the Carmel files. With access to the Stilwell archive and other private collections, and with the amazingly thorough research and documentation by my predecessors, Riley Sunderland and Charles F. Romanus in the military and Herbert Feis in the diplomatic field, and with the publication of the Foreign Relations volumes on China through 1944, what did I need clearance for?

A lawyer who had been consulted on another matter relating to the book was emphatically opposed to my using any clearance that would require submission of the manuscript. By this time, six months after application, owing either to the murkiness of my past or to bureaucratic torpor (I am not sure which), the clearance had not yet come through. The question was, how does one stop a process even if it is not producing anything? The lawyer advised that I simply write to the Adjutant General and ask that my request be canceled on the grounds that I no longer needed it, which was accordingly done, taking a load off my mind. Subsequently, whenever I came across reference to a document I wanted to see for myself, I would write to the very obliging people in the Military Division here at the Archives or at OCMH, and ask if such-and-such a document could be declassified. In all except one instance, I think, it could. In some cases, for example the episode of Colonel McHugh's intervention through Secretary Knox to have Stilwell recalled that so enraged General Marshall, I was able to establish the facts through the simple expedient of going to the private source, in this case the McHugh papers at Cornell, where the top-secret letter to Knox is quietly and innocently—and openly—resting. So much for clearance; it is over-rated.

As to not making a tape-recording of my interviews with participants, I can only say that a machine makes me quail. This may have something to do with being female. A woman is accustomed to entering upon a conversation as a personal thing, even with a stranger—perhaps more so with a stranger—and I can't imagine myself plunking a machine down in front of someone and saying, "Now, talk." Besides, I am quite certain I would not know how to make it work. So I took along a notebook instead, one that fitted into my pocketbook and so was always handy for planned or unplanned need. The loose-leaf pages, being the same size as my index cards, could be filed conveniently along with the other research material.

Interviews, of course, proved some of my most useful sources, but I have told all about that in a speech to the Oral History conference two years ago, and as I have a horror of old speeches, I won't repeat it here. There is one aspect, however, which I was uneasily aware of all along but more acutely since publication, and that is all the associates of Stilwell whom I did *not* talk to. I have now had innumerable letters from CBI (China-Burma-India) veterans and old China hands, some with anecdotes or phrases or bits and pieces of information which I could have used, but none, I think, or only one, that would have changed my thinking.

An incomparable and, I think, indispensable source for historians of World War II is film. I don't mean merely for illustrations but for physical description, for the realities of place and people that one cannot get any other way, and for flashes of insight and understanding through visual means. I think I learned more about Chinese propaganda from a film of the military parade staged for Wendell Willkie in Chungking, and more about Stilwell from a film showing him lying in the dust next to a Chinese soldier at the Ramgarh training ground and demonstrating how to handle a rifle, than I could have any other way. There is a room upstairs in this institution where one can happily spend days among the reels, learning and learning.

On the same principle, there is nothing like research on the spot, but that of course, in the pre-Ping-Pong days, was denied me. As the next best thing, I went to Hongkong and Taiwan to get a feeling of Chineseness and to interview a group of Chinese veterans of the 38th Division who fought under Stilwell. Though not on the mainland, these visits were productive of insights: for instance, into the problem created by the Chinese considering it impolite to say No. I knew this caused Stilwell all kinds of agony, but I never realized how much until the wife of an American officer in Taiwan told me of her difficulty in giving official dinner parties because the Chinese always accepted whether or not they intended to come. She never knew how much food to order or how many places to set. It is equally difficult to conduct a war if your divisional commanders say Yes, they will be ready for action at a time and place, and fail to show up.

So much for research. I would rather talk about the problems of writing, not only because they interest me more but because the average layman underrates writing and is overimpressed by research. People are always saying to me in awed tones, "Think of all the *research* you must have done!" as if this were the hard part. It is not; writing, being a creative process, is much harder and takes twice as long.

The form I use is narrative because that is what comes naturally to me. There is of course another equally important and valid form of history which is written for the purpose of putting the material and the author's conclusions on the record. Such an author is less concerned with communicating than with establishing the facts. He is historian first and writer second, if at all, whereas I am a writer first whose subject is history, and whose purpose is communication. I am very conscious of the reader as a listener whose attention must be held if he is not to wander away. In my mind is a picture of Kipling's itinerant storyteller of India, with his rice bowl, who tells tales of ancient romance and legend to a circle of villagers by firelight. If he sees figures drifting away from the edge of the circle in the darkness, and his audience thinning out, he knows his rice bowl will be meagerly filled. He must hold his listeners in order to eat. I feel just as urgent a connection with the reader.

As a form, narrative has an inherent validity because it is the key to the problem of causation. Events do not happen in categories— economic, intellectual, military—they happen in sequence: When they are arranged in sequence as strictly as possible, down to the week and day, sometimes even time of day, cause and effect which may have been previously obscure will come clear. However, it is not always possible to narrate everything in straight consecutive sequence because there are always times when events are taking place simultaneously in separate places. In August 1914 the developments leading to the Battle of the Frontiers on the Western front and to the Battle of Tannenberg on the Eastern front were unfolding at the same time, putting the narrator in a quandary. The same problem was present with Stilwell when the accelerating deterioration and the launching of the last Japanese offensive took place in China while he was leading the return campaign through Burma. To break off events in one place in order to take up what is happening elsewhere ruins dramatic tension and only accomplishes utter confusion in the mind of the reader—even though that's the way things happen in reality. One has to manipulate reality just a little and carry events through to a natural climax on one scene before moving to the other.

In organization, however, if not always in the finished product, chronology remains the spine. When I started writing *The Guns of August* I planned to begin with the guns going off so people should not think this was yet another book about diplomatic origins—Sarajevo and All That. I had worked out an intricate arrangement of four chapters in which war opened in each country and was followed by an internal flashback in each to explain the background. It was as beautifully designed as a Bach fugue, but when I had finished these chapters my editor didn't know what to make of them. On rereading them, neither did I. He suggested trying it chronologically. This was so simple that I had thought it inartistic, but when the flashbacks were lifted out and put first where they belonged, behold, the result read as simply and naturally as if it had been ordained. I have avoided razzle-dazzle arrangements ever since.

With each book, one encounters new problems of organization and presentation. Obviously the dual theme of *Stilwell*—the biography of a man and the relationship of two countries—was a major difficulty throughout, but it was my choice, and peculiar to this book, so I can't generalize from it—except to say "never again." Every time I started a new chapter I felt like Jacob wrestling with the angel all through the night. Although it was hard work, the dual theme was justified, I think, because the figure of Stilwell as a continuing focus supplies human interest and drama, while the over-all Sino-American relationship gives the subject importance.

The Chinese scene of the book was another problem. It meant, as I was aware all the way through, that the reader had no familiar frame of reference. If you write a book laid in Europe or America, you can count on the reader having a mental picture of the relative location of France and Germany, or of Texas and Alaska, or where the Rockies are, or the Great Lakes. Equally with people. Once introduced let us say to Francis Drake and Walter Raleigh or Robert Oppenheimer and Edward Teller, he will have no great difficulty in keeping them distinct, but what is he going to make of Sun Li-jen and Li Tsung-jen, two prominent persons in my book, or of Yen Hsi-shan and Wang Ching-wei and Wei Li-huang and Chang Tso-lin and Chang Tsung-chang and all those other triple monosyllables—not to mention the provinces: Kwangtung and Kwangsi, which adjoin each other, Kiangsu and Kiangsi, which do not, Honan and Hunan, Shensi and Shansi, and all the rest. I tried at first to avoid using these names, and to locate places in relation to the more familiar rivers and cities, but this soon proved impossible. China's provinces can no more be avoided than America's states.

Especially in an alien setting like China—but the rule should hold true for all historical writing—I try never to introduce a place name without locating it in relation to some place already mentioned, nor introduce a person without describing some attribute that will fix him in the reader's mind. People and places must be given recognizable identities, otherwise the reader flounders in a sea of unknowns; he will miss the point of this or that and sooner or later, bored by incomprehension, will drift away.

The mere parading of names without taking the trouble to locate or personify them is either simple laziness on the part of the writer or else showing-off, in which case it is no trick; anyone can do it just as anyone can double the length of his bibliography if he has a mind to. I never can understand why historians who go in for this name-dropping make themselves great reputations. In D. W. Brogan's *France Under the Republic*, for example, one can count thirty names to a page, all faceless. Michael Howard recently established himself as a leading military historian with a book on the Franco-Prussian War which one can open at random at any page and find sentences like the following: "The Emperor put Failly's 5th Corps under his command and on 5th August while the divisions of 1st Corps concentrated around Froeschwiller and Felix Douay packed off Conseil Dumesnil's division from 7th Corps by train from Belfort, Macmahon summoned Failly to bring his corps south through the Vosges." In the next sentence we learn that Failly's units were spread between Sarreguemines and Bitche and could not be moved until relieved by troops from Rohrbach. On the same page is a sketch map which shows none of these place names. I am sure Mr. Howard knows all there is to know about the Franco-Prussian War, and his book was highly praised, but it left this reader giddy. I did not gather from it a picture of the Battle of Froeschwiller but only how *not* to describe a battle.

Another difficulty peculiar to the Stilwell book, especially to the second half, was over-documentation. Besides Stilwell's diaries and letters, bringing the scale of events down to a daily basis which I did not want, there was a mountainous mass of military and diplomatic records: messages, reports, memoranda, conference minutes, plus all the material of the China controversy—the White Papers, the Foreign Relations series, the interminable testimony before congressional investigating committees in thousand-page volumes. Ever since the advent of mechanical means of duplication there has been a multiplication of material that cannot be dealt with by less than teams of researchers. The twentieth century is likely to be the doom of the individual historian. (Actually, I do not really believe that. Though the doom seems logical, I believe somehow he will illogically survive.) Today we have the opposite problem from that of the researcher in ancient history who suffers from paucity of records and must work from coins, tombs, and artifacts. Beginning with Gutenberg, the sources expand. The nineteenth century is really the great period, with ample information of every kind, yet short of the oversupply of today.

With the appearance of the tape-recorder, a monster with the appetite of a tapeworm, we now have a new problem of what I call artificial survival. The effort needed to write a book, even of memoirs, requires discipline and perseverance which until now imposed a certain natural selection on what survived in print. But with all sorts of people being encouraged to ramble effortlessly and endlessly into a tape-recorder, prodded daily by an acolyte of Oral History, some veins of gold and a vast mass of trivia are being preserved which would otherwise have gone to dust. I should hastily add here that among the veins of gold two of the richest sources I found were two verbal interviews with General Marshall tape-recorded by Army historians in 1949. Marshall, however, was a summit figure worth recording.

As a result of over-documentation I was constantly struggling with the problems of scale in the Stilwell book. It was as if I had been a cartographer trying to draw a map on a scale of 100 miles to the inch while working from surveys detailed to a scale of one mile to the inch. Following in the track of the diary and the official documents, I would get caught up in some issue that was all-absorbing at the time, and spend days writing the developments from Tuesday to Friday when what I should have been doing was the over-all development from, say, May to November. I had to stop short and remind myself: What does this matter in the long perspective?

As a result pages went into the discard—for example, the Henry Wallace mission. Because he was Vice-President, Wallace's visit and conversations with Chiang Kai-shek assumed enormous importance at the time and blew up a swirl of passions, intrigues, and, of course, prolific reports by everyone for miles around. The path of research widened out like the mouth of the Yangtse and the narration likewise in its wake. I had an uncomfortable feeling, however, that something was wrong. Then one day someone asked me what actually had been the significance of the Wallace mission and I heard myself answering, "None." It had really had no effect on the course of events one way or another.

Because of all the quotable reports it spawned, this affair was a good example of the bewitching effect of diplomatic documents. An episode like the Wallace mission exercises the same effect as Everest on Mallory. You write it because it is there. Then it turns out not to mean anything. It would have been false to history to leave out the Wallace mission altogether, so I condensed it as much as I could, even at the cost of cutting a wonderful characterization of Wallace by a man who said, "Henry would cut off his right hand for the sake of an idea—and yours too for that matter." I hated to let that go, but since Wallace no longer appeared as a personality, it no longer belonged.

The larger scale cannot be achieved by blithely skipping over whole episodes or chunks of time; it requires condensing, which is the hardest work I know, and selection, which is the most delicate. Selection is everything; it is the test of the historian. The end product, after all, consists of what the historian has chosen to put in, as well as chosen to leave out. Simply to put in everything is easy—and safe— and results in one of those 900-page jobs in which the writer has abdicated and left all the work to the reader.

Selection is the task of distinguishing the significant from the insignificant. It must be honest, that is, true to the circumstances, and fair, that is, truly representative of the whole, never loaded. It can be used to reveal large meaning in a small sample. As Robert Frost said, "The artist needs only a sample." At Chiang Kai-shek's residence the glimpse of secret-service boots peeking below red curtains, which I took from someone who was present, was a tiny selection that bespoke a whole atmosphere. Likewise the letters of Colonel Carlson to President Roosevelt (which, incidentally, have not before been printed) crystallized, I think, the American idealized view of China at the time.

One must resist the selection that does too much. By that I mean an item or incident which, by the fact of being made part of the narrative, appears representative and leaves the reader with an impression that may not be entirely justified. The author wields tremendous influence in this way which no one superintends but his own conscience.

I remember facing one such choice at the climax of the debacle in Burma when Stilwell was trying desperately to organize transport and food for the retreat before it collapsed into chaos. The Chinese general who was Chiang Kai-shek's personal liaison officer could not be found because, as it happened, he was elsewhere engaged in organizing the retreat to China of a Rolls-Royce which he had delightedly acquired from the British Governor-General in trade for two jeeps. I intended to cap this incident with an aphorism I had picked up from the warlord years in the 1920s: "In Chinese warfare commanding officers have never been known to retire poor." While that may have been reasonably true, it would have left American readers with the impression that all Chinese generals were venal—which is true only in American terms. I am not an authority on China, but I know enough to know that it would be quite false to write about China in the framework of Western values. So I took out the aphorism and the Rolls-Royce too. This illustrates the reasoning behind a negative selection.

I seem to be giving you chiefly examples of what I left out, and this reflects what was a constant struggle. I made a vow when I started that I would keep the finished book under 500 pages, and in the course of that effort I discarded or radically pruned everything I thought could be spared or that was not germane to my main theme. I missed my goal by 51 pages, but it was not for lack of trying.

Which brings me to another working principle: Do not argue the evidence in front of the reader. The author's thought processes have no place in the narrative. One should resolve one's doubts, examine conflicting evidence, and determine motives behind the scenes, and carry on any disputes with one's sources in the reference notes, not in the text. For one thing, this keeps the author invisible and the less his presence is felt, the greater is the reader's sense of immediacy to the events. For another thing, by eliminating discussion one establishes a tone of this-is-the-way-it-was which the reader quickly accepts. He does not want to be bothered by a lot of maybes and perhapses, on-the-one-hand and on-the-other-hand; he wants to follow along with the action, feeling confident this was the way things happened.

In order to identify with the period it is also essential to eliminate hindsight. I try not to refer to anything not known at the time. According to Emerson's rule, every scripture is entitled to be read in the light of the circumstances that brought it forth. To understand the choices open to people of another time, one must limit oneself to what they knew; see the past in its own clothes, as it were, not in ours. To me this is an absolute, although I realize it is one that many historians would fiercely dispute. According to their view, History is properly the interpretation of past events in terms of their consequences, and in the light shed upon them by present knowledge and present values. The history of Kuomintang China, according to this school, is told in the light of the ultimate Communist triumph, although in fact no policy-maker of the 1930s ever seriously considered that within ten or fifteen years China would be ruled by the Communists. An account told in the light of Now must be false to the past, as I see it, whereas the other school maintains that the view from inside the past results in a false judgment for today. The difference is one of philosophic stance and is unlikely to be resolved.

In closing I may say that though I do not think of myself as a military historian, I agree on the need for military history, if only to bring home to the general public that conflict has been a central theme in the human story from pre-history to the present. Except for specialist studies, military history should be treated, I think, not as a separate category, but along with political, economic, and intellectual history, as part of a whole whose object is to exhibit what a given society was like at a given time. That object, it seems to me, should be the historian's purpose. That is what I tried to achieve in *The Proud Tower*, which is the reason I like it the best of my books.

The Houses of Research

To a historian libraries are food, shelter, and even muse. They are of two kinds: the library of published material—books, pamphlets, periodicals, etc.—and the archive of unpublished papers and documents. In the first category, one of the greatest is happily in my home town: the New York Public Library. In resources (not to mention problems) the NYPL has everything: every published work you need to consult on virtually any subject, besides a lot more you do not know you need because you do not know they exist until you come across them by serendipity. In the course of research extending over twenty years on subjects stretching from the Phoenicians of the Bronze Age to the music of Richard Strauss to Americans in China, there were, as I remember, only two books I asked for that the Library lacked. One was in their catalogue but could not be located, and both they were able to borrow for me.

Since most of the work on Stilwell was done in unpublished papers and interviews, I did not spend as much time at the NYPL on this book as on my others; nevertheless, at 42nd Street I made an unexpected strike of the kind that brings the occasional rare thrill in research. In this case it was a full run on microfilm of the *Sentinel*, the weekly journal of the 15th Infantry stationed in Tientsin, to which Stilwell was attached in 1926–9. These were the crucial years when the Kuomintang under Chiang Kai-shek made its bid for control of

Authors Guild Bulletin, March 1972.

China, but up to then I had found almost nothing on the views and attitudes of the American military on what was happening all around them. To my intense disappointment, after winding laboriously through the first reel, scanning every page, I found nothing of interest; the *Sentinel* might have been published at some regimental post in the heart of Kansas for all its notice of China. I was ready to send the box back, but decided as a matter of conscience to look at the second reel. There on the first page of the first issue was an article by Major Stilwell, the regiment's recognized expert on Chinese affairs, inaugurating a *series*, no less, on the personalities and issues of the civil war! His articles continued to appear each week in the *Sentinel* for more than a year, providing me with my protagonist's own judgment of events at a climactic time in which he shared.

The frightening thing was how close I had come to missing them altogether. No one among his family or former colleagues of the 15th Infantry had mentioned to me the existence of the articles; the originals had not been among his papers; and the *Sentinel* was not, of course, indexed in the *Periodical Guide*. With no clue to their existence, I might never have found them, which would have been a serious omission for Stilwell's biographer. This is the kind of thing that makes one shiver to think of what else one may be missing.

How came the 15th Infantry's journal from Tientsin to 42nd Street? It appears that a Library staff member had made a hobby of regimental histories and had acquired a file of the *Sentinel*, which the NYPL, with an admirable sense of time, place, and history, had preserved. Researchers in every field must owe the staff many debts similar to mine.

Unlike the British Museum (BM) and Bibliothèque Nationale (BN), where you cannot penetrate the mysteries of the catalogue (which is written in books and changes system whimsically, say at letter H from 1792–1920 or suddenly at Q in 1898) without the assistance of the staff, at the NYPL you can plunge ahead independently by virtue of its single over-all card catalogue.* The card catalogue, to my mind, is the supreme advantage of being an American; if there are others, they are secondary. One may acknowledge, however, certain drawbacks at 42nd Street: It does not have the marvelously mellow, protected surroundings of the circular Reading Room at the BM or of its replica under the dome of the Congres-

---

* As of the year I wrote, 1972, this was to become a bygone condition. Acquisitions since 1972 are now catalogued in printed books, and in time the entire card catalogue will be photographically reproduced in bound volumes.

sional, nor the pleasant sense of being one among a community of scholars. Although access is open at the Congressional, the drifters do not come there, no doubt because of its location on the Hill rather than in a midtown commercial area like that of the NYPL. In Europe access to the great libraries is controlled by the requirement of written application with a statement of purpose. This is hardly more than a formality in London, but in Paris you should prepare for a week's struggle with French bureaucracy, which regards every applicant as a natural object of suspicion. Supply yourself with passport, birth certificate, university diploma, your mother's marriage license, and a letter from your ambassador. If you can show your return ticket home, that will have a soothing effect.

Apart from the rather heterogeneous types who join you in the NYPL Reading Room—some to come in out of the cold, others to pursue often strange devices (once a lady sat across from me with a large cloth bag from which she extracted a variety of embossed paper napkins, colored pencils with which she decorated the napkins, envelopes into which she stuffed them, an address book which she fiercely leafed for names to write on the envelopes, stamps and a sponge to finish the process)—apart from these distractions, the chief disadvantage of the NYPL is that one cannot enter the stacks, as one can, with authorization, at the Congressional, or at Widener at Harvard (which, suffering from the universal budget squeeze, now sensibly charges outsiders for this privilege). To roam the stacks is of course the most delightful, if not the most disciplined, form of research, and the most productive of discoveries. Collected before you is all the gathered wealth on your subject. You can examine, compare, explore, and choose.

Archives are a resource whose usefulness depends on the knowledge and enthusiasm of their custodians. The searcher is helpless without them. Fortunately, archivists are a genus who seem actually to get their satisfaction from locating for you what you want. At the prototype of them all, the Public Record Office in London, which houses the documents of ten centuries, I once asked for the papers of the English delegation to the Hague Conference of 1899 and received the originals within fifteen minutes. That was another example of serendipity because they were bound in with all the letters from the public to members of the government on the subject of the Peace Conference, and the letters gave an extraordinary glimpse of public opinion at the time; they were something I would never have known to ask for.

The chief disadvantage of the PRO is gastronomical: There is no place to eat a quick lunch in Chancery Lane (or there wasn't when I was there last), and when absorbed in a pile of original papers one hates to waste time by going far afield for food. In these circumstances my solution is a small package of raisins and nuts which can be carried in one's purse and eaten surreptitiously while working. Our National Archives in Washington, the American counterpart of the PRO, suffers from the same disadvantage, except for a cafeteria in the basement; and concerning all cafeterias in American government basements the only polite comment is silence. Maybe libraries and gastronomy do not mix, except, naturally, in Paris, where one can buy a sandwich in a superlative French roll and eat it with mirabelles on a stone bench under a tree in the lovely little park of the Place Louvois outside the BN; that is, if one has arranged to do one's research in summer.

The National Archives and the Manuscript Division of the Library of Congress are our major archival collections, both of them places so seductive that, notwithstanding the nutritional handicaps, historians have been known to enter and never emerge, or at least never publish because they cannot bear to bring their research to an end.

Biography as a Prism of History

Insofar as I have used biography in my work, it has been less for the sake of the individual subject than as a vehicle for exhibiting an age, as in the case of Coucy in *A Distant Mirror*; or a country and its state of mind, as in the case of Speaker Reed and Richard Strauss in *The Proud Tower*; or a historic situation, as in the case of *Stilwell and the American Experience in China*. You might say that this somewhat roundabout approach does not qualify me for the title of biographer and you would be right. I do not think of myself as a biographer; biography is just a form I have used once or twice to encapsulate history.

I believe it to be a valid method for a number of reasons, not the least of which is that it has distinguished precedents. The National Portrait Gallery uses portraiture to exhibit history. Plutarch, the father of biography, used it for moral examples: to display the reward of duty performed, the traps of ambition, the fall of arrogance. His biographical facts and anecdotes, artistically arranged in *Parallel Lives*, were designed to delight and edify the reader while at the same time inculcating ethical principles. Every creative artist—among whom I include Plutarch and, if it is not too pretentious, myself—has the same two objects: to express his own vision and to communicate it to the reader, viewer, listener, or other consumer. (I should add that as regards the practice of history and biography, "creative" does not mean, as some think, to invent; it means to give the product artistic shape.)

Address, Symposium on the Art of Biography, National Portrait Gallery, November 14, 1978. *Telling Lives: The Biographer's Art* (Washington, D.C.: New Republic Books, 1979).

A writer will normally wish to communicate in such a way as to please and interest, if not necessarily edify, the reader. I do not think of edifying because in our epoch we tend to shy away from moral overtones, and yet I suppose I believe, if you were to pin me down, that aesthetic pleasure in good writing or in any of the arts, and increased knowledge of human conduct, that is to say of history, both have the power to edify.

As a prism of history, biography attracts and holds the reader's interest in the larger subject. People are interested in other people, in the fortunes of the individual. If I seem to stress the reader's interest rather more than the pure urge of the writer, it is because, for me, the reader is the essential other half of the writer. Between them is an indissoluble connection. If it takes two to make love or war or tennis, it likewise takes two to complete the function of the written word. I never feel my writing is born or has an independent existence until it is read. It is like a cake whose only *raison d'être* is to be eaten. Ergo, first catch your reader.

Secondly, biography is useful because it encompasses the universal in the particular. It is a focus that allows both the writer to narrow his field to manageable dimensions and the reader to more easily comprehend the subject. Given too wide a scope, the central theme wanders, becomes diffuse, and loses shape. One does not try for the whole but for what is truthfully *representative*.

Coucy, as I began to take notice of him in my early research on the fourteenth century, offered more and more facets of the needed prism. From the time his mother died in the Black Death to his own marvelously appropriate death in the culminating fiasco of knighthood that closed the century, his life was as if designed for the historian. He suppressed the peasant revolt called the Jacquerie; he married the King of England's eldest daughter, acquiring a double allegiance of great historical interest; he freed his serfs in return for due payment (in a charter that survives); he campaigned three times in Italy, conveniently at Milan, Florence, and Genoa; he commanded an army of brigand mercenaries, the worst scourge of the age, in a vain venture in Switzerland, his only failure; he picked the right year to revisit England, 1376, the year of John Wycliffe's trial, the Good Parliament, and the deathbed of the Black Prince, at which he was present; he was escort for the Emperor at all the stage plays, pageantry, and festivities during the imperial visit to Paris; he was chosen for his eloquence and tact to negotiate with the urban rebels of Paris in 1382, and at a truce parley with the English at which a member of the opposite team just happened to be Geoffrey Chaucer; he was agent or envoy to the Pope, the Duke of Brittany, and other difficult characters in delicate situations; he was a patron and friend of Froissart and owned the oldest surviving copy of the *Chronicle*; his castle was celebrated in a poem by Deschamps; he assisted at the literary competition for the *Cent Ballades*, of which his cousin, the Bastard of Coucy, was one of the authors; on the death of his father-in-law, King Edward, he returned his wife *and* the Order of the Garter to England; his daughter was "divorced at Rome by means of false witnesses" by her dissolute husband; he commanded an overseas expedition to Tunisia; he founded a monastery at Soissons; he testified at the canonization process of Pierre de Luxembourg; at age fifty he was challenged to a joust (in a letter that survives), by the Earl of Nottingham, Earl Marshal of England, twenty-three years old, as the person most fitting to confer "honor, valor, chivalry and great renown" on a young knight (though, from what I can gather, Coucy was too busy to bother with him); he was of course in the King's company at the sensational mad scene when Charles VI went out of his mind, and at the macabre "dance of the savages" afterward; it was his physician who attended the King and who later ordered his own tomb effigy as a skeleton, the first of its kind in the cult of death; finally, as "the most experienced and skillful of all the knights of France," he was a leader of the last Crusade, and on the way to death met the only medieval experience so far missing from his record—an attested miracle. In short, he supplies leads to every subject—marriage and divorce, religion, insurrection, literature, Italy, England, war, politics, and a wonderful range of the most interesting people of his time, from Pope to peasant. Among them, I may have rather reached for Catherine of Siena, but almost everyone else in the book actually at some point crossed paths with Coucy.

Once having decided upon him, the more I found out while pursuing his traces through the chronicles and genealogies, the more he offered. The study of his tempestuous dynasty dating back to the tenth century, with the adventures in law, war, and love of his ungovernable, not to say ferocious, forebears, made in itself a perfect prism of the earlier Middle Ages, which I needed for background. When I came upon the strange and marvelous ceremony of the *Rissoles* performed each year in the courtyard of Coucy-le-château, with its strands reaching back into a tangle of pagan, barbarian, feudal, and Christian sources, I knew that there in front of me was medieval society in microcosm and, as I wrote in the book, the many-layered elements of Western man.

As Coucy was a find, so for America at the turn of the twentieth century was Speaker Reed, or Czar Reed as he was called. As soon as I discovered this independent and uncompromising monument of a man, I knew I had what I wanted for the American chapter in *The Proud Tower*, a book about the forces at work in society in the last years before 1914. He was so obviously "writable"—if I may invent a word, which is against my principles—that I could not believe that, except for a routine political biography published in 1914 and an uninspired academic study in 1930, nothing had been written about him since his death in 1902. I now felt he was my personal property and became seized by the fear that someone else would surely see his possibilities and publish something in the years before my book—of which he formed only one part in eight—could appear. Novelists, I suppose, are free of this fear, but it haunts the rest of us from the moment we have found an exciting and hitherto untreated subject. Unbelievably, as it seemed to me, Reed remained invisible to others, and as soon as I had written the chapter I took the precaution of arranging with *American Heritage* to publish it separately a year before the book as a whole was completed.

Reed was an ideal focus, not least because, as an anti-Imperialist, he represented the losers of that era in our history. Usually it is the winners who capture the history books. We all know about Manifest Destiny and McKinley and Teddy Roosevelt and Admiral Mahan, but it is astonishing how much more dramatic an issue becomes if the opponents'—in this case the anti-Imperialists'—views are given equal play and the contest is told as if the outcome were still in the balance.

Though the events of the chapter are confined to less than a decade, I learned more about the ideas that formed our country than I had in all my years since first grade. Reed led, through the anti-Imperialist cause, to Samuel Gompers, E. L. Godkin, Charles Eliot Norton, William James, Charles William Eliot (and what a writable character he was!), Carl Schurz, Andrew Carnegie, Moorfield Storey, and to their attitudes and beliefs about America. All America's traditions were reflected there. Our development up to that time, and indeed since, was caught in the prism of the struggle over expansion.

In form, the piece on Reed is a biographical sketch, which is a distinct form of its own with a long literary history. As a rule such sketches are grouped in a collective volume, often by the dozen, like eggs: *The Twelve Caesars, Twelve Against the Gods, Twelve Bad Men*, and others. The advantage of the form is that one can extract the essence—the charm or drama, the historical or philosophical or other meaning—of the subject's life without having to follow him through all the callow years, the wrong turnings, and the periods in every life of no particular significance. Reed was an excellent choice for many reasons: because of his outsize and memorable appearance —he was a physical giant six foot three inches tall, weighing three hundred pounds, always dressed completely in black, with a huge clean-shaven face like a casaba melon; and, because of his quotable wit, his imposing character, his moral passion, and the tragic irony linking the two great contests of his life—one over the Silent Quorum and the other over the treaty assuming sovereignty over the Philippines. The first in its mad action was a writer's dream, and the second brought into focus the struggle of ideas at the turn of the century that marked the change from the old America to the new.

The Silent Quorum was a custom by which minority members of the House could defeat any legislation they did not like by refusing to answer "present" when called to establish a quorum for the vote. As Republican Speaker of the House, Reed had made up his mind to end once and for all the device that made a mockery of the congressional process. He succeeded in scenes, as a reporter wrote, "of such wild excitement, burning indignation, scathing denunciation and really dangerous conditions" as had never before been witnessed on the floor. Pandemonium reigned, the Democrats foamed with rage, a hundred of them were on their feet at once howling for recognition. One Representative, a diminutive former Confederate cavalry general, unable to reach the front because of the crowded aisles, came down from the rear, "leaping from desk to desk as an ibex leaps from crag to crag." The only Democrat not on his feet at this point was a huge Representative from Texas who sat in his seat significantly whetting a bowie knife on his boot.

Recalling that scene here is for me simply self-indulgence: I had such fun writing it. In the end, after five days of furious battle, Reed triumphed and succeeded in imposing a new set of voting rules that ensured that the will of the majority would thereafter govern. It was a long stride, as he said, in the direction of responsible government. Five years later, when it came to a vote on the annexation of Hawaii, and subsequently, on the treaty taking over the Philippines (which Reed as an anti-Imperialist bitterly opposed), the purpose of the

Quorum battle came to a test with inescapable moral fate, against himself. Still Speaker, he might—by summoning all his authority and manipulating every parliamentary wile of which he was the master— have stifled the vote, but if he did he would nullify the reform he had earlier won. He had to choose between his hatred of foreign conquest and his own rules. Knowing too well the value of what he had accomplished, he could make only one choice. His victory over the Silent Quorum gave the victory to the expansionist sentiment he despised.

To me it seemed a drama of classic shape and I have always thought it would make a good play if only some perceptive playwright would come forward to write it. None has, I suspect because the playwrights of our era prefer to find tragedy in the lives of little people, in pale Laura and her glass menagerie, in the death of a salesman, in loneliness crying for little Sheba to come back. Something about our time does not like the great—though doubtless pathos and frustration are as true for humanity as the theme of *The Trojan Women*.

Another find for *The Proud Tower* was Richard Strauss, who served as a prism for a view of Imperial Germany on the eve of 1914. I did not want to do the usual portrayal of Wilhelmine Germany in terms of Wilhelm II and the militarists and the Agadir Crisis and all that. The business of rewriting what is already well known holds no charm for me. I would find no stimulus to write unless I were learning something new and telling the reader something new, in content or in form. I have never understood how the English manage to interest themselves in turning out all those lives of Queen Victoria, Wellington, Cromwell, Mary Queen of Scots—the large and the hackneyed. For the writer, plowing through the material for such a book must be like sitting down every day to a meal of Cream of Wheat: no surprises.

The choice of Strauss, which meant writing familiarly of music, of which I have no special knowledge, seemed almost too challenging. The reason for it was that, since I knew myself to be frankly prejudiced against Germans, I thought that both for me and the reader it would be fresh and interesting to approach them through the best they had to offer rather than the worst; through the arts, rather than through militarism, and through the one art in which they excelled— music. The result was that I enjoyed myself. Strauss proved satisfactorily Teutonic, and his wife, with her fanatic housekeeping and screams of wrath, even more so. Like Coucy, Strauss led everywhere: through his *Zarathustra* to Nietzsche, a key to the period; through his *Salome* to *fin-de-siècle* decadence; through conductorship of the Berlin Opera to Berlin and the beer gardens and German society and the Sieges Allee with its glittering marble rows of helmeted Hohenzollerns in triumphant attitudes; to Wilhelm II in his fancy as "an art-loving prince"; to Vienna through Strauss's collaborator Von Hofmannsthal; to the brilliant explosion, as the new century opened, of Diaghilev's Russian Ballet, of the Fauves led by Matisse, the dance of Isadora Duncan, the sculpture of Rodin, the *Rite of Spring* of Stravinsky, the scandal of Nijinsky's performance as Debussy's Faun, and to all the frenzy and fecundity of that feverish eleventh hour that was seeking to express itself in emotion and art. I did not have to labor Strauss to carry out the theme; it was all in Romain Rolland's uncanny prophecy after hearing Strauss conduct *Zarathustra*: "Aha! Germany as the All-Powerful will not keep her balance for long. Nietzsche, Strauss, the Kaiser—Neroism is in the air!" Equally perceptive, the Austrian critic Hermann Bahr heard in Strauss's *Elektra* "a pride born of limitless power," a defiance of order "lured back toward chaos." Thus is biography welded to history.

The life of "Vinegar Joe" Stilwell was the nearest I have come to a formal biography, although I conceived of it from the start as a vehicle to carry the larger subject of the American experience in China. Stilwell was not a lucky find like Coucy; he was the natural and obvious choice. His career had been connected with China throughout the period of the modern Sino-American relationship from 1911, the year of the Chinese Revolution, to the penultimate year of World War II, when he was the commanding American in the China Theater. He represented, as I believe, the best that America has tried to do in Asia, and he was in himself a representative American, yet sufficiently non-typical to be a distinct and memorable individual. The peculiar thing about him is that he left a different impression on different readers; some came away from the book admiring and others rather disliking him, which only proves what every writer knows: that a certain number of readers will always find in one's book not what one has written, but what they bring to it.

Or it may be that I failed with Stilwell to achieve a firm characterization, which may reflect a certain ambivalence. I certainly admired him, and critics have said that I was, indeed, too energetically his champion. Yet I was never sure that I would have actually liked him in real life, or that he, to put it mildly, would have approved of me. Perhaps it is fortunate that, although I passed through Peking in 1935 when he was there as military attaché, we never met.

This raises the question: Who is the ideal biographer? One who has known his subject or one who has not? Boswell, I suppose, is generally credited with the most perfect biography ever written (or, rather, personal memoir, for it was not really a biography), and the other biographies that stand out over the ages are mostly those written by friends, relatives, or colleagues of the subject: Joinville's *Memoirs of Saint Louis*; Comines' *Memoirs of Louis XI*; the three monuments by sons-in-law—Tacitus' *Life of Agricola*, William Roper's *Sir Thomas More*, John Lockhart's *Life of Sir Walter Scott*; Lincoln by his two secretaries, John Nicolay and John Hay; Gladstone by his colleague Lord Morley.

Such biographers have a unique intimacy, and if in addition they are reasonably honest and perceptive, they can construct a life that those of us not acquainted with, or not contemporary with, our subject can never match. If the contemporary biographer is blessed with Boswell's genius as reporter and writer, the result may be supreme. On the other hand, he may distort, consciously or unconsciously, through access to too much information, and produce a warehouse instead of a portrait. Lockhart's work fills four thousand pages in nine volumes; Nicolay and Hay's about the same in ten volumes. Unfortunately, in the matter of superabundance, the secondary biographer of today is not far behind.

The most immediate life is, of course, autobiography or diaries, letters and autobiographical memoirs. These are the primary stuff of history: the *Confessions* of St. Augustine and of Jean Jacques Rousseau; Pepys's *Diary*; Ben Franklin's *Autobiography*; the *Memoirs* of Saint-Simon; the letters of the Marquise de Sévigné; the journals of John Evelyn, Charles Greville, and the Goncourt brothers; the *Apologia* of Cardinal Newman; and, I suppose I must add, that acme of self-conscious enterprise, the *Education of Henry Adams*. Even when tendentious or lying, these works are invaluable, but they are in a different category than biography in the sense that concerns us here.

When one tries to think of who the great secondary biographers are, no peaks stand out like the primaries. There are, of course, the four Gospels of Matthew, Mark, Luke, and John, who closely followed but were not acquainted with their subject. Alhough they tell us what we know of the life of Jesus, their motive was not so much biographical as propagandistic—a spreading of the gospel (which means good news) that the Messiah had come. Since then one may pick one's own choice: Carlyle's *Cromwell*, perhaps, Amy Kelly's *Eleanor of Aquitaine*, Sam Morison's *Christopher Columbus*, Cecil Woodham-Smith's *Florence Nightingale*, Leon Edel's *Henry James*, Justin Kaplan's *Mark Twain* and *Steffens*. With apologies to them, however, I think the primary biographers still have the edge.

I shall never be among them because it seems to me that the historian—whether or not the biographer—needs distance. It has once or twice been proposed to me that I write a biography of my grandfather, Henry Morgenthau, Sr., a man of great charm and accomplishment, but though I loved and revered him, I shrink from the very idea. Love and reverence are not the proper mood for a historian. I have written one short piece on a particular aspect of his life,* but I could never do more.

In the subjects I have used I am not personally involved. The nearest I came was in the course of working on the Stilwell papers, then housed in Mrs. Stilwell's home in Carmel, when I became friendly with members of the family, who were, and are, very nice people and, I am happy to say, have remained my friends even *after* publication. Friendly relations, I have to acknowledge, inevitably exerted a certain unspoken restraint on writing anything nasty about the deceased General, had I been so inclined. However, I cannot think of anything I really toned down, except possibly the foul language to be found in Stilwell's diary. Restraint in that case, however, was less concerned with the family's sensibilities than with my own. Not having been brought up with four-letter words and explicit scatological images, I found it impossible to bring myself to repeat them, and yet to omit what I then took to be an indication of character violated my conscience as a historian. I eventually worked around that problem by a generalized, if non-specific, reference to Stilwell's vocabulary. Exposed as we have all been since to the polite and delicate language of the last decade, I think now that I took the problem too seriously. I had no idea then how common and banal these words were in male conversation.

More difficult was Stilwell's horrid reference to Roosevelt as "Rubberlegs," which truly shocked me. That he was a normal Roosevelt-hater of the kind in Peter Arno's famous cartoon, "Let's go

---

* See "The Assimilationist Dilemma: Ambassador Morgenthau's Story," page 208.

to the Trans-Lux and hiss Roosevelt," and that he had a talent for inventing wicked nicknames, I knew, but to make fun of a physical infirmity seemed to me unforgivable. In a real agony over whether to include this usage or not, I conducted considerable research among people of Stilwell's vintage into the phenomenon of Roosevelt-hating, and even found an entire book on the subject. It showed that, compared to many things said in those circles, Stilwell's usage was run-of-the mill, so I put it in, though it felt like picking up a cockroach. Though minor, this episode shows how a biographer can become emotionally involved with her subject.

Whether in biography or straight history, the writer's object is—or should be—to hold the reader's attention. Scheherazade only survived because she managed to keep the sultan absorbed in her tales and wondering what would happen next. While I am not under quite such exigent pressure, I nevertheless want the reader to turn the page and keep on turning to the end. This is accomplished only when the narrative moves steadily ahead, not when it comes to a weary standstill, overloaded with every item uncovered in the research whether significant or not.

Unhappily, biography has lately been overtaken by a school that has abandoned the selective in favor of the all-inclusive. I think this development is part of the anti-excellence spirit of our time that insists on the equality of everything and is thus reduced to the theory that all facts are of equal value and that the biographer or historian should not presume to exercise judgment. To that I can only say, if he cannot exercise judgment, he should not be in the business. A portraitist does not achieve a likeness by giving sleeve buttons and shoelaces equal value to mouth and eyes.

Today in biography we are presented with the subject's life reconstructed day by day from birth to death, including every new dress or pair of pants, every juvenile poem, every journey, every letter, every loan, every accepted or rejected invitation, every telephone message, every drink at every bar. Lytton Strachey, the father of modern biography at its most readable, if not most reliable, and an artist to the last pen-stroke, would have been horrified to find himself today the subject of one of these laundry-list biographies in two very large volumes. His own motto was "The exclusion of everything that is redundant and nothing that is significant." If that advice is now ignored, Strachey's influence on psychological interpretation, on the other hand, has been followed to excess. In pre-Strachey biographies the inner life, like the two-thirds of an iceberg that is underwater, went largely unseen and uninvestigated. Since Strachey, and of course since Freud, the hidden secrets, especially if they are shady, are the biographer's goal and the reader's delight. It is argued—though I am not sure on what ground— that the public has a right to know the underside, and the biographer busies himself in penetrating private crannies and uncovering the failures and delinquencies his subject strove to conceal. Where once biography was devoted to setting up marble statues, it is now devoted, in Andre Maurois' words, to "pulling dead lions by the beard."

Having a strong instinctive sense of privacy myself, I feel no great obligation to pry into a subject's private life and reveal—unless it is clearly relevant—what he would have wanted to keep private. "What business has the public to know of Byron's wildnesses?" asked Tennyson. "He has given them fine work and they ought to be satisfied." Tennyson had a point. Do we really have to know of some famous person that he wet his pants at age six and practiced oral sex at sixty? I suppose it is quite possible that Shakespeare might have indulged in one or both of these habits. If evidence to that effect were suddenly to be found today, what then would be the truth of Shakespeare—the new finding or *King Lear?* Would the plays interest us more because we had knowledge of the author's excretory or amatory digressions?

No doubt many would unhesitatingly answer yes to that question. It seems to me, however, that insofar as biography is used to illumine history, voyeurism has no place. Happily, in the case of the greatest English writer, we know and are likely to know close to nothing about his private life. I like this vacuum, this miracle, this great floating monument of work that has no explanation at all.

II
THE
YIELD

Japan:
A Clinical Note

Ever since the Manchurian incident, Japanese foreign policy has been reaping the world's condemnation. Unlike an individual, a nation cannot admit itself in error; so Japan's only answer has been to tell herself that her judges are wrong and she is right. To strengthen this contention she has built up the belief that she acts from the purest motives which her fellow nations willfully misunderstand. The more they disapprove, the more adamant grows Japan's conviction that she is right.

This conviction of righteousness, and its corollary, the feeling of being misunderstood, find daily expression in the speech and press of the country. An example is the following passage from an editorial on the Ethiopian conflict: "There must be some reasons that justify Italy in attempting to solve the Ethiopian situation by force, but Premier Mussolini seems to have been misunderstood by the other Powers. . . . Our country went through bitter experiences as a result of such misunderstanding at the time of the Manchurian Incident. . . . The world attributed that Incident to the Japanese military and denounced it harshly. This was the outcome of lack of correct knowledge about the situation on the part of the other Powers."[1]

Not only are other nations delinquent in understanding. The next most frequent charge made against them by the Japanese is that they fail to show sincerity. An instance is the stand Japan takes concerning

Foreign Affairs, April 1936.

[1] From the *Jiji*, July 10, 1935. (This and subsequent quotations are taken from the *Japan Advertiser*'s daily translations of editorials appearing in the vernacular press. The sources given, however, refer to the Japanese paper in which the particular passage was originally printed.)

her refusal to sign a non-aggression pact with the Soviet Union. She justifies her position by carrying the attack into the enemy camp. "The Soviet Union is laboring under a mistaken notion about Japan," says an Army spokesman. "If they really want peace in the Far East they should show us the sincerity of their intentions . . . before seeking to conclude a non-aggression pact with this country."[2]

Injured innocence is an attitude which Japan frequently assumes in answer to foreign disapproval. Last summer when the League Council adopted a resolution condemning Germany's denunciation of the Versailles Treaty, the Soviet delegate suggested that a similar resolution might be applied to the Far East. A Japanese editorial on the subject stated: "It is clear that the Soviet representative had Japan in mind," and then asked blandly, "Has Japan done anything in contravention of international treaties?"[3] Needless to note, the editorial made no mention of the Nine-Power Treaty. Again, Japan points with fine indignation at one of her foreign critics who, during the Manchurian Incident, "went so far as to charge Japan with occupying Chinese territory."[4]

With its implied horror at the accusation of having occupied Chinese territory, as if it were an act of which Japan had never dreamed, a statement like the above seems to foreign readers incredible. In real bewilderment the foreigner asks himself what purpose the Japanese believe could be served by such obvious pretense. The only answer is that to the Japanese it is not a pretense. So completely divorced is the Japanese mental process from the Occidental, so devoid of what Westerners call logic, that the Japanese are able to make statements, knowing they present a false picture, yet sincerely believing them. How this is accomplished it is impossible for a foreigner to understand, much less attempt to explain. That appearances mean more than reality to the Japanese mind is the only clue the writer can provide. A fact as such means little to a Japanese; should he be forced to face certain unacceptable facts, he will cut them dead, just as we might cut an unwelcome acquaintance on the street.

Responsible for this attitude is the conception of "face." Everyone has heard of the importance of face to the Oriental, but unless one has lived in the Orient one cannot realize just how vital a part it plays;

[2] Major-General Itagaki, Assistant Chief of Staff of the Kwantung Army, quoted by Rengo News Agency in the *Japan Advertiser*, April 24, 1935.
[3] *Miyako*, April 20, 1935.
[4] *Gaiko Jiho* (*Revue Diplomatique*), August 1935.

how it enters into every word, thought, and act of existence. The appearance put upon an act, and not the act itself, gives or causes loss of face. To draw an example from ordinary life, a Japanese taxi-driver will never ask the way to an address he does not know, although he knows he is lost and you know he is lost. He prefers to cruise around helplessly for hours, using up gasoline and time at his own expense (for in Japan the fare is a flat rate and not by meter), simply for the sake of preserving the appearance of knowledge, thereby saving his face.

It is the ability to disregard facts without feeling any sense of inconsistency which allows them to make statements like the following, apropos of Japan's imminent departure from the League of Nations: "Japan has been a constant supporter of the League and her membership in it has been a powerful factor in maintaining peace in the Far East and on the Pacific."[5] It is not hypocrisy, certainly not deliberate hypocrisy, which is responsible for so strange a remark, any more than it is hypocrisy that allows a devout religious mind to believe in miracles or a child to believe in fairy tales.

Because their mental processes are not alike, Japan and the West find diplomatic intercourse a difficult matter; and what augments the difficulty is the fact that, from the foreign point of view, the Japanese have no understanding of the word "negotiate." Negotiation between two Western states is the mutual attempt to approach common ground. Its essence is compromise. But the concept of compromise is quite foreign to the Japanese. To them, diplomatic negotiation means the effort of each national representative to put over his own plan intact, the end in view being that one shall win and the others shall lose. The Naval Conference this year has been an illustration of Japan's attitude. Arriving at London with a fixed determination to obtain parity or nothing, the Japanese were not prepared to yield a single ton, regardless of what was proposed. So inflexible were their minds that they finally withdrew, having contributed nothing to the Conference and having gained nothing for themselves. The following passage from a pamphlet issued by the Navy shows how the Japanese miss the purpose of international negotiation. "Victory," it says, "is dependent on relative strength, and there is no better way to assure relative strength than to obtain absolute superiority."[6] So irrefutable is the statement that it defies comment, but it helps to reveal how

---

5 *Jiji*, January 5, 1935.
6 Translation of the pamphlet printed by the *Japan Advertiser*, May 28, 1935.

little understanding of the principle of compromise there is in the Japanese mind.

More fundamentally troublesome to Japan's foreign relations than the disability or disinclination to use Occidental tactics in the practice of diplomacy is the combination of an inferiority and a persecution complex which she feels *vis-à-vis* the West. The original cause lies in the fact that at the time the white man first set foot in the Orient, he was able to assume and hold a superior attitude; the attitude of teacher to pupil, of governor to subject. Though in Japan this unjustified relationship no longer exists, traces of its influence will not be obliterated for a long time. Sixty years ago the Japanese made up their minds that the only way to end an unequal association would be to adapt to themselves the civilization of the West. They have succeeded, but at the cost of part of their own integrity. For now the Japanese live under a system not their own; it is one which they have copied. They have become imitators, and an imitator can never feel himself the equal of an originator.

Although well concealed behind an aggressive front, the sense of inequality is always present to make Japan suspect a slight or threat in every act of her neighbors. She is, for instance, extremely sensitive to any possible slur on her position as a major power. With that in mind one realizes that her demand for naval parity is due less to strategical reasons than to a desire to have her status as a major power vindicated before the whole world.

Where her sensitivity is even more acute is in the realm of racial prejudice. Apropos of anti-Japanese activities in the United States, a Tokyo newspaper says: "A contributing factor to this agitation is racial. We, who take pride in the fact that we are one of the three greatest nations in the world, and comparable in any way with any foreign country, cannot tolerate the slight put upon us by the Americans."[7]

Although Japan's racial sensitivity has undoubtedly received provocation from without, especially from the United States, her quickness to see a threat in every act of her fellow nations is born of an inherent feeling of insecurity. This in turn generates a persecution complex which finds expression in Japan's shrill cries of "Danger!" each time one of her neighbors makes a move. For example, American naval maneuvers in the western Pacific last summer were denounced as being actuated by the desire "to dominate over"[8] Japan, and an

[7] *Miyako*, February 19, 1935.
[8] *Ibid.*, May 1, 1935.

announcement of the proposed trans-Pacific air route was described as "exposing to the whole world the United States' aggressive plans against the Far East."[9] And that perennial irritant, the naval ratio system, calls forth this characteristic comment: "It passes the understanding of the Japanese that the equality proposal, so fair and just, should have failed to find the support of Great Britain and the United States, except on the theory that the Anglo-Saxon races are bent on arresting the advance of the Yamato race."[10]

In these conditions the relations between Japan and the West will continue to present most difficult problems of diplomacy.

[9] *Nichi Nichi*, April 26, 1935.
[10] *Kokumin Domei*, February 13, 1935.

Campaign Train

"Here comes the boss now," said one of the newspapermen indifferently. It was dark on the station platform, with only a few lights shining through the rain. Reporters and photographers who were going along on the campaign tour stood around in slickers, talking in small groups. The President climbed on board in silence. There were no greetings; no one said anything. Only a Secret Service man standing on the rear platform, every muscle alert, his head turning this way and that, his eyes darting over the groups of men below as if to ward off any hostility, gave one a sense of excitement.

Our first stop the next morning was Thomas, a little mining town in West Virginia. Because of the rain none of us knew whether the President would take the drive through the hills that had been planned. Dr. Ross McIntire, his physician, came out on the platform, looked worriedly at the sky, shook his head as he held out his hand to the rain, and went in again. "Old Doc Mac doesn't like it," said one of the reporters. "He gets worried sick if the President gets his feet wet." But Roosevelt came out anyway, and as he climbed into the open car shrill cheers broke from the hillside, where people from miles around had been waiting patiently in the rain to see the President. Their faces as we drove by were all slightly agape with a look of delighted wonder at being visited by the nation's number-one celebrity.

We made five stops at mining towns, each one bigger and grimier than the last. The crowds, too, grew in size and enthusiasm till we reached Fairmont, where there were over fifteen thousand massed in the station, the streets, on the bridge and housetops. At one stop I shoved in among the crowd, hoping to hear revealing comments, but all I heard was, "There he is! No, that ain't him. Sure that's him,"

The Nation, October 10, 1936.

which was no help in predicting how West Virginia's eight electoral votes would go. No distinguished guests were in our party, but just before each station we would make a short stop and several cigar-smoking, well-fed gentlemen in thick overcoats would climb on. These, in the words of the irreverent press, were the "local boll weevils"; they would then appear on the rear platform, smiling and graciously waving to the crowd, which was so proud to see its home-state leaders traveling with the President.

At these stops the newspapermen would rush back to hear the President express his joy at seeing smoke coming out of the chimneys again and tell about that telegram he had "just received" announcing the first year in fifty-five with no national-bank failures. As he finished, everyone would clamber back on board, disappear into separate compartments, and immediately fill the train with the sound of clicking typewriters. Nearing Pittsburgh, we wondered why no release of the speech was forthcoming, the delay, some said, being to safeguard against a possible Landon spy wiring its contents on to Al Smith in New York. As a matter of fact, although there were many pro-Landon papers represented, there were very few pro-Landon journalists. One reporter told me that while eighty percent of the newspaper owners are Republican, eighty percent of the individual journalists are pro-Roosevelt. And there is the story of the still unpublished poll taken by the *Herald Tribune* of fifty editorial employees, which showed forty-four for the President. When one of the correspondents said he was going to stay on the train and listen to the Pittsburgh speech over the radio in order that the enthusiasm of the crowd might not color his story, I asked why he wanted to be so objective. "When you're a New Dealer writing for a Republican paper," he said, "you have to be as objective as hell."

Judging from the reception Pittsburgh gave to Roosevelt, Pennsylvania, which has been steadfastly Republican in every election since Lincoln, stands a good chance to go Democratic for the first time this November. Hardly listening to what the President said, the crowd cheered their heads off, blew whistles, and jangled cowbells whenever he paused for breath. Once when he said, "And during the late war we piled up a national debt of twenty-five billions," the crowd answered, "Hooray!" And when Governor Earle gave his list of Pennsylvania bad men—the Mellons, Pew, Ware—the crowd delightedly roared back "Boo!" to each name, ending with the richest, fruitiest boo of all when the Governor, drawing out the final *s* into a long hiss, cried, "the du Ponts!" As the band played "The Star-Spangled

Banner" at the end, and the President stood erect, his profile immobile and stern, he looked (consciously perhaps?) not unlike one of those heads of Washington carved out of a mountain. Just then an aide nudged him, and without looking down the President reached for his hat and folded it across his bosom in the proper gesture of patriotic reverence. An almost imperceptible move, but it made him once more a mortal. Everywhere we went, with his sumptuous voice and dominating presence, he was invariably the best speaker on the program.

In Jersey City the next morning the reporters' theme song, "Hey, Bill, what do you estimate the crowd?" was brought into full play as we drove through the incredible demonstration staged by Mayor Hague, who was making show of his loyalty to the man he called a "weakling" when he led the "Stop Roosevelt" movement in Chicago in 1932. As we crawled through the three miles of shrieking, flag-waving schoolchildren (half of Hague's turnout was below voting age), we were heckled with such remarks as "Aw, it's oney de press . . . say, ya got it pretty soft . . . gimme a lift, mister? . . . hey, mister, take my pitcha . . . ooh, lookit, a woman repawter, hiya, toots."

Back in New York no machine organization turned out the crowds which sprang up impromptu to cheer the President. Except on Park Avenue. There the sidewalks were no more crowded than usual, and the only heads peering out the windows were the servants'. It called to mind the story, which no one would swear was not apocryphal, of Knox in San Francisco. As he was driving through the streets, someone in the crowd yelled, "Hurrah for Roosevelt!" The cry was taken up and Knox began to get red in the face until a Republican committeewoman driving with him leaned over and said, "Never mind, Colonel, they're only working people."

What Madrid Reads

"And so Puss-in-Boots made the miller's son into a marquis and he married the Princess Violet Ink, the daughter of the king of that country who was called Saxofon XIII. Soon afterward the king died from having eaten a rice pudding made of pearls instead of rice and the miller's son inherited the crown. But he kept his promise to Puss-in-Boots and published a royal decree handing over the country to the workers. Then the workers of all classes formed a council and elected a president of the republic. And they gave the crown to the dentists to make gold fillings for the poor people who had lost their teeth."

So runs the Madrid, 1937, version of the old fairy tale. Little Red Riding Hood, too, has suffered a war change. She has become a worker in a chocolate factory. After her tragic end her fellow workers get together and kill the wolf and chase all his rich and powerful friends out of the country forever. But Madrid's literature has become Marxist only in spots. The Army, which through the efforts of the Cultural Militia is learning to read as fast as it is learning to fight, has an extraordinarily eclectic literary taste. At the Escorial, where the 3rd Division is in training, the soldiers' library contains a collection of works ranging from Homer to Elinor Glyn, the latter, it should be added, represented by *La Filosofía del Amor*. Among the authors in between are Plato, Sophocles, St. Augustine, Spinoza, Francis Bacon, Descartes, Machiavelli, Shakespeare, Rousseau, Kant, Victor Hugo, Dostoevski, Marx, Henry George, Freud, Jules Verne, Lenin, Gals-

The Nation, November 6, 1937.

worthy, Ortega y Gasset, Dos Passos, García Lorca, and Sinclair Lewis.

At the rear, the effect of the war on the printed word is apparent everywhere. It is dark inside the big bookstore on the Gran Via because all the windows have been blocked up with sandbags. But it is not too dark to see the blaze of civil-war literature spread out on the front tables. Because prices must meet hard times, most of it is in the form of paperbacks and pamphlets with covers that are vivid and striking: raised fists, broken chains, and bombs bursting. Guernica in flames proclaims "the torch of fascism"; Marx's beard flows over innumerable volumes; the sandaled foot of the Spanish worker crushes the swastika; Stalin's profile is uplifted to a fleet of conquering airplanes; Lenin's fist pounds the table; Durutti, the fallen Anarchist hero, summons Spanish comrades to victory. Soldiers, for the most part, are buying these books, for the trenches have been fertile soil for the growth of political curiosity.

But behind the front tables the regular stock is still displayed and still sought. You can find *El Mundo de Guermantes* of Proust, *La Montaña Mágica* of Thomas Mann, *Contrapunta* of Aldous Huxley, and the collected works of H. G. Wells, Pierre Loti, Oscar Wilde, Jack London, the last a tremendous favorite.

Secondhand books are sold in stalls and from pushcarts in the streets. As the war literature has not had time to simmer down to the secondhand stage, the civil war is ignored here as completely as if the bookstalls were in Fourth Avenue or 59th Street. You find chiefly dime novels, detective stories, and Mexican "Westerns." Edgar Wallace, E. Phillips Oppenheim, S. S. Van Dine, and James Oliver Curwood lead the field in translation. I did see two books on Russia, but they could hardly be said to indicate a trend. One, with a picture of Lenin on the cover, was *Santa Rusia* by Jacinto Benavente. The other was *Esplendor y Ocaso de los Romanof* (*Glory and Decadence of the Romanoffs*) by Ana Wyrubova, "la favorita de la Zarina."

Newsstand dealers have found it necessary to move so often because of the shelling that they no longer have permanent stalls. Newspapers and magazines are spread out on the sidewalks or on soapboxes. At first you are surprised to find the smooth-paper movie, fashion, theater, and art magazines still displayed. Looking closer, you find they are pre-war issues, and the news dealer tells you that all the smooth paper was imported and is no longer obtainable. Katharine Hepburn's portrait adorns the July 1936 issue of *Cinelandia*, the last movie magazine to be published in Spain.

In the place of the luxury reviews a number of thin but lively weeklies have sprung up, each dealing in its own fashion with some aspect of the war. Some are political, some satiric, some pictorial, some literary. The paper is sleazy, the ink smells, the print comes through on the wrong side, but the writing is vigorous. A favorite subject of the caricaturists is Queipo de Llano with his Kaiser Wilhelm mustache and his bottle. Known as the "Lion of the Subway" because of his preference for the rear guard, he is generally shown swaying uncertainly before the microphone. Parodies of his nightly broadcasts from Seville accompany the sketches.

For photographers the war is a golden opportunity. *Life* would envy the series in the rotogravure weekly *Crónico* on "Blood and Fire in the Mediterranean," dealing with the torpedoing of the British oil tanker *Woodford*. Even the comic strips have become war-minded. Weekly the terrible tale is unrolled, in rhymed couplets and color, of "Don Tadeo Bergante, Un fascista repugnante."

But if the war has permeated ninety percent of the newsprint, some pages still remain untouched by it. In one of the new weeklies, between two articles on "The Magnificent Discipline of the Republican Army" and "The New Workers' Institute in Valencia," appears a fiction serial entitled "Marion: Neither Maid, Wife, nor Widow." Marion is a pure anachronism. She hails taxis and wears evening dresses, two things that might belong to the Stone Age, so vanished are they from the Madrid of today. Even the daily papers leave a corner open to matters outside the war. The siege of Gijon, the speeches of Dr. Negrin in Geneva, the problems of evacuation and food, the machinations of the "Fifth Column," the disputes of the CNT and the UGT occupy the news and editorial columns. But you can still turn to the back page of *El Liberal* and find an agony column overflowing with ardor. "Single lady, serious, would like to become acquainted with gentleman of position and education." "Gentleman, thirty-eight, cultivated, well-employed, would like to become acquainted, object matrimony, with lady thirty to thirty-five, not tall, good-natured." That is the quality of Madrid. A year of siege and shells has shattered the surface of life, but underneath the old wheels are still turning. Life conforms to civil war where it must and clings to the old ways where it can.

"Perdicaris Alive or Raisuli Dead"

On a scented Mediterranean May evening in 1904 Mr. Ion Perdicaris, an elderly, wealthy American, was dining with his family on the vine-covered terrace of the Place of Nightingales, his summer villa in the hills above Tangier. Besides a tame demoiselle crane and two monkeys who ate orange blossoms, the family included Mrs. Perdicaris; her son by a former marriage, Cromwell Oliver Varley, who (though wearing a great name backward) was a British subject; and Mrs. Varley. Suddenly a cacophony of shrieks, commands, and barking of dogs burst from the servants' quarters at the rear. Assuming the uproar to be a further episode in the chronic feud between their German housekeeper and their French-Zouave chef, the family headed for the servants' hall to frustrate mayhem. They ran into the butler flying madly past them, pursued by a number of armed Moors whom at first they took to be their own household guards. Astonishingly, these persons fell upon the two gentlemen, bound them, clubbed two of the servants with their gunstocks, knocked Mrs. Varley to the floor, drew a knife against Varley's throat when he struggled toward his wife, dragged off the housekeeper, who was screaming into the telephone, "Robbers! Help!," cut the wire, and

American Heritage, August 1959.

shoved their captives out of the house with guns pressed in their backs.

Waiting at the villa's gate was a handsome, black-bearded Moor with blazing eyes and a Greek profile, who, raising his arm in a theatrical gesture, announced in the tones of Henry Irving playing King Lear, "I am the Raisuli!" Awed, Perdicaris and Varley knew they stood face to face with the renowned Berber chief, lord of the Rif and last of the Barbary pirates, whose personal struggle for power against his nominal overlord, the Sultan of Morocco, periodically erupted over Tangier in raids, rapine, and interesting varieties of pillage. He now ordered his prisoners hoisted onto their horses and, thoughtfully stealing Perdicaris' best mount, a black stallion, for himself, fired the signal for departure. The bandit cavalcade, in a mad confusion of shouts, shots, rearing horses, and trampled bodies, scrambled off down the rocky hillside, avoiding the road, and disappeared into the night in the general direction of the Atlas Mountains.

A moment later Samuel R. Gummere, United States Consul General, was interrupted at dinner by the telephone operator, who passed on the alarm from the villa. After a hasty visit to the scene of the outrage, where he ascertained the facts, assuaged the hysterical ladies, and posted guards, Gummere returned to confer with his colleague Sir Arthur Nicolson, the British Minister. Both envoys saw alarming prospects of danger to all foreigners in Morocco as the result of Raisuli's latest pounce.

Morocco's already anarchic affairs had just been thrown into even greater turmoil by the month-old Anglo-French entente. Under this arrangement England, in exchange for a free hand in Egypt, had given France a free hand in Morocco, much to the annoyance of all Moroccans. The Sultan, Abdul-Aziz, was a well-meaning but helpless young man uneasily balanced on the shaky throne of the last independent Moslem country west of Constantinople. He was a puppet of a corrupt clique headed by Ben Sliman, the able and wicked old Grand Vizier. To keep his young master harmlessly occupied while he kept the reins, not to mention the funds, of government in his own hands, Ben Sliman taught the Sultan a taste for, and indulged him in all manner of, extravagant luxuries of foreign manufacture. But Abdul-Aziz's tastes got out of bounds. Not content with innumerable bicycles, six hundred cameras, twenty-five grand pianos, and a gold automobile (though there were no roads), he wanted Western reforms to go with them. These, requiring foreign loans, willingly supplied by the French, opened the age-old avenue of foreign penetration.

The Sultan's Western tastes and Western debts roused resentment among his fanatic tribes. Rebellions and risings had kept the country in strife for some years past, and European rivalries complicated the chaos. France, already deep in Algeria, was pressing against Morocco's borders. Spain had special interests along the Mediterranean coast. Germany was eyeing Morocco for commercial opportunities and as a convenient site for naval coaling bases. England, eyeing Germany, determined to patch up old feuds with France and had just signed the entente in April. The Moroccan government, embittered by what it considered England's betrayal, hating France, harassed by rebellion, tottering on the brink of bankruptcy, had yet one more scourge to suffer. This was the Sherif Mulai Ahmed ibn-Muhammed er Raisuli, who now seized his moment. To show up the Sultan's weakness, proportionately increase his own prestige, and extract political concessions as ransom, he kidnapped the prominent American resident Mr. Perdicaris.

"Situation serious," telegraphed Gummere to the State Department on May 19. "Request man-of-war to enforce demands." No request could have been more relished by President Theodore Roosevelt. Not yet forty-six, bursting with vigor, he delighted to make the Navy the vehicle of his exuberant view of national policy. At the moment of Perdicaris' kidnapping he faced, within the next month, a nominating convention that could give him what he most coveted: a chance to be elected President "in my own right." Although there was no possibility of the convention's nominating anyone else, Roosevelt knew it would be dominated by professional politicians and standpatters who were unanimous in their distaste for "that damned cowboy," as their late revered leader, Mark Hanna, had called him. The prospect did not intimidate Roosevelt. "The President," said his great friend Ambassador Jean Jules Jusserand of France, "is in his best mood. He is always in his best mood." The President promptly ordered to Morocco not one warship but four, the entire South Atlantic Squadron—due shortly to coal at Tenerife in the Canaries, where it could receive its orders to proceed at once to Tangier. Roosevelt knew it to be under the command of a man exactly suited to the circumstances, Admiral French Ensor Chadwick, a decorated veteran of the Battle of Santiago and, like Roosevelt, an ardent disciple of Admiral Alfred Thayer Mahan's strenuous theories of naval instrumentality.

Roosevelt's second in foreign policy was that melancholy and cultivated gentleman and wit, John Hay, who had been Lincoln's private secretary, wanted only to be a poet, and was, often to his own disgust, Secretary of State. On the day of the kidnapping he was absent, delivering a speech at the St. Louis Fair. His subordinates, however, recognized Gummere, who was senior diplomatic officer in Tangier in the absence of any American minister and had six years' experience at that post, as a man to be listened to. The victim, Perdicaris, was also a man of some repute, whose name was known in the State Department through a public crusade he had waged back in 1886–7 against certain diplomatic abuses practiced in Tangier. His associate in that battle had been Gummere himself, then a junior member of the foreign service and Perdicaris' friend and fellow townsman from Trenton, New Jersey.

"Warships will be sent to Tangier as soon as possible," the Department wired Gummere. "May be three or four days before one arrives." "Ships" in the plural was gratifying, but the promised delay was not. Gummere feared the chances of rescuing Perdicaris and Varley were slim. Nicolson gloomily concurred. They agreed that the only hope was to insist upon the Sultan's government giving in to whatever demands Raisuli might make as his price for release of his prisoners. Most inconveniently, the government was split, its Foreign Minister, Mohammed Torres, being resident at Tangier, where the foreign legations were located, while the Sultan, Grand Vizier, and court were at Fez, which was three days' journey by camel or mule into the interior. Gummere and Nicolson told Mohammed Torres they expected immediate acquiescence to Raisuli's demands, whatever these might prove to be, and dispatched their vice-consuls to Fez to impress the same view urgently upon the Sultan.

The French Minister, St. René Taillandier, did likewise, but since the Anglo-French entente was still too new to have erased old jealousies, he acted throughout the affair more or less independently. France had her own reasons for wishing to see Perdicaris and Varley safely restored as quickly as possible. Their abduction had put the foreign colony in an uproar that would soon become panic if they were not rescued. The approach of the American fleet would seem to require equal action by France as the paramount power in the area, but France was anxious to avoid a display of force. She was "very nervous," Admiral Chadwick wrote later, at the prospect of taking over "the most fanatic and troublesome eight or ten millions in the world"; she had hoped to begin her penetration as unobtrusively as possible without stirring up Moroccan feelings any further against her. Hurriedly St. René Taillandier sent off two noble mediators to

Raisuli; they were the young brother sherifs of the Wazan family, who occupied a sort of religious primacy among sherifs and whom France found it worthwhile to subsidize as her protégés.

While awaiting word from the mediators, Gummere and Nicolson anxiously conferred with an old Moroccan hand, Walter B. Harris, correspondent of the London *Times*, who had himself been kidnapped by Raisuli the year before. Raisuli had used that occasion to force the Bashaw, or local governor, of Tangier to call off a punitive expedition sent against him. This Bashaw, who played Sheriff of Nottingham to Raisuli's Robin Hood, was Raisuli's foster brother and chief hate; the two had carried on a feud ever since the Bashaw had tricked Raisuli into prison eight years before. The Bashaw sent troops to harass and tax Raisuli's tribes and burn his villages; at intervals he dispatched emissaries instructed to lure his enemy to parley. Raisuli ambushed and slaughtered the troops and returned the emissaries—or parts of them. The head of one was delivered in a basket of melons. Another came back in one piece, soaked in oil and set on fire. The eyes of another had been burned out with hot copper coins.

Despite such grisly tactics, Harris reported to Gummere and Nicolson, his late captor was a stimulating conversationalist who discoursed on philosophy in the accents of the Moorish aristocracy and denied interest in ransom for its own sake. "Men think I care about money," he had told Harris, "but, I tell you, it is only useful in politics." He had freed Harris in return for the release of his own partisans from government prisons, but since then more of these had been captured. This time Raisuli's demands would be larger and the Sultan less inclined to concede them. Sir Arthur recalled that on the last occasion Mohammed Torres had "behaved like an old brute" and shrugged off Harris' fate as being in the hands of the Lord, when in fact, as Nicolson had pointed out to him, Harris was "in the hands of a devil." Sir Arthur had suffered acutely. "I *boil*," he confessed, "to have to humiliate myself and negotiate with these miserable brigands within three hours of Gibraltar." Gummere thought sadly of his poor friend Perdicaris. "I cannot conceal from myself and the Department," he wrote that night, "that only by extremely delicate negotiations can we hope to escape from the most terrible consequences."

Back in America, the Perdicaris case provided a welcome sensation to compete in the headlines with the faraway fortunes of the Russo-Japanese War. A rich old gentleman held for ransom by a cruel but romantic brigand, the American Navy steaming to the rescue—here was personal drama more immediate than the complicated rattle of unpronounceable generals battling over unintelligible terrain. The

President's instant and energetic action on behalf of a single citizen fallen among thieves in a foreign land made Perdicaris a symbol of America's new role on the world stage.

The man himself was oddly cast for the part. Digging up all available information, the press discovered that he was the son of Gregory Perdicaris, a native of Greece who had become a naturalized American, taught Greek at Harvard, married a lady of property from South Carolina, made a fortune in illuminating gas, settled in Trenton, New Jersey, and served for a time as United States Consul in his native land. The son entered Harvard with the class of 1860, but left in his sophomore year to study abroad. For a young man who was twenty-one at the opening of the Civil War, his history during the next few years was strangely obscure, a fact which the press ascribed to a conflict between his father, a Union sympathizer, and his mother, an ardent Confederate. Subsequently the son lived peripatetically in England, Morocco, and Trenton as a dilettante of literature and the arts, producing magazine articles, a verse play, and a painting called "Tent Life." He had built the now famous Villa Aidonia (otherwise Place of Nightingales) in 1877 and settled permanently in Tangier in 1884. There he lavishly entertained English and American friends among Oriental rugs, damasks, rare porcelains, and Moorish attendants in scarlet knee-pants and gold-embroidered jackets. He was known as a benefactor of the Moors and as a supporter of a private philanthropy that endowed Tangier with a modern sanitation system. He rode a splendid Arab steed—followed by his wife on a white mule—produced an occasional literary exercise or allegorical painting, and enjoyed an Edwardian gentleman's life amid elegant bric-a-brac.

A new telegram from the State Department desired Gummere to urge "energetic" efforts by the authorities to rescue Perdicaris and punish his captor—"if practicable," it added, with a bow to realities. Gummere replied that this was the difficulty: Raisuli, among his native crags, was immune from reprisal. The Sultan, who had a tatterdemalion army of some two thousand, had been trying vainly to capture him for years. Gummere became quite agitated. United action by the powers was necessary to prevent further abductions of Christians; Morocco was "fast drifting into a state of complete anarchy," the Sultan and his advisers were weak or worse, governors were corrupt, and very soon "neither life nor property will be safe."

On May 22 the younger Wazan returned with Raisuli's terms. They demanded everything: prompt withdrawal of government troops from the Rif; dismissal of the Bashaw of Tangier; arrest and imprisonment of certain officials who had harmed Raisuli in the past; release of Raisuli's partisans from prison; payment of an indemnity of $70,000 to be imposed personally upon the Bashaw, whose property must be sold to raise the amount; appointment of Raisuli as governor of two districts around Tangier that should be relieved of taxes and ceded to him absolutely; and, finally, safe-conduct for all Raisuli's tribesmen to come and go freely in the towns and markets.

Gummere was horrified; Mohammed Torres declared his government would never consent. Meanwhile European residents, increasingly agitated, were flocking in from outlying estates, voicing indignant protests, petitioning for a police force, guards, and gunboats. The local Moors, stimulated by Raisuli's audacity, were showing an aggressive mood. Gummere, scanning the horizon for Admiral Chadwick's smokestacks, hourly expected an outbreak. Situation "not reassuring," he wired; progress of talks "most unsatisfactory"; warship "anxiously awaited. Can it be hastened?"

The American public awaited Chadwick's arrival as eagerly as Gummere. Excitement rose when the press reported that Admiral Theodore F. Jewell, in command of the European Squadron, three days' sail behind Chadwick, would be ordered to reinforce him if the emergency continued.

Tangier received further word from the sherifs of Wazan that Raisuli had not only absolutely declined to abate his demands but had added an even more impossible condition: a British and American guarantee of fulfillment of the terms by the Moroccan government.

Knowing his government could not make itself responsible for the performance or non-performance of promises by another government, Gummere despairingly cabled the terms to Washington. As soon as he saw them, Roosevelt sent "in a hurry" for Secretary Hay (who had meanwhile returned to the capital). "I told him," wrote Hay that night in his diary, "I considered the demands of the outlaw Raisuli preposterous and the proposed guarantee of them by us and by England impossible of fulfillment." Roosevelt agreed. Two measures were decided upon and carried out within the hour: Admiral Jewell's squadron was ordered to reinforce Chadwick at Tangier, and France was officially requested to lend her good offices. (By recognizing France's special status in Morocco, this step, consciously taken, was of international significance in the train of crises that was to lead through Algeciras and Agadir to 1914.) Roosevelt and Hay felt they had done their utmost. "I hope they may not murder Mr. Perdicaris," recorded Hay none too hopefully, "but a nation cannot degrade itself to prevent ill-treatment of a citizen."

An uninhibited press told the public that in response to Raisuli's "insulting" ultimatum, "all available naval forces" in European waters were being ordered to the spot. Inspired by memory of U.S. troops chasing Aguinaldo in the Philippines, the press suggested that "if other means fail," marines could make a forced march into the interior to "bring the outlaw to book for his crimes." Such talk terrified Gummere, who knew that leathernecks would have as much chance against Berbers in the Rif as General Braddock's redcoats against Indians in the Alleghenies; and besides, the first marine ashore would simply provoke Raisuli to kill his prisoners.

On May 29 the elder Wazan brought word that Raisuli threatened to do just that if all his demands were not met in two days. Two days! This was the twentieth century, but as far as communications with Fez were concerned it might as well have been the time of the Crusades. Nevertheless Gummere and Nicolson sent couriers to meet their vice-consuls at Fez (or intercept them if they had already left) with orders to demand a new audience with the Sultan and obtain his acceptance of Raisuli's terms.

At five-thirty next morning a gray shape slid into the harbor. Gummere, awakened from a troubled sleep, heard the welcome news that Admiral Chadwick had arrived at last aboard his flagship, the *Brooklyn*. Relieved, yet worried that the military mind might display more valor than discretion, he hurried down to confer with the Admiral. In him he found a crisp and incisive officer whose quick intelligence grasped the situation at once. Chadwick agreed that the point at which to apply pressure was Mohammed Torres. Although up in the hills the brigand's patience might be wearing thin, the niceties of diplomatic protocol, plus the extra flourishes required by Moslem practice, called for an exchange of courtesy calls before business could be done. Admiral and Consul proceeded at once to wait upon the Foreign Minister, who returned the call upon the flagship that afternoon. It was a sight to see, Chadwick wrote to Hay, his royal progress through the streets, "a mass of beautiful white wool draperies, his old calves bare and his feet naked but for his yellow slippers," while "these wild fellows stoop and kiss his shoulder as he goes by."

Mohammed Torres was greeted by a salute from the flagship's guns and a review of the squadron's other three ships, which had just arrived. Unimpressed by these attentions, he continued to reject Raisuli's terms. "Situation critical," reported Chadwick.

The situation was even more critical in Washington. On June 1 an extraordinary letter reached the State Department. Its writer, one

A. H. Slocumb, a cotton broker of Fayetteville, North Carolina, said he had read with interest about the Perdicaris case and then, without warning, asked a startling question, "But is Perdicaris an American?" In the winter of 1863, Mr. Slocumb went on to say, he had been in Athens, and Perdicaris had come there "for the express purpose, as he stated, to become naturalized as a Greek citizen." His object, he had said, was to prevent confiscation by the Confederacy of some valuable property in South Carolina inherited from his mother. Mr. Slocumb could not be sure whether Perdicaris had since resumed American citizenship, but he was "positive" that Perdicaris had become a Greek subject forty years before, and he suggested that the Athens records would bear out his statement.

What blushes reddened official faces we can only imagine. Hay's diary for June 1 records that the President sent for him and Secretary of the Navy Moody "for a few words about Perdicaris," but, maddeningly discreet, Hay wrote no more. A pregnant silence of three days ensues between the Slocumb letter and the next document in the case. On June 4 the State Department queried our Minister in Athens, John B. Jackson, asking him to investigate the charge—"important if true," added the Department, facing bravely into the wind. Although Slocumb had mentioned only 1863, the telegram to Jackson asked him to search the records for the two previous years as well; apparently the Department had been making frenzied inquiries of its own during the interval. On June 7 Jackson telegraphed in reply that a person named Ion Perdicaris, described as an artist, unmarried, aged twenty-two, had indeed been naturalized as a Greek on March 19, 1862.

Posterity will never know what Roosevelt or Hay thought or said at this moment, because the archives are empty of evidence. But neither the strenuous President nor the suave Secretary of State was a man easily rattled. The game must be played out. Already Admiral Jewell's squadron of three cruisers had arrived to reinforce Chadwick, making a total of seven American warships at Tangier. America's fleet, flag, and honor were committed. Wheels had been set turning in foreign capitals. Hay had requested the good offices of France. The French Foreign Minister, Théophile Delcassé, was himself bringing pressure. A British warship, the *Prince of Wales*, had also come to Tangier. Spain wanted to know if the United States was wedging into Morocco.

And just at this juncture the Sultan's government, succumbing to French pressure, ordered Mohammed Torres to accede to all Raisuli's demands. Four days later, on June 12, a French loan to the government of Morocco was signed at Fez in the amount of 62.5 million francs, secured by the customs of all Moroccan ports. It seemed hardly a tactful moment to reveal the fraudulent claim of Mr. Perdicaris.

He was not yet out of danger, for Raisuli refused to release him before all the demands were actually met, and the authorities were proving evasive. Washington was trapped. Impossible to reveal Perdicaris' status now; equally impossible to withdraw the fleet and leave him, whom the world still supposed to be an American, at the brigand's mercy.

During the next few days suspense was kept taut by a stream of telegrams from Gummere and Chadwick reporting one impasse after another in the negotiations with Raisuli. When the Sultan balked at meeting all the terms in advance of the release, Raisuli merely raised his ante, demanding that four districts instead of two be ceded to him and returning to the idea of an Anglo-American guarantee. "You see there is no end to the insolence of this blackguard," wrote Hay in a note to the President on June 15; Roosevelt, replying the same day, agreed that we had gone "as far as we possibly can go for Perdicaris" and could now only "demand the death of those that harm him if he is harmed." He dashed off an alarming postscript: "I think it would be well to enter into negotiations with England and France looking to the possibility of an expedition to punish the brigands if Gummere's statement as to the impotence of the Sultan is true."

No further action was taken in pursuit of this proposal because Gummere's telegrams now grew cautiously hopeful; on the nineteenth he wired that all arrangements had been settled for the release to take place on the twenty-first. But on the twentieth all was off. Raisuli suspected the good faith of the government, a sentiment which Gummere and Chadwick evidently shared, for they blamed the delay on "intrigue of authorities here." Finally the exasperated Gummere telegraphed on the twenty-first that the United States position was "becoming humiliating." He asked to be empowered to deliver an ultimatum to the Moroccan government claiming an indemnity for each day's further delay, backed by a threat to land marines and seize the customs as security. Admiral Chadwick concurred in a separate telegram.

June 21 was the day the Republican National Convention met in Chicago. "There is a great deal of sullen grumbling," Roosevelt wrote that day to his son Kermit, "but they don't dare oppose me for the nomination. . . . How the election will turn out no one can tell." If a poll of Republican party leaders had been taken at any time during the past year, one newspaper estimated, it would have shown a majority opposed to Roosevelt's nomination. But the country agreed with Viscount Bryce, who said Roosevelt was the greatest President since Washington (prompting a Roosevelt friend to recall Whistler's remark when told he was the greatest painter since Velázquez: "Why drag in Velázquez?"). The country wanted Teddy and, however distasteful that fact was, the politicians saw the handwriting on the bandwagon. On the death of Mark Hanna four months before, active opposition had collapsed, and the disgruntled leaders were now arriving in Chicago prepared to register the inevitable as ungraciously as possible.

They were the more sullen because Roosevelt and his strategists, preparing against any possible slip-up, had so steamrollered and stage-managed the proceedings ahead of time that there was nothing left for the delegates to do. No scurrying, no back-room bargaining, no fights, no trades, no smoke-filled deals. *Harper's Weekly* reported an Alabama delegate's summation: "There ain't nobody who can do nothin'" and added: "It is not a Republican Convention, it is no kind of a convention; it is a roosevelt."

The resulting listlessness and pervading dullness were unfortunate. Although Elihu Root, Henry Cabot Lodge, and other hand-picked Roosevelt choices filled the key posts, most of the delegates and party professionals did not make even a pretense of enthusiasm. The ostentatious coldness of the delegation from New York, Roosevelt's home state, was such that one reporter predicted they would all go home with pneumonia. There were no bands, no parades, and for the first time in forty years there were hundreds of empty seats.

Roosevelt knew he had the nomination in his pocket, but all his life, like Lincoln, he had a haunting fear of being defeated in elections. He was worried lest the dislike and distrust of him so openly exhibited at Chicago should gather volume and explode at the ballot box. Something was needed to prick the sulks and dispel the gloom of the convention before it made a lasting impression upon the public.

At this moment came Gummere's plea for an ultimatum. Again we have no record of what went on in high councils, but President and Secretary must have agreed upon their historic answer within a matter of hours. The only relevant piece of evidence is a verbal statement made to Hay's biographer, the late Tyler Dennett, by Gaillard Hunt, who was chief of the State Department's Citizenship Bureau during the Perdicaris affair. Hunt said he showed the correspondence about Perdicaris' citizenship to Hay, who told him to show it to the President; on seeing it, the President decided to overlook the difficulty and instructed Hunt to tell Hay to send the telegram anyway, at once. No date is given for this performance, so one is left with the implication that Roosevelt was not informed of the facts until this last moment—a supposition which the present writer finds improbable.

When Roosevelt made up his mind to accomplish an objective, he did not worry too much about legality of method. Before any unusual procedure he would ask an opinion from his Attorney General, Philander Knox, but Knox rather admired Roosevelt's way of over-riding his advice. Once, when asked for his opinion, he replied, "Ah, Mr. President, why have such a beautiful action marred by any taint of legality?" Another close adviser, Admiral Mahan, when asked by Roosevelt how to solve the political problem of annexing the Hawaiian Islands, answered, "Do nothing unrighteous but . . . take the islands first and solve afterward." It may be that the problem of Perdicaris seemed susceptible of the same treatment.

The opportunity was irresistible. Every newspaperman who ever knew him testified to Roosevelt's extraordinary sense of news value, to his ability to create news, to dramatize himself to the public. He had a genius for it. "Consciously or unconsciously," said the journalist Isaac Marcosson, "he was the master press agent of all time." The risk, of course, was great, for it would be acutely embarrassing if the facts leaked out during the coming campaign. It may have been the risk itself that tempted Roosevelt, for he loved a prank and loved danger for its own sake; if he could combine danger with what William Allen White called a "frolicking intrigue," his happiness was complete.

Next day, June 22, the memorable telegram "This Government wants Perdicaris alive or Raisuli dead" flashed across the Atlantic cable over Hay's signature and was simultaneously given to the press at home. It was not an ultimatum, because Hay deliberately deprived it of meaningfulness by adding to Gummere, "Do not land marines or seize customs without Department's specific instructions." But this sentence was not allowed to spoil the effect: It was withheld from the press.

At Chicago, Uncle Joe Cannon, the salty perennial Speaker of the House, who was convention chairman, rapped with his gavel and read the telegram. The convention was electrified. Delegates sprang upon their chairs and hurrahed. Flags and handkerchiefs waved. Despite Hay's signature, everyone saw the Roosevelt teeth, cliché of a hundred cartoons, gleaming whitely behind it. "Magnificent, magnificent!" pronounced Senator Depew. "The people want an administration that will stand by its citizens, even if it takes the fleet to do it," said Representative Dwight of New York, expressing the essence of popular feeling. "Roosevelt and Hay know what they are doing," said a Kansas delegate. "Our people like courage. We'll stand for anything those two men do." "Good hot stuff and echoes my sentiments," said another delegate. The genius of its timing and phrasing, wrote a reporter, "gave the candidate the maximum benefit of the thrill that was needed." Although the public was inclined to credit authorship to Roosevelt, the Baltimore *Sun* pointed out that Mr. Hay too knew how to make the eagle scream when he wanted to. Hay's diary agreed. "My telegram to Gummere," he noted comfortably the day afterward, "had an uncalled for success. It is curious how a concise impropriety hits the public."

After nominating Roosevelt by acclamation, the convention departed in an exhilarated mood. In Morocco a settlement had been reached before receipt of the telegram. Raisuli was ready at last to return his captives. Mounted on a "great, grey charger," he personally escorted Perdicaris and Varley on the ride down from the mountains, pointing out on the way the admirable effect of pink and violet shadows cast by the rising sun on the rocks. They met the ransom party, with thirty pack mules bearing boxes of Spanish silver dollars, halfway down. Payment was made and prisoners exchanged, and Perdicaris took leave, as he afterward wrote, of "one of the most interesting and kindly-hearted native gentlemen" he had ever known, whose "singular gentleness and courtesy . . . quite endeared him to us." At nightfall, as he rode into Tangier and saw the signal lights of the American warships twinkling the news of his release, Perdicaris was overcome with patriotic emotion at "such proof of his country's solicitude for its citizens and for the honor of its flag!" Few indeed are the Americans, he wrote to Gummere in a masterpiece of understatement, "who can have appreciated as keenly as I did then what the presence of our Flag in foreign waters meant at such a moment and in such circumstances."

Only afterward, when it was all over, did the State Department inform Gummere how keen indeed was Perdicaris' cause for appreciation. "Overwhelmed with amazement" and highly indignant, Gummere extracted from Perdicaris a full, written confession of his forty-year-old secret. He admitted that he had never in ensuing years taken steps to resume American citizenship because, as he ingenuously explained, having been born an American, he disliked the idea of having to become naturalized, and so "I continued to consider myself an American citizen." Since Perdicaris perfectly understood that the American government was in no position to take action against him, his letter made no great pretension of remorse.

Perdicaris retired to England for his remaining years. Raisuli duly became governor of the Tangier districts in place of the false-hearted Bashaw. The French, in view of recent disorders, acquired the right to police Morocco (provoking the Kaiser's notorious descent upon Tangier). The Sultan, weakened and humiliated by Raisuli's triumph, was shortly dethroned by a brother. Gummere was officially congratulated and subsequently appointed minister to Morocco and American delegate to the Algeciras Conference. Sir Arthur Nicolson took "a long leave of absence," the Wazan brothers received handsomely decorated Winchester rifles with suitable inscriptions from Mr. Roosevelt, Hay received the Grand Cross of the Legion of Honor, and Roosevelt was elected in November by the largest popular majority ever given to a presidential candidate.

"As to Paregoric or is it Pericarditis," wrote Hay to Assistant Secretary Adee on September 3, "it is a bad business. We must keep it excessively confidential for the present." They succeeded. Officials in the know held their breath during the campaign, but no hint leaked out either then or during the remaining year of Hay's lifetime or during Roosevelt's lifetime. As a result of the episode, Roosevelt's administration proposed a new citizenship law which was introduced in Congress in 1905 and enacted in 1907, but the name of the errant gentleman who inspired it was never mentioned during the debates. The truth about Perdicaris remained unknown to the public until 1933, when Tyler Dennett gave it away—in one paragraph in his biography of John Hay.

The Final Solution

Review of *Justice in Jerusalem* by Gideon Hausner

Not again! Are we never to have done with it? Never be allowed to forget? Once more those six million dead? We have had the pictures of the naked emaciated corpses, the accounts of concentration-camp survivors, the Nuremberg testimony, the Warsaw Ghetto, the genocide debates, the filmed documentaries, the Eichmann trial and its reverberating controversies. Must we now go over it all again? Faced with this vast and terrifying, yet noble book by Gideon Hausner, former Attorney General of Israel and prosecutor of the Eichmann trial, the answer is an inescapable "Yes."

Hausner has compiled the record not only of the trial and its protagonist but of the total German program for the extermination of the Jews, plus a third record in Chapter 12 dealing with what the Powers did not do. Like the unwilling Wedding Guest, we must listen whether we want to or not, for Mr. Hausner's book has to do not simply with Germans and Jews, with war crimes and unimaginable atrocities but, like the tale of the Ancient Mariner, fundamentally with the human soul. We must listen because what we are confronting here is the soul of man in the twentieth century.

The "Terrible Twentieth," it was called by Winston Churchill. Until it opened, the idea of progress had been the most firmly held conviction of the nineteenth century. Man believed himself both improvable and improving. Then, twice in twenty-five years, or the

New York Times Book Review, May 29, 1966.

space of one generation, came the Gadarene plunge into world war, accompanied the second time by the Germans' actual physical killing —pursued with fanatic zeal for more than five years amidst the simultaneous demands of foreign war—of six million people in the area they occupied. For sheer size and deliberate intent, this episode of man's inhumanity to man was unprecedented. It is time to ask what was its historical significance.

A possible answer is that in vitiating our idea of human progress, the experience inflicted a moral damage upon mankind. It scarred man's image of himself horribly, with effects that society is now showing. It may be that the offense against humanity committed by the Germans and permitted by the rest of the world was such that a moral barrier like the sound barrier was broken through, with the result that man, at this moment in history, may no longer believe in his capacity to be good or in the social pattern that once contained him. Disillusioned and without certainty or sense of direction, he appears afflicted and fascinated by self-disgust, as if, having lost sight of the Delectable Mountains, he must wander joylessly in the Cities of the Plain.

This is not a proposition that can be sociologically supported within the limits of a book review. In the book itself Hausner, drawing from all the available evidence, builds up an account which shows how the implausible figure of six million was actually reached. To read the minutes of the Wannsee Conference of 1942 at which the grandiose plan for the Final Solution—extermination of Europe's Jews —was adopted, is hardly to believe the printed page. No one of the thirteen departments of the German government represented at the meeting questioned the goal, only the methods.

The developing process only becomes believable by watching it happen in these pages, and the immensity of the task suggests the numbers of Germans involved in it: lawyers to draw up the decrees, civil servants to administer them, virtually the whole of the SS to carry out the program, police and certain sections of the Army to assist them, trainmen and truck-drivers to transport the victims, clerks to keep the statistics, bank tellers to tabulate the gold teeth and wedding rings salvaged from the millions of corpses, not to mention the fortunate citizens who received Jewish property, businesses, and belongings.

Amnesia has intervened and our own is no less bland. The role of the free world in this affair, with the exception of the epic Danish rescue and the shelter offered by Sweden and Switzerland, was largely one of omission. In assembling the evidence of repeated opportunity and repeated turning away, Hausner in Chapter 12 reveals the governments of Western democracies in a conspiracy of official silence much as *The Deputy* revealed the Pope. It forces us to recognize that omission can be an act which must be taken into the final account.

Much of the material of this book has appeared before—most recently in *The Destruction of the European Jews* by Raul Hilberg and in the more polemic work of Mr. Hausner's colleague Jacob Robinson, *And the Crooked Shall Be Made Straight*—but nowhere more exhaustively. Mr. Hausner has combined hundreds of accounts by both predators and prey into a towering monument of a book. Its special quality is the reality infused into the incredible facts by the terrifying testimony of survivors. Caught up with them, the reader feels with personal immediacy what it meant to be a Jew, without recourse or exit, in Gestapo-controlled Europe.

The task of having to assemble the case against Eichmann and conduct it under the hot spotlight of world attention, often critical, clearly left Mr. Hausner a ravaged and passionate man, fired by a need to make the public know. What is regrettable is that, writing in a language not his own and ill-served by his editor, he reaches, particularly at the start, for overblown prose to express strength of feeling. This is unfortunate, as it tends to arouse resistance in the reader. However, by skipping the first two chapters, which are unnecessary, the reader will find that the deeper the author gets into his material, the more he lets it speak for itself. All one needs to know is here; the total is overwhelming.

The central and dominant figure is, of course, Lieutenant Colonel Eichmann himself, chief, under Heydrich and Himmler, of the Jewish Affairs bureau of the SS, executive arm of the Final Solution. The evidence shows him pursuing his job with initiative and enthusiasm that often outdistanced his orders. Such was his zeal that he learned Hebrew and Yiddish the better to deal with the victims. When even one threatened to escape him, as in the case of Jenni Cozzi, Jewish widow of an Italian officer, he fanatically and successfully resisted her release from the Riga concentration camp against the reiterated demands of the Italian Embassy, the Italian Fascist party, and even his own Foreign Office.

When the Dutch made difficulties, he had to, as he put it, "fight for more [deportations]." His record in Hungary, where, even under the threat of the advancing Soviet Army, deportations were pressed with such urgency that at times five trains loaded with fourteen thousand people were arriving at Auschwitz daily, was climaxed by a maniacal effort, conceived and organized in minute detail by himself, to round up the four hundred thousand Jews of Budapest in a single day. "It needed something like genius," wrote one observer at the trial, the English historian Hugh Trevor-Roper, "for a mere SS lieutenant-colonel to organize in the middle of war . . . and in fierce competition for the essential resources, the transport, concentration and murder of millions of people."

Eichmann was an extraordinary, not an ordinary man, whose record is hardly one of the "banality" of evil. For the author of that ineffable phrase—as applied to the murder of six million—to have been so taken in by Eichmann's version of himself as just a routine civil servant obeying orders is one of the puzzles of modern journalism. From a presumed historian it is inexplicable.

Any historian with even the most elementary training knows enough to approach his source on the watch for concealment, distortion, or the outright lie. To transfer this caution to live history—that is, to journalism—should be instinctive. That he was just an ordinary man, a "banal" figure, was of course precisely Eichmann's defense, his assumed pose desperately maintained throughout his interrogation and trial. It was the crux of his lawyer's plea. Hannah Arendt's acceptance of it at face value suggests either a remarkable naïveté or else a conscious desire to support Eichmann's defense, which is even more remarkable. Since simple caution warns against ascribing naïveté to the formidable Miss Arendt, one is left with the unhappy alternative.

The question that has raised further controversy—the extent of the Jews' cooperation in their own destruction—is clarified here for anyone who wishes to understand rather than judge. Indeed, the dispute, it seems to me, is a matter of attitude rather than facts. There is a peculiar stridency about those who, having remained safe outside, now seize eagerly on the thesis that the Jews submitted too easily and were somehow responsible for their own slaughter. The attractiveness of the thesis is that by shifting guilt onto the victim, it relieves everyone else.

If by cooperation is meant that the Jews, at gunpoint and outside the ordinary protections of society, went where they were told and did what was ordered without organized resistance, then certainly they cooperated because this was their traditional means of survival. It was bred in the bone during two thousand years as an oppressed minority without territory, autonomy, or the ground of statehood under their feet.

Always helpless against the periodic storms of hate visited upon them, they chose compliance rather than hopeless battle out of the strongest instinct of their race—survival. Their only answer to persecution was to outlive it. Who was to know or believe that this time death was deliberately planned for all of them? At what stage is finality accepted? When as in the Warsaw Ghetto, it *was* accepted, the Jews fought as fiercely and valiantly as their own ancestors had against the Romans—and as hopelessly.

Inside the camps what motive was there for resistance or revolt when there was no place to go, no chance of friendly succor, no refuge? At the very edge of the grave, at the door of the gas chamber, they obeyed orders to undress, unwilling to invite death a moment earlier by refusal. One's mind revolts at this submission. Yet it was the brothers and cousins and uncles of these same people who, in Palestine when their situation was changed, fought against the longest odds ever known in war, to win, at long last, independence.

Mr. Hausner makes the additional point that lack of resistance inside the death camps was not unique. The Germans massacred literally millions inside the Soviet POW camps without resistance that we know of. And he recalls the American paratroop company inside the Bulge, executed after being ordered to dig their own graves. They too complied.

To convey to Israel's younger generation an understanding of this issue and of the nature of the tragedy that overtook their lost people was a main objective of the Eichmann trial. Among the many letters Hausner received when it was over was one from a girl of seventeen: "I could not honor all my relatives about whom I heard from my father. I loathed them for letting themselves be slaughtered. You have opened my eyes to what really happened." In a larger context the trial was undertaken by the state that was wrenched into life out of the aftermath of the tragedy, from a sense of responsibility to its people, to the dead, and to history.

Israel: Land of Unlimited Impossibilities

No nation in the world has so many drastic problems squeezed into so small a space, under such urgent pressure of time and heavy burden of history, as Israel. In a country the size of Massachusetts, all included in one telephone book, it must maintain national existence while subject to the active hostility of four neighbors jointly pledged to annihilate it. Under their boycott it is cut off from trade, transportation, and communication across its entire land frontier. In this situation it must perform three vital functions at once: maintain a state of military defense at constant alert, forge a coherent nation out of a largely immigrant population, and develop an economy capable both of supporting defense and absorbing the continuing flow of newcomers who now outnumber the founders of the state by two to one. It speaks a language, Hebrew, distinct from any other both in grammatical structure and alphabet, which must be learned on arrival by virtually all immigrants. To become self-sufficient in food, or by trade in food, it must restore fertility to the soil and reclaim the desert. Half of its land is non-arable except by irrigation, and its water supply is both inadequate and under threat of diversion by the Arabs. It must create industry where there was none and compete with more developed countries for foreign markets. It must operate with two official languages, Hebrew and Arabic, plus a general use of English; two sets of schools, religious and lay; and three

Saturday Evening Post, January 14, 1967.

forms of law, Ottoman, English, and rabbinical. While carrying the living memory of the mass murder of European Jewry who would have been its reservoir of population, and whose survivors and sons and daughters are among its citizens, it must, out of necessity, accept financial "restitution" and economic assistance from the nation of the murderers.

The drama of the struggle is in the atmosphere and in the facts of life. It is in the half-finished buildings of poured concrete going up on every hand, the most ubiquitous sight in Israel; in the intense faces of a class in an *ulpan* where adults from twenty countries learn Hebrew in five months; in the draft for military service, which takes every citizen of both sexes at eighteen; in the barbed wire dividing Jerusalem and in the empty house in no-man's-land still standing as it was left eighteen years ago with shattered walls and red-tiled roof fallen in; in the sudden sound of shots on a still Sabbath morning from the northern shore of the Sea of Galilee; in the matter-of-fact underground shelter dug in the yard of a *kibbutz* kindergarten near the Syrian border, with two benches against earth walls and a concrete door always open; in the fantastic machinery and belching smokestacks of phosphate works in the Negev; in the weed-grown dirt streets and emergency shacks of a new village where a bearded Jew from Morocco stares out of dull eyes at a strange land, and a Hungarian Jew with more hope has hung out a sign: SALON BUDAPEST—HAIRDRESSING; in the compulsive talk of plant manager, government official, or school principal as they explain to a visitor what conditions were like five years ago and what they will be five years hence; in the energy of marching youth groups on a mass hike, singing and swinging as they walk, with a purposefulness almost too arrogant; in plant nurseries with millions of pine and cypress seedlings for reforestation of the barren hills; in two figures on the wharf at Haifa after a ship has come in—an immigrant father locked in the arms of a waiting son as if all the deaths and griefs of the lost six million were enclosed in their wordless long embrace.

The landscape too is dramatic, both in Israel and Jordan, which together make up the country of the Bible. Seeing it at first hand, one realizes it was no accident that God was invented and two religions originated here. In the desert with its endless horizon by day and brilliance of stars at night, the vastness of the world would make a man lonely without God. The grotesque pillars of basalt and eroded sandstone on the shores of the Dead Sea, the red mountains of Edom, the weird gulfs and crags and craters of the Negev could not have failed to make him wonder what immortal hand or eye had shaped them. If he saw God in a burning bush, one recognizes the bush today in the blaze of yellow blossoms on the broom, as well as the origin of another story in the extraordinary brightness of the star hanging over Jerusalem (and over Bethlehem five miles away in Jordan). To Abraham and his progeny the supernatural would have seemed close at hand in the sudden ferocity of cloudbursts that can wipe out a village, or in rainbows of startling vividness with all the colors and both ends visible. Even the sun does not set reasonably here, as it does in the Western hemisphere, but drops all at once in what seems less than a minute from the time its lower rim first touches the Mediterranean horizon. Visions like miracles occur in the constant play of moving clouds across the sun, as when a hilltop village or ruined crusaders' castle will suddenly be picked out in a spotlight of sunshine and then, when a passing cloud blots out the light, as suddenly fade into the shadowed hills and vanish. A suffused pale light, sometimes luminous gray, sometimes almost white, constantly changing, shines always on Jerusalem, and when the sun's rays shoot skyward from behind a cloud, one sees instantly the origin of the halo.

The past lies around every corner. Herod's tomb is next door to one's hotel in Jerusalem. And at Megiddo, the site of Armageddon that dominates old pathways from Egypt to Mesopotamia, archeologists have uncovered the strata of twenty cities, including Solomon's with its stalls for four thousand horses and chariots. The past is seen from one's car on the way to Tiberias, where workmen cutting into the road bank have laid bare a row of Roman sarcophagi. It lies on the beach at Caesarea, where one's shoe crunches on a broken shard of ancient pottery. One is sitting on it when picnicking on a grass-covered *tel*, or mound, thought to be the site of Gath, where Goliath came from. One walks on it along the crusaders' ramparts of Acre, where Richard the Lion-Heart fought Saladin, or on the hill of Jaffa overlooking the harbor besieged by Napoleon. It is present, if somewhat obscured by cheap souvenirs, at Nazareth.

Archeology is a national occupation, hobby, and, in a sense, the national conscience. The government maintains a department for the exploration and study, preservation and display of ancient sites and monuments. Students in summertime volunteer for "digs." Although private digging is forbidden, a national hero like General Moshe Dayan, who is not easily restrained, pursues it with the intensity he applied to the Sinai campaign, piecing together amphorae from fragments in his studio and dragging home two entire Roman columns to set up in his garden—not without stirring up the usual wrangling in the newspapers, another favorite Israeli sport. The most spectacular recent work, under the direction of another wartime hero, General (now Professor) Yigael Yadin, is the uncovering of Massada, high on the cliffs above the Dead Sea, where in 73 A.D., after the fall of Jerusalem, 960 Jewish zealots holding out against Roman siege with the energy of despair finally committed mass suicide rather than surrender. Not far away, in Dead Sea caves reached by rope and helicopter, Yadin's team found further reminders of ancient valor in the letters of Simon Bar Kochba, who in 132–5 A.D. raised the remnants of Palestinian Jewry and maintained for three years the last battle for independence against Roman rule.

To feel itself a nation, a people must have not only independence and territory but also a history. For Israelis, so long and so widely dispersed, the distant past is important and the recent past even more so. Both the mass disaster, or Holocaust as they call it, suffered under Hitler, and the War of Independence against the Arabs in 1948 pervade the national consciousness and have their memorials on every hand. For Arabs the memory of 1948 is full of gall, but for Israelis it is heroic, and they leave its mementoes in place with deliberate pride. Along the road up to Jerusalem, so bitterly fought for in 1948, the rusted relics of their homemade armored cars have been left where they fell under fire. A captured Syrian tank stands in the village of Degania and a Bren-gun carrier in the garden of the *kibbutz* Ayelet Hashachar. A ship named *Af-Al-Pi-Chen* ("In Spite of Everything"), one of those which ran the British blockade to bring in illegal immigrants, has been hauled up as a monument where it landed at the foot of Mount Carmel, on the road a few miles south of Haifa.

Unforgotten and unforgettable, the memory of the Germans' extermination of the majority of Europe's Jews is no less a part of the nation's history. Six million trees to reforest the Judean hills have been planted as a "Forest of Martyrs" in the name of the six million dead, as well as an avenue of trees for each of the "Righteous Gentiles" who, at risk to themselves in Gestapo-controlled Europe, saved and hid Jewish neighbors. A central archive of material on the extermination has been established, and it supplied much of the evidence for the Eichmann trial. In itself the trial was a form of memorial, for its main object was perhaps less to bring a war criminal to justice than to solidify the historical record. The archive is housed in the dark new memorial to the dead called the Yad Vashem, unquestionably the most impressive building in Israel. Nowhere has architectural form more clearly and unmistakably expressed an idea and an emotion. It stands on a hill outside Jerusalem—a low, square, forbidding structure on a stark plaza, with walls of huge rounded stones, each like a dead man, surmounted by a heavy lid of wood that seems to press down with the weight of centuries. The building is unadorned by lettering or decoration of any kind. Indoors a raised walk behind a railing surrounds a bare stone floor. Flat on its surface, so that one looks down on them, lie in metal letters the names of the concentration camps: Auschwitz, Buchenwald, Dachau, Bergen-Belsen, Theresienstadt, and the others. A memorial flame burns in one corner. There is nothing else, and nothing else is needed. The building is a coffin and a grave, a monument to death.

Groups of visitors, Israeli and foreign—Americans, Scandinavians, Italians, French—come daily to stand at the railing, shaken, or silently weeping, or just uneasy. Like the seated Lincoln brooding in his marble hall on the Potomac, the Yad Vashem leaves no one unmoved. Israel, as the state whose people were the immediate victims, is the nearest heir of the tragedy (apart from Germany, which is another matter). As such it keeps the memory alive, not merely to mourn but with a sense, perhaps, of some mission to history.

Jerusalem, the Washington of Israel as compared to Tel Aviv, the country's New York, still exerts the same magnetism as it did on pilgrims through the long centuries of the Middle Ages. There is something heartbreaking in its division between Israel and Jordan. One can stand at one's window and look out on the wall of the Old City in the Jordanian half, under the lovely and mystical light, and feel as sad as if one had lived here all one's life, instead of having just arrived for the first time two days before.

At night the city is still and dark. In the stillness one can hear the wail of the muezzin calling Moslems to prayer in the Old City. Broadcast nowadays by loudspeaker to save the muezzin from climbing the minaret five times a day, it has a harsh sound, yet eerie and full of nostalgia for something one has never known. It is so close, yet from another country—one from which attacks sporadically erupt onto Israeli territory. Mostly these are sabotage raids on pump houses and irrigation pipes by marauders of al-Fatah, an Arab terrorist organization with headquarters in Syria, or they may be haphazard rifle fire by a nervous or fanatic sentry at the border. The Israelis have not submitted meekly to these attacks, and in recent weeks the U.N. Security Council censured Israel for its reprisal action against Jordan. These incidents, together with serious episodes involving artillery and jet aircraft on the Syrian and Egyptian borders, numbered about forty last year and caused more than thirty-five deaths.

The pressure of the Arab threat is constant. No place in Israel is beyond artillery range from its borders with Egypt, Syria, Jordan, and Lebanon. In their own countries the Arabs are gracious and attractive people, friendly and courteous to strangers, possessing dignity, charm, and even humor. On the subject of Israel, however, they are paranoid. Israel does not appear on Arab maps. The Arabs keep up, at violent cost of common sense and convenience, an elaborate pretense that it does not exist, or if it does, that somehow, by refusal to deal with it in any way whatsoever, it can be choked off by isolation. At intervals, when Arab unity flags or internal politics demand a bellicose posture, they make explicit threats. "We could annihilate Israel within twelve days," announced President Nasser of Egypt last March 26, "were the Arabs to form a united front and were they prepared to join battle."

The depth of Arab bitterness stems, one suspects, from humiliation. Much of the land they lost in Palestine had been sold as worthless to the early Zionist settlers who, draining the swamps in spite of malaria, and building on sand dunes, made it livable. The Jews became in the process a reminder of Arab failings. Then in 1948 an astonished world watched as the assembled military forces of five sovereign Arab states were fought off by the Jewish colonists of Palestine, who declared themselves a state, held their ground, and, to put an end to infiltration and border raids, reaffirmed the verdict in the Suez campaign of 1956. The Arabs were left, like a woman scorned, with a fury matching hell's, while the Israelis for the time being could afford to feel satisfied with their performance, if never off guard. They have put territory under their feet at last in the land they once ruled, and they do not intend to be uprooted again. The Arabs' undying intransigence in the face of accomplished fact has a quality of Peter Pan faced with growing up. Territory lost through the fortunes of war is a commonplace of history. What is Texas but 267,339 square miles of Mexico settled by Americans and then forcibly declared independent? In any event, the territory never formed part of an Arab state in modern times, having passed from Turkish sovereignty to the British Mandate.

With their enormous preponderance in size and manpower, why do the Arabs *not* attack? Partly because from previous experience they have a rather nervous respect for Israel's powers of retaliation; further, because of fear of one another and of internal opponents given to bloody *coups d'état*. Yet, since acceptance of reality does not always prevail in dealings among nations, Israel can never be sure that the Arab inundation will *not* roll, nor free themselves of the thought that someday—next month, next year, or tomorrow—they may wake to the sudden scream of a hostile air force in their skies. They must live and plan in that constant expectation. Meanwhile, from day to day the small pressures continue. Yellow signs proclaiming DANGER! FRONTIER mark an erratic curve through the countryside. Visitors to the Knesset, Israel's parliament, must pass through a maze of guards and precautions before entering the visitors' gallery, and ladies must leave their handbags, presumably capable of concealing a bomb or pistol, outside. Driving down through the Negev along the new highway that skirts the bleak, eroded slopes of Jordan to the east, the chauffeur stubbornly refuses to stop for a visit to the Nabatean ruins of Avdat or other sights along the way, and when finally pressed for an explanation, admits, almost apologetically, to a desire to reach Eilat before sunset. Why? Well, in case of—the word comes reluctantly—"trouble" from over there, nodding toward the somber mountains on the left. A startled American, unused to thinking in these terms, is reminded of covered wagons and Indian ambush.

At Almagor, a hilltop settlement in northern Galilee where clashes with Syria involving machine guns, tanks, and aircraft took place during the past two summers, one looks down on a silver stream winding through a green delta to the lake. The stream is the River Jordan where it enters the Sea of Galilee (otherwise Lake Tiberias). The land on its far bank, backed by a range of hills, is Syria, with snow-capped Mount Hermon looming hugely in the distance. On one of the hills is a cluster of the Arabs' characteristic flat-topped sandstone huts, many of them painted pale blue to ward off evil. Down on the delta black cattle graze, white egrets stand on the sand flats of the river, Arab families and farmers go about their business. The air is filled with a spring breeze and the twittering of birds, the hillside with weeds and wild flowers blossoming as profusely as a garden. Lavender thistle mixes with blue gentian, daisies with wild mustard and wild pink geranium, and scarlet poppies are scattered everywhere. A solitary young soldier sits with binoculars on a pile of stones, intently scanning the hills opposite.

Almagor is a settlement founded by Nahal, a pioneer corps in which military training and land cultivation are combined in a system Israel has developed to defend and simultaneously settle the frontier. The young recruit points to a long straight scar on the side of the hill opposite and says it is the track of the Arabs' attempted diversion of the headwaters of the Jordan. Involving seventy-five miles of open ditch, the scheme could hardly be carried out secretly, and is not an operation that Israel could idly watch. After the Syrians started shooting in August 1965, the Israelis' answering fire, according to their communiqué, damaged "tractors at work in Syria on the diversion of the Jordan headwaters," after which the work "appeared to cease for the time being." When I was there in March before last summer's battle, the hillside scar, from what anyone could tell through binoculars, was quiescent.

Down on the lake, which is wholly Israeli territory, two fishing boats were moving out from the Syrian shore. The soldier remarked without heat that last year Syrian guns in the hills fired on an Israeli fishing boat and a cruising police patrol boat. Handing me the binoculars, he pointed to two black dots far out in the center of the lake. Slowly moving into vision, they took shape as Israeli police boats. The Syrians kept on fishing, and the patrols approaching. Gripping the binoculars, I waited, feeling as if the air had suddenly gone still. The police were within hailing distance when, unhurriedly, the Syrians rowed back to shore, beached their boats, and wandered off. Equally without fuss the patrol boats turned back the way they had come. Almagor remained quiet for that day.

The hillside scar, mentioned on return to Jerusalem, aroused no excitement. "It could be a road," they said. Israel so desperately needs peace—to divert taxes from the crushing defense budget to other vital needs, to rejoin the continent of which it is a part, to live with neighbors on reasonably neighborly terms, above all to breathe normally— that it has usually leaned over backward to avoid cause for quarrel. It tries to remain suave and, for as long as possible, unprovoked, in the effort to leave room for whatever tiny chance of negotiation might appear. Israel too has its hotheads of irredentism, the "adventurists" who clamor to "take the west bank," but this is largely lip-service to old slogans. They know, or if not, the country's leaders know, that to swallow western Jordan with nearly a million Arab inhabitants (or equally the Gaza Strip), thus increasing Israel's existing Arab minority of twelve percent who already outbreed the Jews, would be to court disaster. What Israel needs is not more land populated by Arabs but more people to populate its own empty Negev, a problem which in turn depends on water to make the desert habitable.

Even the wound of the Old City's loss is not so fresh anymore. For Jews its essence was the Wailing Wall for bewailing lost Zion, but since restoration of the state, who needs to wail? From long association, many still yearn for the Wall, but the native-born generation are not wailers. On their own land the Jews have successfully become what they were never allowed to be in the ghetto—farmers and soldiers. The transformation has literally changed the Jewish face. Complexion and lighter hair-color can no doubt be explained by sun and climate; blue eyes one must leave to the geneticists, but the fundamental change is one of expression. The new face has an outdoor look and, more noteworthy, it is cheerful. This is not of course true of the immigrant settlements, where the look among the adults is compounded of bewilderment, strangeness, difficulties, and resentments, nor of Tel Aviv, which has been unkindly (if not inaccurately) described as a mixture, on a smaller scale, of New York and West Berlin. The Tel Aviv look, compounded of traffic, shops, business deals, and culture, with a sprinkling of beatniks, is no different from Urban the world over.

The new face is elsewhere, notably in the army. At the officers' training school outside Tel Aviv it was visible in students, instructors, and in the commandant, Colonel Meier Paeel, a tall, vigorous, smiling man. Colonel Paeel had smile crinkles at the corners of his eyes, a characteristic I noticed among many of the other officers, although someone else might say it came from squinting at the sun.

The school had pleasant tree-lined quarters inherited from the British Army, which was always accustomed to do itself well. The tradition continues in one respect, for the secretaries, all girl soldiers in khaki, were so invariably pretty, without makeup, that it was hard to believe they had been chosen at random. Because of its essential role in the creation of the state, the army's prestige is high, and it attracts the best. It has a noticeably breezy air. The open shirt collar —spotless and correctly starched—prevails. Saluting is casual, but there is an underlying seriousness and sense of tension. At the general-staff school, where virtually all the students wore the two campaign ribbons of 1948 and 1956, there was once again the outdoor face, and a commandant, Colonel Mordecai Goor, no less handsome and confident. "You are making a new breed," I said to one officer. He looked around thoughtfully at his colleagues and searching for the right English words, replied deliberately, "Yes. Jewish sorrow has gone out of their eyes."

Reclamation of the land, after centuries of being strangers and rootless in the lands of others, has helped to achieve that result as much as anything. The Jews are at home: not a home taken over ready-made, but one they had to clear, clean, repair, and reconstruct by their own labor. Palestine, under Arabs and Turks during the thousand years before 1900, reverted to the nomad, and for lack of cultivation was left to the desolation predicted by Isaiah: a "habitation of dragons and a court for owls." English explorers in the nineteenth century found it a stony goat pasture with "not a mile of made road in the land from Dan to Beersheba." To be made livable again, reported the Palestine Exploration Fund in 1880, the land required roads for wheeled transport, irrigation and swamp drainage, restoration of aqueducts and cisterns, sanitation, seeding of grass and reforestation to check soil erosion. This was the task that faced, and all but overwhelmed, the early Jewish colonists. Internal dissension and self-made problems, as prevalent then as today, did not help. While they starved, they engaged in furious dispute over whether to keep the commandment of a sabbatical year during which no work on fields or among livestock could be done.

The issue survives. At Kfar Yuval, a little colony in northern Galilee settled by an Orthodox group of Indian Jews, a schoolteacher apologized for the weed-grown yard that could not be cultivated because it was sabbatical year for the village. When I asked, "What do they eat?" my guide shrugged and said, "They pray and eat less." The fossilized rules of Orthodoxy hamper progress and convenience in the nation out of all proportion to the number who take them seriously. Because the Orthodox party holds the political balance of power, it has an official grip on the country, and Orthodoxy strikes a visitor as the most stultifying of Israel's self-made problems.

Yet the Jews have made the land bloom—with terraced hills and delicate orchards, hedges of rosemary and the thick lush green of orange groves. Everywhere around the groves in springtime the pungent sweet fragrance of orange blossom hangs in the air like smoke. Yellow mimosa and feathery, pine-like tamarisks grow along the roadside, punctuated by great cascades of purple bougainvillaea. Away from the urban strips and gas stations and industrial plants and somewhat shoddy emergency settlements, Israel has an extraordinary beauty. Cypresses like dark green candles point upward against the blue sky, and windblown olive trees shimmer as if their leaves were tipped with silver. When the wind blows, the palms bend like reeds over Lake Tiberias, and from western Galilee one can see, far in the distance between the hills, the whitecaps of the Mediterranean glint in the sun.

It is no wonder the Jews have grown a new face. Perhaps what accounts for it most of all is that Israel is theirs; here they are not a minority; they are on top. Which is not to say they will live happily ever after, or even now, for they are the most contentious people alive, and Orthodoxy is not their only self-made problem. Their quarrels are legion, they abuse each other incessantly and without compunction, and settle differences of opinion within any group by splitting instead of submitting to majority rule. The Haifa Technion, Israel's MIT, was recently plunged in battle over the teaching of architecture. The issue, roughly one between scientific and humanistic schools of thought, exists in other countries as well, but the solution in Israel was radical. By dictate of the Technion's president, the faculty of architecture was split into two faculties—a decision which enraged the students, since they would have to choose between one or the other, and many wanted elements of both. Carried over to political life, the habit causes factionalism which Israelis explain as the natural consequence of long centuries without political power or responsibility. They consider that the experience of self-government is gradually providing an enforced cure.

Israel is not an affluent society; it is hard-working, with the six-day week still in force. Until last March Israel had no television. This circumstance grew from the strong puritan strain of the early settlers, who were founders of Histadrut, the labor federation, and of the *kibbutzim.* Although the *kibbutz* system of communal ownership is neither predominant nor spreading, the influence of its people is out of proportion to their numbers because they came early, were self-motivated, and, to survive at all, had to have vigor and grit. *Kibbutz* members in government took the view, violently disputed, that TV would distract from work, disrupt family life, and intensify economic and class differences between settled residents and the newcomers who could not afford to buy television sets. Besides, it would cost money, and the government had none to spare on a luxury. The awkward result is that anyone who buys a TV set, and that includes a large number of Arab citizens, tunes in Cairo or Beirut. Since last March educational television is being tried.

Because Israel is a small country, the individual is able to feel that what he does counts. No more powerful incentive exists. It will make a man work even at a job he dislikes. One government official, who detested going abroad to beg for funds for an essential operation, told me he continued to go because he felt "on the front line of defense." Seeking something of this feeling, students from abroad, particularly Scandinavian refugees from too much welfare, come every summer to work in the *kibbutzim*.

With all its problems, Israel has one commanding advantage—a sense of purpose: to survive. It has come back. It has confounded persecution and outlived exile to become the only nation in the world that is governing itself in the same territory, under the same name, and with the same religion and same language as it did three thousand years ago. It is conscious of fulfilling destiny. It knows it must not go under now, that it must endure. Israelis may not have affluence or television or enough water or the quiet life, but they have what affluence tends to smother: a motive. Dedication is not necessarily total, and according to some who see materialism displacing the idealism of the early days, it is already slipping. Israelis are not all true, honest, loyal, industrious—a nation of Boy Scouts. Many (an estimated total of 80,000 to 90,000 so far) leave for more pay (Israeli salaries are low and taxes high), more comfort, wider opportunities and contacts, a life of less pressure, or for a variety of reasons which add up to one: to escape geography. But on the whole and for the present, the pacesetters of the nation have what Americans had at Plymouth Rock, a knowledge of why they are there and where they are going. Even the visitor begins to feel that there may be a design to history after all, a purpose in the survival of this people who, ever since Abraham came out of Ur to mark the turn to monotheism, have fertilized civilization with ideas, from Moses and Jesus to Marx, Freud, and Einstein. Perhaps survival is their fate.

Paradoxically, Arab hostility has been useful in forcing Israel to face westward, to find her contacts and competition with the West, including a trade agreement with the European Common Market. While this exacerbates the problem of acclimating her growing proportion of Oriental Jews from Iraq, Iran, and North Africa, it also drives her to greater enterprise, to "think deeper," as the manager of the Timna Copper Mines said. "Of course," he added a little wistfully, "if we had the whole of the Middle East to trade with, we would have an easier life." As it is, necessity has required the development of such enterprises as his own, the former mines of King Solomon, unexploited under the Turks or the British Mandate, and now restored to production by Solomon's descendants.

Timna is one of those projects, like almost everything in Israel, undertaken against the soundest advice of practical persons who declared it "impossible." Originally the resettlement of Palestine was impossible, the draining of malarial swamps impossible, the building on sand dunes (where Tel Aviv now has a population of over 600,000) impossible; the goal of statehood, partition, self-defense, the Law of Return, absorption of a million immigrants, then of two million immigrants—all impossible. The country has been created out of impossibilities, embraced sometimes from idealism, more often because there was no other choice.

Since no one would invest in a dead copper mine, Timna was subsidized and its shares taken up by the government; during the first three years of effort to begin operations, the project drew sarcastic press comment about "putting gold in the ground to get out copper." Now with production booming, and a convenient world shortage caused by strikes in Chile and by Rhodesia's troubles, it is exporting ten thousand tons of copper cement a year, at explosively profitable prices, to Spain, Japan, and Hungary, while the public offers to buy the government's shares. No one expects this happy condition to last forever, but future, even present, limitations frequently fail in Israel to have a limiting effect. If Israelis looked ahead at the stone wall or ditch looming up, they would stop dead from sheer fright; instead, they go on out of optimism or necessity, and trust that God, or their own inventiveness, or some unforeseen development will provide.

Out of such necessities the country finds its resources. To compete with Italy in the export of oranges, for example, an Israeli fruit-grower joined with a village farm-machinery factory to invent an ingenious motorized orange-picking machine that consists of two raised platforms on a wheeled hoist and permits faster, cheaper harvesting. The Arid Zone Research Center in Beersheba has shown that the warm, sheltered climate of the Wadi Araba in the southern Negev can, with careful utilization of rain runoff from the hills, produce four crops a year. This makes possible the export to Europe of luxury out-of-season vegetables and fruits, such as the strawberries that are flown to European ski resorts.

A rather more major enterprise is Israel's "dry Suez," the pipeline which brings Iranian oil from Eilat on the Red Sea to Haifa and Tel Aviv on the Mediterranean. Built in answer to Nasser's exclusion of

Israel from the Suez Canal, one eight-inch and one sixteen-inch line, with a capacity of 4.5 million tons a year, already exist. They were chiefly financed by Baron Edmond de Rothschild on condition of a guaranteed return; he has since made two and a half times his original investment. The ditch for a third line can be seen cutting its way through the Negev toward a terminus on the Mediterranean at the new deep-sea port of Ashdod, opened in 1965. Chiefly for the use of foreign oil companies as a supplement to the tanker route through the Suez Canal, the new Israeli pipeline may, depending on eventual size of the pipe and cost of service, one day undercut Suez rates.

The Negev itself, known in the Bible as the Wilderness of Zin, is the prime "impossible." Although it accounts for more than fifty-five percent of Israel's land area, its capacity to absorb any increase of population was said by the Peel Commission, the most authoritative of the many which investigated Palestine's troubles during the Mandate, to be nil. Nevertheless from 1948 through 1964 the number of people supported by the area has risen from 21,000 to 258,000, including the cities of Beersheba and Ashkelon, which are not strictly in the desert but on its northern edge. The rest are scattered among some 130 settlements, including Sde Boker, a *kibbutz* established in the middle of the desert as a magnet and an example, where Ben-Gurion has chosen to live. This population is greater than the estimated 30,000 to 60,000 which the Negev supported at its height in Roman and Byzantine times, when the system of guiding rainwater through man-made channels to cisterns was brought to engineering perfection. The Israelis consider themselves capable of no less, up to the limit of the rains from heaven. But modern man uses more water than the ancients; moreover, to bring more people to the Negev necessitates the finding of new sources by any means creative intelligence can devise. Investigators are testing methods of inducing artificial rainfall; of using unpotable brackish water for irrigating salt-resistant crops; of enforcing water-saving by metering water; of reducing evaporation in reservoirs by coating the surface with a fatty substance. But the ultimate answer for populating the Negev must be desalinization of seawater. A joint Israeli-American study is now under way for a future plant which, one is confidently told, will be ready by 1971. Powered by a nuclear reactor, it is expected to produce more than thirty billion gallons a year at reasonable cost. On the other hand, a recent report of the Weizmann Institute states that while it is possible by desalinization to provide fresh water in limited amounts for users "not sensitive" to the cost, "it is still an open question whether methods suitable for large-scale and *cheap* production of fresh water will ever be found."

Beersheba, once a dusty market town with an Arab population of 3,000 (who decamped in the war of 1948), began with a Jewish population of zero. Two hundred families came in 1949. As a result of the opening of the Negev by road and railroad, the development of chemical industries in the Dead Sea area, and a mass influx of immigrants, Beersheba has so exploded that a harried municipal councilor hastily scribbled new figures on a fact sheet before handing it to me. The population is, or was last spring, 72,000, of whom eighty-five percent are immigrants, half Orientals and half from Europe and South America. The city still serves as a center for some 16,000 Bedouin citizens of Israel who live in the desert in their long black goat-hair tents. Everyone rushes, everyone is harried (except the Bedouin and the inevitable "tourist" camel who waits inappropriately in front of a filling station). Trash flies about in the wind, streets are half paved, rubble and debris of building construction lie around, tattered posters advertise the city's seven movie houses, and the shell of an empty, circular, concrete building with a crenelated top, looking something like a child's cardboard crown, excites one's curiosity. "It's the synagogue," I am told with an impatient shrug. "The funds ran out. There are other things more important."

Schools, for instance. Beersheba has thirty-two elementary schools, each with a kindergarten, two high schools, and three trade schools, as well as a training school for teachers and one for nurses, an *ulpan* for immigrant adults, a *yeshiva*, and a music school. In order to keep students in the area, it has even last year started a university. Not degree-granting yet, it operates without a campus or faculty of its own but with visiting professors lent by other institutions. Courses in the humanities and social sciences, one in biology, and a postgraduate course in engineering are offered to 260 students—a figure which, according to the regular Israeli refrain, "will be doubled next year." Nevertheless a problem remains: There are not enough high schools in the Negev to fill up a university.

Beersheba is a microcosm—or it might be called a hothouse—of the nation's immigration problem, which cannot be envisaged without a few figures. In three and a half years from May 1948 to the end of 1951, while the new state was struggling to its feet under a new government, 685,000 persons entered Israel, or slightly more than the population existing at the time the state was proclaimed. In 1950 the Knesset (parliament) enacted the Law of Return, confirming the right of every Jew to enter the country unless he has been guilty of offenses against the Jewish people or is a danger to public health or security. (The law was soon to raise interesting questions of what is a Jew, as in the case of Brother Daniel, a monk who demanded the right of entry, claiming that though converted to Christianity he was a Jew under the rabbinical definition—that is, a person born of a Jewish mother. The court rejected his claim, a decision that raised other interesting questions: Is Judaism a religion or, so to speak, a condition? Can a Jew, like Brother Daniel, abandon his religion and yet remain a Jew? He could, of course, have acquired Israeli citizenship after three years' residence, like any Moslem or Christian, but he wanted it as his right under the Law of Return. The doctrine established by his case may in the long run, as cases continue to arise, undergo a change. Perhaps someday that old question, What is a Jew? may find an answer, although one thing is certain—if Israelis remain Jews, they will continue to dispute it.)

On July 30, 1961, the millionth immigrant since statehood arrived. Of these million, 431,000 came from Europe (beginning with 99,000 escapees and survivors from the concentration camps), with the largest groups coming from Romania and Poland; about 500,000 came from Asia and North Africa, including 125,000 from Iraq, 45,000 from Yemen, 33,000 from Turkey, others from Iran, India, and China, and 237,000 from Morocco, Tunisia, Libya, and Algeria. Thirteen thousand came from North and South America. The influx was never regular or planned, but came in waves or rushes in response to political crises and pressures. Airlifts brought the exodus from Iraq and Yemen under a time deadline. Groups surged out from Poland and Romania, and a few from Russia, between sporadic liftings and lowerings of the Iron Curtain. In 1956 the number rose sharply in response to the revolt in Hungary and to the Suez campaign, which brought about the expulsion of 15,000 to 20,000 Jews from Egypt, many of them of the professional classes. Since 1961 another quarter of a million have come. Boats arrive at Haifa every week. Reception, examination, registration for first papers, arrangements for transportation and housing, and an initial grant of cash and food all take place on board. Every Jew admitted becomes a citizen with the vote at once; every non-Jew, once admitted, may become a citizen after three years' residence. It requires a visual effort of the imagination to picture what the settlement of almost 1.5 million strangers, nearly all requiring social and financial assistance, involves, not only physically in terms of housing, job-finding, adaptation, and schooling, but in the psychological strains on society, and the tensions and frictions both among the immigrants themselves and between them and the earlier residents. By contrast, the 500,000 Arab refugees of 1948, who have since doubled their number and remain an undigested lump and a charge on the U.N., could merge into the host countries with no barriers of language or custom, if the will to absorb them were present. Much of the cost of the operation in Israel, being beyond the powers of the state, is raised by contributions from Jews abroad and administered by a form of state within a state—the Jewish Agency. The origins, nature, and role of this remarkable institution, which is the residual office of the World Zionist Organization that virtually governed the Jews of Palestine under the Mandate, are complex, but it can be said that the work of the Agency for the time being is indispensable, while its implications are unresolved.

The effort on behalf of the immigrants is not of course purely eleemosynary. Israel needs these people to fill the vessel of the state. Besides filling the villages vacated by the Arabs in 1948, they create new settlements on land formerly non-arable. Twenty-one new towns and 380 new rural villages have been established since—and because —they began to arrive, and it is their increase of the manpower of Israel that now enables it to produce over three quarters of its own food as well as enough food exports to pay for the balance. The immigrants' labor is needed for defense purposes as well. The settlements are of every kind. Some are small, struggling communities with outhouses, weeds, and a few cows; others, multiple housing developments with streets, flung down on what was last month an empty hillside.

The greatest difficulty is providing income-producing work, especially among the Jews from North Africa, who despise manual labor— unlike the early European settlers, who idealized it and made it the cult of the *kibbutz*. Whereas they came to Palestine drawn by an ideal, the present Orientals have come as more or less passive victims of circumstance. To adapt at all, they must learn a new manner of living, a new language, how to read, and new agricultural or manual skills they never knew before, a task beyond the capacity of most of them. For teenage immigrants, however, the period of military service, which provides as much classwork as drill, is an effective forcing house. Mixing with the native-born *sabras*, they learn to speak Hebrew and feel Israeli very soon.

Antagonism between Orientals and Europeans certainly exists. The latter, who led the return and reclaimed the country, have made

Israel, despite geography, predominantly Western in ideas and habits. They are not particularly happy about the flood of darker-skinned people, whom they yearn to see balanced by a portion of their three million compatriots still locked up in Russia. (The Soviet government refuses to allow a general exit, because it would annoy their Arab friends and because voluntary departure would reflect poorly on the Soviet paradise.) The Orientals resent the fact that the earlier comers hold the better houses and jobs and, on the whole, the direction of the country (although there are two Cabinet ministers of Oriental origin). They are burdened with all the frustrations and troubles of a group which feels itself inferior. Israel has an integration problem, but it does not have a deep or hardened segregation pattern to overcome. With both will and need working for a rapid solution, Israelis talk of absorbing their Oriental citizens into the society within two generations.

Efforts are concentrated on the children, whose problems are many but whose inner transformation into Israelis can be quick and visible. When I visited a school in Beersheba, the woman principal, a Bulgarian by origin, showed me her classes with the pride of a creator, although the way had been rough. The absolutism of the Oriental father, particularly the Moroccan, collapses in Israel, she explained. The parents lose prestige, and the children, quickly feeling ashamed of them, look for revenge and become discipline problems. During her first year as a teacher, she said, her classes were so unruly that she cried every day for a year and wanted to quit, but her principal would not let her go. In a torrent of anguished reminiscence, she poured out all the difficulties of the past years, including, as an example of the immigrants' adjustment troubles, cases of stealing among children. When I suggested that this was not unknown in the private school my daughters attended in New York, not to mention every other American school I ever had any acquaintance with, she brushed aside the interruption, unimpressed. The problem is always bigger and better— or in this case, worse—in Israel.

As the teacher talked, the end-of-period bell rang, as it was doubtless doing all over the world. The corridors flooded with noisy youngsters, and the yard outside in the warm sun filled with groups kicking soccer balls. It could have been anywhere. The children all dressed much alike in slacks and colored shirts and cotton dresses, and one could not tell a Persian from a Pole or Moroccan from Hungarian.

Education is Israel's greatest internal task and absorbs the largest share, after defense, of the national budget. At the peak of the system stands the pride—or the wonder—of Israel: the reincarnated Hebrew University of Jerusalem. Opened in 1925, its original campus on Mount Scopus, one of the eastern hills behind the Old City, was left inside Jordanian territory by the war of 1948, a loss that seemed almost as irreconcilable as the loss of the Wailing Wall. Under the terms of the truce the Israelis were to retain ownership and have access to the University and the adjoining Hadassah Hospital as a kind of enclave within Jordan, but as things have worked out, the only access that Jordan has permitted is a ritual inspection twice a month by Israeli officials in a sealed car escorted by the U.N. For a while after the war, classes were conducted in various buildings and rented premises, but the situation became too chaotic, and the hard decision to build a new home, giving up hope of regaining Mount Scopus, had to be taken.

Begun in 1954 with money raised by Jews abroad, a new university has risen on the western edge of the city on a hill called Givat Ram. Accommodating over 10,000 students, it is a handsome complex of modern functional buildings whose straight lines contrast with the pool and curves and artful landscaping of a wide, open terrace. It seems to command its domain, but in fact the Hebrew University lives on impossibles, of which the chief, of course, is money. The government supplies a little over half its budget, tuition fees supply about one-tenth, income from gifts another tenth, and the rest is a harassed look on the face of the president. While battling what is said to be the largest deficit of any university in the world, the Hebrew University runs because it must, as the pump of the intellectual and professional life of the country. Besides the undergraduate college, it operates professional schools of medicine, law, social work, agronomy, and education as well as a university press. Already overcrowded, its lecture halls stay open thirteen hours a day to accommodate all classes. It can house as yet only a small proportion of students in dormitories, so the majority must find rented rooms in Jerusalem, which has a housing shortage. Most of them, in addition, must find full- or part-time employment to pay their way through. Out of the struggle come the skills the country needs.

Under the shadow of Arab enmity, Israel's need for friends and relationships with the outside world has drawn her into a program of quite surprising proportions that provides technical assistance to the underdeveloped countries. Last year 832 Israeli technicians were serving in sixty-two countries, mostly in the emerging African states, but also in Burma, Ecuador, and other Asian and Latin American countries. They teach agriculture, irrigation, road construction, cost accounting, office management, and other essentials for a new country pulling itself into the modern stream. Students from the client countries—over 2,000 in 1965—come to Israel to learn on the job as well as to take academic courses at the university and professional schools. The flourishing program gives the Israelis immense satisfaction. It makes them feel they are putting back into the world the help they themselves have received, and it feeds their strong sense of mission. They are great improvers of mankind, and the noble sentiments expressed in the technical-assistance program are sometimes overpowering.

Of all enterprises to which Israel has been driven by need for an outlet to the world, the Red Sea port of Eilat is the most dramatic. Ten years ago it did not exist except as a name on the map and in the misty past as the Eziongeber of the Bible, where the people of Exodus halted on the flight from Egypt, and where later the Queen of Sheba disembarked. In 1949 when the first Israeli jeeps rolled in from the desert to occupy it, the only habitation was a deserted stone hut on the beach. Today Eilat is a functioning port for ocean-going ships, an airport, and a city of 13,000 with plans for expansion to 60,000. It might be Jack's Beanstalk except that human hands made it, not magic. Squeezed in between Egypt on the west and Jordan on the east, with the coast of Saudi Arabia below Jordan only four miles away, it sits on a seven-mile stretch of shoreline at the head of the Gulf of Aqaba. Only through this tiny slit could Israel open a door to the east and south for contact with the countries of Africa and the Orient. Although Eilat was allocated to Israel under the U.N. Partition plan of 1947, the right to use it had to be affirmed by force of arms, because Egypt blocked egress through the straits at the bottom of the Gulf. This was accomplished by the Sinai campaign of 1956, when, by taking possession of the land controlling the straits, Israel made their permanent opening a condition of the armistice which ended that adventure.

Given that development, Eilat burst like a racehorse from the starting gate. Its lifeline, the highway to Beersheba, was opened in 1958. As the artery of the Negev's future, the road has made possible the expansion of the desert and Dead Sea chemical industries whose products, borne on diesel-powered fifty-ton trucks with eight pairs of wheels, now rumble into the docks of the new port. The port can accommodate four ships at the pier and three tankers at the oil jetty.

Plans have been drawn up to double present capacity. Goods leave Eilat bound for Abyssinia, Iran, Burma, Singapore, Vietnam, Japan, and Australia. Rubber imported from Singapore is manufactured into tires at Petah Tikvah in the north, to be re-exported from Eilat to Iran as finished product. The manager of the port is a young man of twenty-four who came to Eilat three years ago after his army service. To improve his command of English for dealing with shipmasters, he was going to England for two and a half months. Accustomed to government grants and the largesse of foundations, I asked who was sending him. "I send myself," he replied haughtily.

In addition to being a port, Eilat is booming as a tourist resort for sun-seekers and skin divers. It has twelve hotels of varying size and luxury, a tour by glass-bottomed boat to view the exotic fishes of the Red Sea, three museums, including a *"musée de l'art moderne,"* a library, an aquarium, a zoo, a park, a shopping plaza, a municipal hall of immodest proportions obviously designed for a town three times the present size, a 120-bed hospital under construction, two movie houses and a third under construction, a Philip Murray Community Center jointly established by the CIO and Histadrut, Israel's labor federation, two local airlines serving Tel Aviv, Haifa, and Beersheba, a bus line, three banks, three filling stations, two synagogues, two bars, and one mayor of dynamic capacity.

He is Joseph Levy, aged forty-three, a native of Egypt who in 1948 was arrested in Cairo as a Zionist youth leader and sent to a prison camp in the Sinai peninsula. Held there for a year, he planned an escape to the nearest point in Palestine, which happened to be Eilat, but was released before he could make the attempt. Reaching Israel, as it had now become, by way of Marseilles, he made for Eilat, having on the way talked himself into a job as manager of an airline branch office about to be opened there. He arrived in 1949, one of Eilat's Mayflower generation, and ten years later was mayor.

A dark-haired, dark-skinned, quiet-mannered man, he wore when I saw him recently an air of enforced calm, as if he felt that were he to let himself go in reaction to all the demands, pressures, and harassments of his job, he might fly apart in a thousand pieces. He was entirely self-possessed, with the self-assurance that comes from having tackled and, if not solved, at least come through a chronic multiplicity of problems, and from acquiring the knowledge *en route* that no one of them need be fatal. Besides Hebrew and Arabic, he spoke English, French, and Italian, all of which he had been taught as a boy at the Jewish school in Cairo because, as the headmaster had explained to protesting parents, "Who knows today what may happen in the world? I must do what I can to prepare these children for anything."

Mayor Levy knew all about Mayor Lindsay of New York, kept similar hours, and left us after dinner to attend a meeting at ten-thirty. He had just been re-elected for a second term by an increased majority and was supported by what he called a "wall-to-wall coalition" in the municipal council—that is, without other-party opposition on the council, a condition virtually unique in Israel. He ascribed it to the pioneers' sense of solidarity in Eilat. Out on the perimeter, too distant from the rest of the country to draw either water from the national carrier or electricity from the national grid, Eilat feels thrown on its own resources, a kind of fortress on the frontier.

The mayor recalled the hard early days when no one had any faith in the town's future. Businessmen would not invest capital there; no one would build a hotel until Histadrut put up the first; water would give out in the middle of a shower; power would fail. Families left after a few months, citing all sorts of reasons: Schools were inadequate, hospitals non-existent, provisions erratic, the summer's heat unbearable. "It was terrible to see them go." To keep at least the bachelors on the job, Histadrut was persuaded to build a girls' youth hostel ("We had to go to Histadrut for girls too"), but few girls came. Yet bit by bit, with subsidies and from small beginnings, industry and tourism got started, gradually bringing in money, people, and developing facilities.

Water was, and remains, the major problem. Rainfall collected in cisterns, plus underground desert water that is too saline to be potable unless diluted by pure water, can together supply about seventy percent of requirements. The remaining thirty percent must be provided by desalinization, which, however uneconomic, the government subsidizes, since Eilat could not exist without it. Air-conditioning makes an extra demand, but because of the extreme summer heat it is considered necessary in order to hold the population. The desalinization process is operated in conjunction with Eilat's independent power plant. Nearby, a second desalinization plant, using a refrigerating process, has proved ineffective. Mayor Levy shrugged when asked how water would be found to match the city's proposed expansion. "We can't let the water problem limit our plans," he said. "It will be found somehow." Perhaps he operated from some race-memory of the water that gushed when Moses tapped the rock.

One alteration of nature already figured in his plans: to increase artificially the coastline available for tourist facilities by cutting a number of lagoons and canals inland from the sea, and eventually to sell property along the banks of this "little Venice" for more hotels. The creeping shadow of Hilton could be felt over one's shoulder; already a Sheraton is being talked about. Doubtless in the course of that relentless advance, Eilat will one day become Israel's Miami. Such is progress.

Meanwhile, water or no water, Eilat plants as it builds. Fast-growing eucalyptus trees already give shade and a green rest for the eye, shrubs and grass plots battle sand, scrawny saplings border a newly paved street, looking as if they had been planted yesterday. Waking early, I went for a walk before eight in the morning when the air was fresh, before the dust and heat would rise. A street cleaner on his knees was sweeping up the leftover dirt with a small brush, singing a melancholy Oriental chant while he worked. Over grass and shrubs, sprinklers were whirling as if no one had ever heard of a water shortage. They seemed symbols of the Israelis' refusal to accept limits, a living example of unlimited impossibility. In the sprinklers of Eilat one could see what the professors call a "future-oriented society."

Woodrow Wilson on Freud's Couch

Since Americans are not, by and large, a people associated with tragedy, it is strange and unexpected that the most tragic figure in modern history—judged by the greatness of expectations and the measure of the falling off—should have been an American. During the two climactic years of one of the world's profound agonies, 1917–19, Woodrow Wilson was the receptacle of men's hopes. He personified the craving of men of good will to believe that some good would come of it all, that the immense suffering, turmoil, and disruption would not be for nothing, that the agony must prove to have been the birth pangs of a better world. In a series of pronouncements that seemed to pluck out men's best desires and give them shape, Wilson supplied the formula for that better world (which must be read not as a stale slogan but in the first fine rapture of its promise) as one made "safe for democracy," safe from war ever again, safe from tyranny, hunger, and injustice, safe from the oppression of one people by another. It was felt he had made the world a promise; nor was it only simple people who believed in him, but also the sophisticated—men of affairs and intellectuals. It was these whom the subsequent disillusion most embittered, for they felt they had been made to look like fools. When the Treaty of Versailles made a fiasco of their hopes, they felt personally deceived and betrayed.

Two men acutely afflicted by this anger and resentment were Sigmund Freud and William Bullitt. Their collaboration seems at first sight wildly improbable: the old famed weary European, a genius, one of the rare authentic pathfinders of all time, and the young Amer-

The Atlantic, February 1967.

ican, a person of courage, independence, and good will but volatile and "adrenal" (to use the word of a shrewd observer), a picaresque adventurer in politics, a Tom Jones of diplomacy. This seemingly bizarre combination has produced a fascinating but distorted book. As an analysis of the deep mainsprings of motivation in one of the most complex and puzzling public characters who ever lived, it is sharply illuminating and, with certain reservations, convincing; it makes the contradictions in Wilson's behavior fall into place with an almost audible click. But as an over-all estimate of the whole man it is lamentable, and as an interpretation of events it falls to pieces. It is good psychology but bad history; bad because it is invalid, dangerous because it misleads us as to where the responsibility lies.

Past circumstances have a direct bearing on content. As a twenty-eight-year-old specialist for the State Department on Eastern European affairs, Bullitt, previously a participant in the Ford Peace Ship, went with the American delegation to the Paris Peace Conference in 1919 in the same mood expressed by his contemporary and colleague Harold Nicolson on the British delegation: "We were preparing not Peace only, but Eternal Peace. There was about us the halo of some divine mission. . . . We were bent on doing great, permanent noble things." For Bullitt the opportunity came when he was sent to Russia to ascertain terms of settlement with the Bolshevik regime, which Wilson acknowledged to be "the acid test of good will." Accompanied by Lincoln Steffens and sharing his conclusion, "I have seen the future and it works," Bullitt returned with Lenin's offer of incredibly favorable peace terms. His reception was a stunning blow.

Because the treaty with all its faults, after agonizing delay, was at that moment on the edge of conclusion and the Bolshevik problem seethed with cause for dissension, Wilson, who habitually evaded reality by refusing to look at it, refused to receive Bullitt, to read his report or hear what he had to say. Although it meant inviting attack as pro-German and a Bolshevik, Bullitt resigned in a public letter to the President stating that "effective labor for a new world order" was no longer possible as a servant of his government. He then left for the Riviera telling reporters he intended "to lie on the beach and watch the world go to hell." Subsequently called to testify before the Senate, he supplied Senator Lodge with potent material to aid in defeating American ratification, thus earning denunciation as a traitor to his party and finishing off, as it seemed, his public career. True, Bullitt had a private income, but not everyone who can afford the courage of conviction exercises it.

Freud, too, had had high hopes of Wilson which had turned sour. It was "one of those numerous cases" in his life, according to his biographer Dr. Ernest Jones, where his "optimism and credulity" led to inevitable disappointment and resentment. The experience confirmed Freud's existing displeasure with America, a country which he regarded as a "gigantic mistake." "Your Woodrow Wilson," he told Max Eastman in 1926, "was the silliest fool of the century, if not of all centuries. And he was probably one of the biggest criminals—unconsciously I am quite sure." When Dr. Jones, in a similar conversation, pointed out that the complexity of the problems after the war precluded an ideal peace being dictated by any one man, Freud replied tartly, "Then he should not have made all those promises." In this preface he writes that from the start of the undertaking Wilson "was unsympathetic to me," and this aversion increased the more he learned about him and "the more severely we suffered from the consequences of his intrusion into our destiny." The last four words are highly revealing of a point of view, perhaps a natural one to a national of the Central Powers.

In the 1920s when Bullitt's second wife was a patient of Freud's, the doctor helped Bullitt through a difficult period, and the two became friends. Their joint study of Wilson was begun in 1930 when, on learning from Bullitt that he was planning a book on the Treaty of Versailles and its authors, Freud eagerly offered to collaborate on the chapter on Wilson. The project soon grew into an analysis of Wilson alone. No more tempting subject for the exercise of the Freudian method could have offered itself. Wilson had combined world power with extraordinary contradictions of character which to Freud bespoke some torturing inner conflict. What was the nature of the conflict, and was it in fact the source of Wilson's power as well as of his failure? The challenge of the question was obviously irresistible. Although, in the usual procedure, psychoanalysis takes two, the couch in this case would not be quite as silent as in the case of Moses, on whom Freud also tried analysis without the patient. Wilson had been dead only six years, not three thousand, and had left a mass of contemporary evidence.

Although work on the manuscript was completed in 1932, certain unspecified differences between the authors kept it from publication at that time. It was not until 1938, after Freud's safe removal from Vienna to London, in which Bullitt, by then Ambassador to France, was directly instrumental, that agreement between them was reached. A contract authorizing publication by Bullitt was then signed, whether under a sense of obligation to Bullitt felt by Freud, who was then in his last illness and was to die in the following year, is impossible to say. Publication was mysteriously delayed for nearly thirty years, according to Bullitt as a matter of courtesy until after the death of Mrs. Wilson. The explanation seems inadequate since Mrs. Wilson died in 1961 (Bullitt survives), and in any case the authors originally intended to publish in 1932. Undeniably, certain questions are left unanswered, but not such, it seems to this reviewer, as to justify the current anguish of the psychoanalytic fraternity, who have greeted this posthumous work of the Master as if it were something between a forged First Folio and the Protocols of Zion. The sinister doubts they cast upon the authenticity of Freud's share in the book seem groundless. The writing may or may not be largely Bullitt's, but even if Freud only talked his share, characteristic ideas and prejudices affirm his presence. Moreover, his estate is sharing in the royalties.

The authors' basic premise is that the Treaty of Versailles was the Great Betrayal, from which the world has suffered ever since; that as such it was the result of Wilson's failure to make the Allies live up to the promise of the Fourteen Points and other Wilsonian principles; that he had the power to do so but exhibited a moral collapse and "mental degeneracy" at Paris which were the outcome of his inner psychological conflicts; ergo, that all of us thereafter have suffered from Wilson's neuroses.

Despite a gaping hole in this argument, which I shall come to later, it has the simple appeal of all personal devil explanations of history. Blaming Versailles on Wilson's personal faults is the easy way out, which J. M. Keynes, among others, followed in his *Economic Consequences of the Peace*. It has taken enough hold to justify a deeper look at the President whose Secretary of War, Lindley M. Garrison, said he could never understand him and doubted if anyone could. "He was the most extraordinary and complex character I ever encountered."

The central neurosis, unearthed by the authors, which established its deep unconscious grip on the whole course of Wilson's life and caused him, like Whittier's Daniel Webster, to be "fiend-goaded down the endless dark," was his fixation on his father. The relationship was, in fact, sufficiently remarkable to have attracted notice by others, notably Alexander and Juliet George in their study *Woodrow Wilson and Colonel House*, published in 1956. Recognizing in Wilson "some consuming inner difficulty for which he paid a terrible price," the Georges used the father fixation as an informing symptom. Freud and Bullitt break it down into its Freudian components and show how these determined Wilson's development and explain his frequent episodes of self-defeating behavior, which have always seemed so incomprehensible. They draw on the known facts of Wilson's passionate adulation of and unbroken subservience to his father, his chronic headaches, indigestion, "breakdowns," and other psychosomatic symptoms, his exaggerated friendships, hates, and quarrels, and other evidence.

Briefly, the analysis discovers a man in whom manifest submissiveness toward his father warred with unconscious hostility, which had to find release in acted-out hostility toward substitute father figures such as Dean West at Princeton and Senator Lodge, while the submissiveness had to be compensated by a torturing super-ego whose excessive demands "required of him such God-like achievements that no actual accomplishment could satisfy it." On the jangling Freudian battlefield of the id, the conflict rages in many forms: There are the complicated shapes of narcissism—identification with the father, a Presbyterian minister, becoming identification with God, and, conversely, as little "Tommy" Wilson, with Jesus; there are over-devoted friendships with small, slight "son" figures—Hibben, Tumulty, House—always ending in a sense of betrayal; there is identification with the mother, prompting or requiring "feminine" concessions and submissions to father figures in the case of Lloyd George and Clemenceau; there are the compulsions to repeat, and, over all, the unrelenting super-ego.

Born of his deep inferiority as a small child *vis-à-vis* his father, which itself was part cause and part effect of the startling and almost unbelievable circumstance that Wilson did not learn the alphabet until the age of nine or read easily until eleven, his tyrannical super-ego could never be satisfied with any success. No rung up the ladder was high enough, not even Presidency of the United States; he had to become Savior of the World. The League of Nations was to be the Grail, proof of his title as Savior. The treaty's inequities did not mater as long as it embodied the League, for the existence of the League would solve all problems. The League was "the rationalization which made it possible for him to believe he had indeed saved the world." Wilson *had* to gain the League to save his soul, yet in the fight with Lodge he himself set up the conditions which made the gain impossible. In Freudian terms this becomes the death wish, which to this reviewer seems supererogatory, for the battle with his father in the shape of Lodge, plus the demands of his super-ego and the terrible truth in his heart that the treaty, even including the League, was not the peace he had promised the world, was enough to destroy any man. On October 2, 1919, came the paralytic stroke by thrombosis in the brain, even as thirteen years earlier, in the midst of his frenzied struggle with West at Princeton, his arteries reacted with the bursting of a blood vessel in the eye.

Thus foreshortened, the analysis is less persuasive than in the book, where all the details, examples, and corroborative evidence from episode to episode build up an inherent logic which has the same quality as certain dream interpretations: When they are right they fit, and one knows it at once. Otherwise no bell rings. The bell rings here. One feels that Wilson, himself so like a queer dream, is explained.

Certain aspects seem slighted: for one, the fact of Wilson's late reading, whose repercussions for a mentally gifted child in an intellectual family could not fail to have been devastating, and for another, oddly enough, Wilson's relations with women. The easy references to mother identification and to his wives as "mother substitutes" are coupled with the flat statement that until the first Mrs. Wilson's death Wilson "had not the slightest sexual interest in any other woman." I am perfectly prepared to believe it, but, to quote my own marginal notes at this point, "how on earth do they know?" What is the evidence for or proof of this negative? (The book, incidentally, is without notes or references of any kind, and quotations are given without attribution.) As regards the second Mrs. Wilson: "Let us content ourselves," the authors say airily, that Wilson "again found a mother's breast on which to rest." In view of rather more genial aspects of this relationship not mentioned in this book, including the fact that Wilson habitually referred to his second wife as "Little Girl," the authors' reliance on mother seems a bit glib.

Sex in lay terms in fact receives surprisingly little explicit emphasis in a work co-authored by the progenitor of the sexual revolution. (I note this less in complaint that in wonder.) Even the male friendships are treated as facets of the father-son problem, not as latent homosexuality, a relief to anyone whose cup of ennui has been filled by that particular strain in our current literary supply.

Up to this point the authors' exploration of Wilson's unconscious is enlightening and valuable, despite an irritating style. Among other faults is a habit of maddening repetition, not only of phrases but of whole episodes, recounted two or three times in identical language as if the reader were some sort of nitwit who could not be trusted to retain what he is told from one chapter to the next. More fundamental is the basically irresponsible approach. The authors have allowed emotional bias to direct their inquiry, which has led to undisciplined reasoning, wild overstatement (the Treaty of Versailles was "the death sentence for European civilization"), and false conclusions.

A writer dealing with the world of actuality as distinct from fiction has, it seems to me, an obligation to the reader to deal as honestly with the facts as he knows how. It is easy enough with even a minimum skill in words to leave a loaded impression on the reader while evading the responsibility of being explicit, but the temptation is one that most writers who respect their profession will try to resist. Freud and Bullitt indulge it. They repeatedly, for instance, use the suggestive but loose terms "mental degeneracy" and "degeneration" ("the mental degeneration which led him to sign the Treaty of Versailles"), and sidle up to psychosis while avoiding a precise statement which could be challenged ("he nearly plunged into psychosis" or "he was rapidly nearing that psychic land . . . in which an asylum chair may be the throne of God"). This is pretty, but is it historical? The fact may be historical; indeed, the evidence adduced by the authors, especially the truly frightening quotations from Wilson's last frenetic speeches on the League, suggests that he *was* psychotic in the final period from Versailles to his collapse. But the historian's duty, especially in a matter of such moment as the psychosis of a President, is to state plainly, not to evade responsibility by the blurring of metaphor.

Freud says in his preface that as he studied Wilson's life "a measure of sympathy developed . . . mixed with pity" which grew until it "was so overwhelming that it conquered every other emotion," and he vouches the same for Bullitt. If so, the pity does not penetrate into print. Dislike and contempt dominate these pages. So highly charged is the authors' bias that it is a constant astonishment to realize that they seem unaware of its effect on their thinking. Watching Dr. Freud exhibiting overtones of the Freudian unconscious is a faintly eerie experience, like watching a Pirandello play within a play. The authors, for instance, describe Wilson as "ugly," though, judging by the hundreds of pictures one has seen of him, he was reasonably presentable. They depict him from youth onward with decayed teeth, "disfiguring" eyeglasses, putty-colored, unhealthily blotched skin, protuberant ears, short legs, "sour" stomach, a priggish, sickly, nervous, rather repulsive hypochondriac. Is this the man two women loved devotedly? I do not know whether Mrs. Galt was in love or beglamoured by the Presidency, but of Ellen Axson's feelings there is no doubt. "He is the most wonderful man in the world," she wrote, "and the best."

Dislike shows too in borrowings from William Bayard Hale's clever but venomous *Story of a Style*, published in 1920. Although, according to Dr. Jones, Freud had read this book "with gusto," Bullitt in his preface carefully omits it from the list of books they consulted.

Kept under control, bias can direct and inform an inquiry, but Freud allows himself the undisciplined prejudices of a Personage— with sometimes ludicrous results. The passage on America is certainly his. According to this, Wilson was able to flourish in America because America was a nation "protected from reality during the nineteenth century by inherited devotion to the ideals of Wyclif, Calvin and Wesley" and because the "Thou shalt not!" of the "Lollard" tradition produced an atmosphere congenial to women and feminine men but "intolerable" to a masculine man. Had Wilson been brought up in "the comparative freedom of European civilization," the argument continues, he would have had to face up to his inner conflicts.

One is almost helpless before this concoction. Besides twice using "Lollard" where he means "Puritan" (a very different thing), and assuming that Puritanism was alien to masculine men (Cotton Mather? Oliver Cromwell?), and transferring in one magnificent swoop the entire Protestant tradition of Europe to the United States, and picturing Europe in the Victorian age as a place where screens of rationalizations fell "early," the passage also imagines an America that is the never-never land of Peter Pan. It exemplifies a characteristic of the psychoanalytic method that is its own worst enemy, the habit of rapid expansion from the perceptive and profound to the fatuous.

The authors give Wilson no credit for ideas. They absurdly claim that his legislative program as President was derived from Colonel House's novel *Philip Dru*, evidently themselves suffering from total ignorance of the Progressive movement and its ideas. When Wilson takes a definite stand, they gave it a minimizing explanation; they ignore or underrate his positive policies; they are lavish with sarcasm. When forced to allow that Wilson's super-ego drove him to "considerable accomplishments," they hurriedly add that it made him in the end "not one of the world's greatest men but a great fiasco." Their emphasis is always on the failure, not the achievement. True, Wilson's end, from the Peace Conference on, was a fiasco, but not the totality of his life and not what he is remembered for.

How do the authors account for his "considerable accomplishments"? Easily. It was a matter of rhetoric. Superb oratory was the secret of his influence. They present Wilson as obsessed by speechmaking, as no doubt he was. (In Freudian terms speechmaking, it appears, is a "pleasure of the mouth," and the mouth is a "feminine weapon." They have lost me here.) But that his speeches were merely verbal emperor's clothes, the pretense of a vacant mind, hardly suffices to explain a man whose collected papers are now being issued in forty volumes, who had the stuff to fill an eight-volume official biography thirty years ago, plus a new one of equal length now under way, as well as countless other appraisals and studies over a period of fifty years. Behind Wilson's speeches were thought and profound belief and ideas which pierced through to men's hearts, aroused minds, and awakened hopes. That he was also weak, self-deceiving, rigid, sometimes hypocritical, even dishonest, self-defeating, insufferably self-righteous, ruthless, unforgiving, and mean is equally true but not the whole truth.

In allowing their bias to control their judgment, what the authors have come up with is Mencken's "the perfect model of a Christian cad"—with headaches. This is inadequate. It does not account for Wilson's enduring influence or for the devotion, adoration, and respect of good men that he was able to inspire. The puzzle of Wilson remains.

More serious than their one-sided picture of the man is the authors' twisting of history. The most startling example is their claim that for eight months, from October 1915 to May 1916, Wilson's "supreme desire was to lead the United States into war" on the basis of an agreement to be reached with the Allies allowing him to dictate the peace. This is their analysis of the negotiations surrounding the House-Grey Memorandum. It supposes that the combined lure of being leader in war and arbiter of peace was irresistible to Wilson because the first would release his hostility to his father and the second would satisfy the super-ego's demand to become Savior of the World. The argument is compelling if one grants the Freudian premise that unconscious drives invariably *control* conscious acts, but the human record suggests rather that sometimes they do and sometimes they do not. It is quite possible that a subconscious desire for war as a vent for hostility may have been rumbling around in Wilson's interior, but the historical fact is that his conscious determination to stay neutral maintained control. Undoubtedly Colonel House, out of strong personal conviction, was trying at this time to maneuver the United States into the war. By playing upon the President's ambitions and weaknesses and judiciously misinforming him, he may have lured Wilson for a time into believing that the Allies' acceptance of his terms was possible (being ignorant of the Allies' secret treaties, House may have thought it was). But that American entry into the war was Wilson's "supreme desire," or that he was "doing his best" to bring it about, is, to put it politely, hokum.

To reveal Wilson as warmonger, the opposite of what he professed and everyone has believed him to be, is the kind of magicianship Freud delighted in. He always "took a special interest," says Dr. Jones, "in people not being what they seemed to be." He was convinced that Shakespeare was really Bacon or the Earl of Oxford and discovered to his own satisfaction that Moses was not Hebrew but Egyptian. Giving free rein to intuitive flashes may be fun, but it is not history and it is not science. These disciplines require that the intuitive flash must stand the test of evidence. Freud, by reason of the change he wrought on habits of thought, with effect on art, literature, philosophy, medicine, social relations, and indeed almost any aspect of modern life, is one of the world's outstanding figures, but when he called his method "the science of the unconscious" he was setting a standard that it does not live up to.

We come now to the gaping hole in the argument. It is the assumption that in the conditions prevailing after the Armistice, in the passion of anti-German feeling, in the wounds of the victors, in the antagonisms and nationalisms released by the breaking up of three empires, an ideal peace was possible; that, in short, Wilson had the power to dictate a just peace and failed to exercise it.

All he need have done, the authors announce, was to have faced Clemenceau and Lloyd George with "masculine" weapons: threaten to leave the Conference, to publicly denounce the Allies as the "enemies of peace," and to withdraw American financial and economic aid. In fact, as Wilson well knew, to have risked such an open rupture was impossible, if only for his own sake, for with it would have gone glimmering any hope of the League. Rather than being hailed as Savior, he would have been denounced as a destroyer, and pro-German besides. But, careless of history, the authors rush on. "One crack of Wilson's financial whip," they inform us with characteristic restraint, might have brought Lloyd George "to heel." "One threat" to leave France to face Germany alone might have brought Clemenceau "to compromise" (which suggests a capacious ignorance of the

Tiger). Wilson, they state, "still had more men ready to answer his call and follow him to battle than any man has had before or since. He was still the leader of all the idealists of the world." Two sentences less translatable into reality or more empty of hard fact would be difficult to imagine. The idealists of the world, if the authors are referring to the crowds who cheered Wilson in ecstasy when he arrived in Europe, were now, if French, shouting for reparations and the Saar; if Italian, for Trentino and Fiume; if English, to "hang the Kaiser" and "squeeze the orange till the pips squeak."

The authors' version of a Peace Conference with Wilson cracking the whip that would have brought the Allied powers "to heel" is another never-never land. It ignores those who had done most of the fighting. It presents the Allies as scheming plotters against the noble "idealists of the world," rather than, nearer to the truth, as the battered, exhausted survivors of terrible war who had lost the best part of a generation and, in the case of France, suffered the wreck, pillage, and ruin of a large part of its territory, and who were determined to make victory produce gains to pay for the long bleeding years. It supposes that Wilson, by the simple exertion of a little masculinity, would have had no problem in extracting a "just" peace out of the rival claims of a dozen nationalities, the redrawing of boundaries, the conflicting promises of secret treaties, the allocating of mandates, the dividing of the spoils of the German colonies and the Turkish dominions, the arranging of areas of sovereignty among Arab claimants, the adjudicating of claims to the coal of Silesia, the oil of Mosul, and the other rich prizes, the application of "self-determination" to Austrians in the Italian Tyrol, Sudeten Germans in Bohemia, Armenians in Turkey, Montenegrins in Yugoslavia, and a score of other groups inside alien frontiers, the settlement of such ancient insolubles as Constantinople and the Straits, Danzig and the Polish Corridor and the status of Palestine, the quarrels of Greeks and Yugoslavs over Salonika, of Poles and Czechs over Teschen, of Romanians and Serbs over Transylvania, of British and French over Syria, of Chinese and Japanese over Shantung, and even of Zionists and anti-Zionists over the National Home, all of whom and many more were at Paris pressing their demands while the specter of the Bolsheviki and the revolution in Germany loomed in the background.

It was not only Wilson's psyche that failed in this situation, nor his fault alone that the Treaty of Versailles was less than ideal. The fault was humanity's.

It could have sufficed the authors to have analyzed the nature of

Wilson's neuroses, which they have done brilliantly and convincingly. It was not necessary to have claimed it as the historical cause of what they see as the "evil peace" of Versailles. They are addicted to the oversimplified single explanation of great events. There was in Bullitt, writes his fellow New Dealer Raymond Moley, "a deep somewhat disturbing strain of romanticism." As ambassador he saw foreign affairs as "full of lights and shadows, plots and counterplots, villains and a few heroes"; a dangerous state of mind if not subjected to "the quieting influence of some controlling authority." It can be dangerous to the historian as well as the ambassador.

On a grander scale Freud had something of the same quality. As an originator, powered by extraordinary energy of mind, he was capable of great forward bounds, so that he habitually extrapolated a whole system from a single item: saw the ocean in a drop of water, perceived a law of human behavior in a dropped handkerchief. These marvelous leaps of his from observation to deduction, from the particular to the general, opened for the world a whole new area of thought, but they were not subjected to that "controlling authority." Freud was an adventurer of the mind, and the truest thing ever said of him he said himself: "I am not really a man of science. . . . I am by temperament a *conquistador*—an adventurer if you want to translate the word—with the curiosity, the boldness and the tenacity that belong to that type of being." The Conquistador and the Romantic made natural collaborators.

The undoubted insights of this book into the motivation of a crucial figure in our past raise the question, What can the Freudian method do for history? The answer must be that as an instrument of illumination it can do much—on one condition: Let it for God's sake be applied by a responsible historian.

How We Entered World War I

On April 2, 1917, the United States as a new contender entered the tournament of world power from which we have not since, despite wishful attempts, been able to withdraw. Up to then, notwithstanding our hearty belligerence in the Spanish-American War, we were not regarded as one of the Great Powers, either by them or, on the whole, by ourselves. American participation in the Great War was the beginning of our majority in world affairs.

In the half-century that has since elapsed, a fundamental shift of the international balance has taken place, with the sites of power spreading outward from Europe to the periphery. The governing seat vacated by the collapse of Britain has been taken—not without kicking and protesting against our fate—by this country. Risen from newcomer to one of the world's two dominant powers in fifty years, we are once again at war, no longer fresh and untrained but an old hand, skilled, practiced, massively equipped, sophisticated in method, yet infirm of purpose, and without a goal that anyone can define. Is this the destiny to which that first experience has led us? How did the United States become involved and had she a choice? "God helping her," said President Wilson on that April 2 fifty years ago, "she can do no other." Could we have done other?

The Great War has never been for us so embedded a part of our national tradition as the Civil War or World War II. It is somehow less "ours." The average person thinks of it in terms of air aces who

New York Times Magazine, May 5, 1967.

flew in open cockpits, a place called Château-Thierry, a song called "Over There," a form of transport called "40 and 8," and a soldier in leggings who became President Truman—but what it means in our history he could not easily say. When this writer in 1955 proposed to a prospective publisher a book on the Zimmermann telegram, a major factor in precipitating America's involvement, the advice received was to abandon the idea because it was the "wrong war"; the public was interested only in the Civil and the Second. This was in fact a justifiable assessment, much the same as that reached by a historian in 1930 who, a decade after the end of the war, found the American people still "irritated and bewildered" by it.

These words, which describe so aptly our attitude toward the war in Vietnam, establish a link between the two experiences. The first experience was governed by an old illusion, and the present experience by a new one. World War II, on the other hand, with the imperative of Pearl Harbor supplying an understood cause and purpose, did not sow doubt and self-mistrust. It was clear why we had got in and what was the end in view. But as will certainly be the case with Vietnam, so for twenty years after World War I historical controversy raged over how and why we got into it, and the question is still being probed and re-examined.

The revisionists of the 1920s and '30s, fueled by post-war disillusion, discarded the accepted view of our involvement as the unavoidable consequence of German aggression toward neutral shipping, in favor of conspiracy theories of one kind or another. They discovered the causative factor in British propaganda, capitalist profit, and other concealed and sinister forces. Burrowing into statistics of trade and finance, private correspondence, and all manner of inner workings, the revisionists brought to light much significant material and fresh insights. But their self-accusatory thesis required a compensatory leaning-over-backward in favor of Germany, and just as they were most vigorously making their case, Germany, returning to the offensive under Hitler, unmade it for them.

Since then, as is the circular fashion of history, counter-revision is leading the way back to what was obvious at the start. The somersaults of revisionists—whether it be that Roosevelt plotted Pearl Harbor or that the Third Reich, as held by England's antic historian A. J. P. Taylor, was pushed into aggression by the democracies—enjoy the notoriety of the sensational, but the facts roll over them in the end.

On the outbreak of war in 1914 the prevailing American attitude was one of self-congratulation that it was none of our affair; and there was a fixed intention that it should not become so. In classic summary —appropriately from a small town in the heart of the Midwest—the *Plain Dealer* of Wabash, Indiana, stated: "We never appreciated so keenly as now the foresight of our fathers in emigrating from Europe." Newspaper cartoons habitually depicted Uncle Sam separated by a large body of water from a far-off, furiously squabbling group of little figures; in one case reminding himself that the chance of his life was to "sit tight, keep his hands in his pockets and his mouth shut"; in another case standing shoulder to shoulder with President Wilson with backs firmly turned on Europe's gore-dripping "barbarians."

The belief in our safe isolation was reinforced by Wilson, who, bent on pursuing the New Freedom through domestic reform, was irritated by the threatened interference with his program from overseas. He declared in December 1914 that the country should not let itself be "thrown off balance" by a war "with which we have nothing to do, whose causes cannot touch us." (The familiar ring can be traced to a more famous echo twenty-five years later in Neville Chamberlain's reference to Czechoslovakia as "a far-away country of which we know nothing.")

For Wilson it was justifiable in August 1914 to ask the American people to be "impartial in thought as well as in action . . . neutral in fact as well as name." But by December, when the expectation of a short war had vanished at the Marne and the armies were locked in the deadly stalemate of the trenches, the war was already touching us. Forced to recognize that American business could not be held immobile, Wilson had already in October reversed his earlier ban on loans to belligerents. This was the foundation for the economic tie which thereafter in ever-increasing strength and volume attached the United States to the Allies. By permitting extension of commercial credit it enabled the Allies to buy supplies in America from which the Central Powers, by virtue of Allied control of the seas, were largely cut off. It opened an explosive expansion in American manufacture, trade, and foreign investments and bent the national economy to the same side in the war as prevailing popular sentiment.

For the country on the whole was as pro-Allied in sympathy as it was anti-belligerent in wish. The President shared the sentiment. "I found him," wrote Colonel House after the first month of war, "as unsympathetic with the German attitude as is the balance of the country." Counselor Von Haniel of the German Embassy in Washington, trying to disabuse his principals of certain illusions, reminded them that American feeling was the outgrowth of a natural connection with England "in history, blood, speech, society, finance, culture," and that "in the present case commercial instinct and sentiment point in the same direction." He had hit upon the essence of the situation.

At the same time as he lifted the ban on loans, Wilson agreed to permit unrestricted trade in munitions, contrary to an earlier proposal for their embargo. The two measures were not taken in the Allied interest (although they were to work to the Allies' advantage) but in the American interest—for the Administration, no less than Von Haniel, knew the strength of the country's "commercial instinct" and feared that an embargo would turn Allied orders to Canada, Australia, and Argentina. To ban loans and embargo munitions would have been to give realistic expression to the isolation that the people and their President believed they enjoyed. But it would have closed off the wealth of unlimited orders, and Americans did not wish to suffer for their neutrality. Rather they hoped to make a good thing of it. With these two economic measures taken before the war was three months old, the fact, if not the illusion, of isolation was dead.

In February 1915 Germany declared a submarine blockade of Britain, to be carried out by a policy of "unrestricted" undersea warfare, which meant attack without warning on merchant ships found in the war zone. As a violation of traditional neutral rights to freedom of the seas, this was, said Wilson, outraged, "an extraordinary threat to destroy commerce." An American President was obliged to resist it even though a quarrel would heighten the risk of involvement. Quarrels with the British were continuous over their incursions on freedom of the seas in the form of the Declaration of London, the doctrine of continuous voyage, elaboration of contraband, the right of search, Prize Court procedures, and other annoyances which together added up to that old conflict between the belligerent's right to blockade and the neutral's right to trade. But Britain's measures, however infuriating to legalists of the State Department, did not threaten life or touch the public mind or seriously hamper the flow of goods, of which by far the major share was directed to the Allies in any case.

By contrast, acquiescence in the role claimed for the U-boat would have meant the end of overseas trade. The explicit threat to neutral civilian lives meant either that Americans must stay off the public highway of the ocean or the American government must exert enough pressure, without tipping the precarious balance of neutrality into open rupture, to make the Germans draw back. Either way, with this development, the war had not only touched but entangled us.

During the next two years German activities on the seas, in Belgium, and in the plots of spies and saboteurs in the United States operated relentlessly to weaken American neutrality, with results that would have been the same with or without Allied propaganda.

Germany's violation of Belgium's guaranteed neutrality, the opening act of the war, had aroused American indignation and put Germany in the wrong from the start. It established the image of bully in the public mind. This was no sudden reversal, for the image of the kindly German professor personified by Dr. Bhaer, who married Jo in *Little Women*, had long since given way, under the influence of Wilhelmine Germany, to the arrogant Prussian officer. Initial American indignation would doubtless have subsided into indifference if, before the first month was out, it had not been re-excited and confirmed by the burning of Louvain and its ancient library. The horror engendered by this act was profound, for the time, it must be remembered, was on the far side of the gulf of 1914–18, when people permitted themselves simple and sentimental reactions and society was believed to be advancing in moral progress.

With the American Minister to Belgium, Brand Whitlock, former reform mayor of Toledo, remaining in Brussels in constant contact between the occupying power and the population, Americans felt a particular concern for Belgium's misfortunes, from the shooting of hostages to the developing starvation that evoked the Hoover Relief Commission. The Bryce Report on atrocities issued by England and signed, not by accident, by the Englishman best known to the United States, the former Ambassador to Washington and author of *The American Commonwealth*, fell on prepared ground. It gave rise to many exaggerated atrocity stories, but it was not British propaganda that staged the trial and execution of Edith Cavell. This shooting of a woman, a nurse, a humanitarian, accomplished with the unfailing German affinity for the act that would most successfully outrage world opinion, sealed the concept of the Hun.

Above all, the mass deportations, begun in 1916, of ultimately three hundred thousand Belgians to forced labor inside Germany aroused more anger than anything since the *Lusitania*. Whether or not because of sensitivity on the subject of slavery, Americans—at least of that day—found something peculiarly shocking about citizens of a white Western nation being carried off to forced labor. The revulsion, reported Von Haniel, "is general, deep-rooted and genuine."

The sinking in May 1915 of the Cunard Line's *Lusitania*, which carried, in addition to a full complement of non-combatant passengers, a part-cargo of small-arms ammunition, besides enhancing

German "frightfulness," had brought to a head the issue of submarine warfare. Regarded by the Germans as a munitions carrier using its non-combatant status as protection, the ship was sunk without warning; that is, without ordering passengers off in lifeboats before loosing the torpedo. Of the nearly 2,000 persons aboard, 1,195 were lost, including 124 Americans. In the previous week two American ships had been attacked with two American deaths.

Thus the rights of both neutrals and non-combatants were at stake. Tense and protracted negotiations followed in which Wilson's almost impossible task was to force Germany to acknowledge these rights without the ultimate threat of war, which was the last thing he wanted. He had to pick his way along a narrow ridge between the precipice of war on one side and that of abdication of neutral rights, as advocated by his Secretary of State, William Jennings Bryan, on the other. Representing the pacifist position that no interest was worth defending at the risk of war, Bryan became spokesman of the demand that Americans be warned not to (or, as some insisted, forbidden to) travel on belligerent ships.

In this demand was crystalized a central issue that transcended the matter of American trade or neutral rights. The real issue was our position as a great power. The United States could not allow the U-boats to keep her nationals off the sea lanes without forfeiting the respect of other nations, the confidence of her own citizens, and her prestige before the world. She could not forbid her own people to exercise their rights, Wilson wrote to Senator Stone, chairman of the Foreign Relations Committee and a leading isolationist, "without conceding her own impotence as a nation." This was the crux, the more so as to concede impotence now would undercut the ambition which the President already had in mind: to mediate the war and save the world from its own wickedness.

Wilson rejected the proposal to keep American citizens off belligerent ships as a gesture "both weak and futile" which, by revealing the United States posture to be one of "uneasiness and hedging," would "weaken our whole position fatally." Bryan, finding his insistent and reiterated advice as Secretary of State overridden, accordingly resigned to become thereafter a trumpeting voice of the pacifist wing. While his going relieved Washington's diplomatic dinners from the temperance of grape juice, imposed by the Secretary's edict, it hardly eased matters for Wilson, who had still to make good his stand against the submarine without going to war. The pressure of the dilemma brought forth those memorable words: "There is such a thing as a nation being so right that it does not need to convince others by force that it is right. . . . There is such a thing as a man being too proud to fight."

Although the speech aroused tirades of disgust by the interventionists at Wilson's "poltroonery," it reasserted the strength of the "sit-tight" sentiment in the nation which the *Lusitania* had so nearly dissipated.

Wilson, in note after note to Berlin, fencing, countering, reiterating, rejecting, ultimately won his point. After another ship crisis over the sinking of the *Arabic* in August 1915, with the loss of forty-four lives, including two Americans, he extracted a German promise not to sink without warning. But the whole issue was revived again by the sinking of the *Ancona* in November and the *Sussex* in March 1916, and was only resolved by Germany's renewal of her promise upon the President's notice that without it the United States would have no recourse but to sever relations. In fact, this result was due less to Wilson's firmness than to Germany's recognition that she had too few submarines to sink enough shipping to make the risk of American belligerency worthwhile. Her shipyards meanwhile worked round the clock to correct that inadequacy.

Each time during these months when the torpedo streaked its fatal track, the isolationist cry to keep Americans out of the war zones redoubled. When a resolution to that effect was introduced in Congress by Senator Gore of Oklahoma and Representative McLemore of Texas in February 1916, Champ Clark of Missouri, Speaker of the House, led a delegation to the White House to inform Wilson that it would pass two to one. After absorbing four and a half million words of debate, it was, however, ultimately tabled, although not without 175 votes in its favor.

As the war lengthened and hates and sufferings increased, with repercussions across the Atlantic, American public opinion lost its early comfortable cohesion. The hawks and doves of 1916, equivalent to the interventionists and isolationists of the 1930s, were the preparedness advocates and the pacifists, with the great mass of people in between still stolidly, though not fanatically, opposed to involvement.

The equivalency to the present, however, is inexact because of the sharp ideological reversal in our history that took place after 1945. The attitude of the American people toward foreign conflict in the twentieth century has been divided between those who regard the enemy or potential enemy as a threat to American interests and way of life and are therefore interventionists, and those who recognize no such danger and therefore wish us to stay at home and mind our own business. Who belongs to which group is decided by the nature of the enemy. When, as in the years before 1945, the enemy was on the right, our interventionists by and large came from the left. When, as in the years since 1945 the Soviet Union and Communist China replaced the right-wing powers of Germany and Japan as our opponents, American factions switched roles in response. The right has become interventionist and the left isolationist. Former advocates of America First, who used to shriek against engagement outside our frontiers, are now hawks calling for more and bigger intervention (otherwise escalation). Former interventionists who once could not wait to fight the Fascists now find themselves doves in the unaccustomed role of isolationists. It is this regrouping which has made most people over twenty-five so uncomfortable.

In 1916 ideologies of right and left were less determining. The most vigorously anti-German interventionists came from the upper and educated classes especially on the East Coast, where Prussian militarism (the term then in use) was regarded as the ultimate foe of democracy which could not be allowed to triumph. President Emeritus Eliot of Harvard, "the topmost oak of New England," declared the defeat of the Central Powers to be "the only tolerable result of this outrageous war." Chief Justice White of the Supreme Court said, "If I were thirty years younger, I would go to Canada to enlist."

Distinguished clergymen like Henry Van Dyke and Lyman Abbott felt no less warmly, and the president of the American Historical Association, William Roscoe Thayer, announced in response to Wilson's original advice to be impartial in thought, that only a "moral eunuch" could be neutral in the sense implied by the "malefic dictum" of the President. The new Secretary of State, Robert Lansing, was convinced that a German victory "would mean the overthrow of democracy in the world" by the forces of military despotism, an opinion shared by his Republican predecessor, Elihu Root, not to mention by the President's closest adviser, Colonel House, and his bitterest despiser, ex-President Theodore Roosevelt.

The opinions of the articulate East, however, were more influential than representative. The rest of the country, with its center of gravity a thousand miles from any ocean, still bore the stamp "Keep out of it." Isolationism naturally centered in, although was not confined to, the largely Republican Midwest, with its "hyphenated" settlements of German-Americans in Milwaukee, Chicago, St. Louis, and other cities, its Populist traditions, and its agrarian radicals called sons-of-the-wild-jackass. The home states of congressional isolationist leaders tell the tale: Speaker Champ Clark and Senator Stone of Missouri, Senators Hitchcock and Norris of Nebraska, La Follette of Wisconsin, Gore of Oklahoma, and, from the South, Vardaman of Mississippi and Representative Claude Kitchin, chairman of the Ways and Means Committee, from North Carolina.

Ideological divisions cut across the geographical. Progressives and Socialists, though hating the autocracies, were largely (though by no means all) isolationist, partly because they did not want war to interfere with domestic reform and partly from inherited dislike of Europe. They shunned foreign entanglements with the Old World from whose quarrels and standing armies and reactionary regimes their fathers had escaped to the promise of America. Regardless of background or position, they all joined in one dominant argument: Sentiment for war was manufactured for profit by bankers and businessmen. David Starr Jordan, pacifist president of Stanford, pictured Uncle Sam "throwing his money with Morgan & Co. into the bottomless pit of war," La Follette denounced profiteers as the real promoters of preparedness, and Eugene Debs, leader of the Socialist party, declared he would rather be shot as a traitor than "go to war for Wall Street."

Foreseeing that we might, and believing that we should, enter the war, pro-Allied groups opened a preparedness campaign in 1915. Supported by the Army and Navy Leagues, they formed committees for national security and American rights, organized parades, distributed books, films, and leaflets identifying preparedness with patriotism, introduced a bill in Congress to expand the Reserve into a continental army of 400,000, and called for a congressional appropriation of $500 million to build an "adequate Navy." As the agitation mounted, vociferously led by Theodore Roosevelt, the administration forces took alarm lest in resisting it, in a diehard grip on neutrality, they allow a partisan issue to develop in which the Republicans would become the party of patriotism and the Democrats be identified with "weakness."

Wilson accordingly embraced preparedness, marched straw-hatted in parades, supported the Army Bill for increasing the Regulars from 80,000 to 140,000 and the Reserves to 400,000, and approved a five-year program of naval construction to provide 10 battleships, 16 cruisers, 50 destroyers, and 100 submarines. He undertook a speaking tour through the Midwest on behalf of the Army Bill, but failed to persuade the hard core of isolationists of the need for adequate armed forces. This outcome was not surprising since he balanced every eloquent plea to prepare "not for war but for adequate national defense" with an equally eloquent avowal of his and the country's "deep-seated passion for peace."

In the spring of 1916 debate raged in Congress and country over the Army Bill. Progressives thundered against militarism as the spawn of capitalist greed and the destroyer of the American dream. Interventionists insisted America must join in the battle of the democracies against tyranny (a cause embarrassed by the inconvenient alliance of the Czar) if political freedom was to survive anywhere. Preparedness parades grew louder and longer, a mammoth example on Fifth Avenue lasting twelve hours with 125,000 civilian men and women marchers, two hundred brass bands and fifty drum corps, thousands of cheering observers on the sidewalks, and floodlights on the last squadrons as they marched on into the night. Impervious, a majority of Republican Representatives in the House voted to warn American citizens off armed merchant ships, indicating their firm preference for discretion over neutral rights.

A stunning and unexpected testimony to the depth of pacifist feeling emerged at the Democratic convention at St. Louis in June. Wilson's managers had planned to make patriotism the theme, with bands concentrating on the national anthem instead of "Dixie" and bursts of "spontaneous" enthusiasm for the flag. These demonstrations proved uninspired, but the keynote speech of ex-Governor Martin Glynn of New York, which argued that the American tradition was to stay out of war whatever the provocation, produced a frenzied outburst and a "delirium of delight." Designed to appeal to the peace sentiment, it had been approved in advance by the President, who, no less than any other practicing politician in search of re-election, was interested in consensus. As Glynn cited each historical precedent, his audience took up the chant, "What did we do? What did we do?" and the speaker roared in reply, "We did not go to war!" Delegates cheered, waved flags, jumped on their seats. When Glynn, becoming somewhat dismayed at what he had aroused, tried to slide over his prepared text, they yelled, "No! No! Go on! Give us more! More! More!" They danced about the aisles, "half mad with joy . . . shouting like schoolboys and screaming like steam sirens."

Glynn had shown that pacifism, instead of being something not quite manly, was right, patriotic, and American. The effect was "simply electrifying." Convention leaders were appalled. Chairman McCombs hastily scribbled on a sheet of paper, "But we are willing to fight if necessary," signed his name, and passed it to Glynn, who nodded and called back, "I'll take care of that." But by now fascinated with his own effect on the crowd, he never did. Political plans were deranged. Wilson's campaign was revised to make peace the main issue; the Republicans, repudiating Roosevelt, nominated Hughes on a platform of "straight and honest neutrality" and lost in November to the slogan promoted by Wilson's managers, "He kept us out of war."

It was this use of the peace sentiment which accomplished the close victory through a notably sectional vote of the Western states in new alliance with the South. It enabled Wilson to recover for the Democratic party what Bryan had three times failed to win, the support of the majority of predominantly agricultural states.

The final four months leading up to U.S. belligerency began with Wilson's concerted effort through December and January to end the war through mediation. His concept of a "peace without victory," although called by Senator La Follette "the greatest message of the century," did not appeal to the belligerents. Since neither side wanted the American President to arrange the terms of a settlement and each was bent on total victory, Wilson's attempt to negotiate a peace failed.

In the meantime Germany, having built up a fleet of two hundred submarines, took the decision to risk American hostility for the sake of an all-out effort to end the war her way. On January 31, 1917, she formally notified Washington of intent to resume unrestricted submarine warfare beginning next day. All neutral ships would be "forcibly prevented" from reaching England. A single exception in the form of one U.S. passenger ship a week would be allowed provided that it carry no contraband, dock only at Falmouth and only on a Sunday, be marked by three vertical stripes each a meter wide painted alternately white and red, and fly at each mast a large flag checkered white and red.

At the prospect of funnels "striped like a barber's pole and a flag like a kitchen tablecloth," the American historian J. B. McMaster could hardly contain his indignation. The insult implied in such orders addressed to the major neutral indicated that Germany had no doubts of America's answer. "We are counting on the probability of war with the United States," Field Marshal von Hindenburg had said at Supreme Headquarters when the decision was taken, but "things cannot be worse than they are now. The war must be brought to an end by whatever means as soon as possible." Headquarters had convinced itself that in the time before the submarine could knock out the Allies, American military assistance would "amount to nothing." But the civilian Chancellor Bethmann-Hollweg believed the entry of America meant "*finis Germaniae.*"

In the vortex of the conflict, America had become, willing or not, a major power: as arsenal and bank of the Allies, to whose cause our economy no less than our political system was now attached, and as obstacle, so long as we continued to supply the Allies, to any German hope of victory. To yield freedom of the seas now after two years' hard-fought maintenance of the principle was incompatible with first-class status. Wilson was left with no choice but to declare the long-avoided rupture of relations. At once pacifist groups were roused to feverish action in mass meetings to demand that American ships stay out of war zones, while interventionists agitated equally loudly for the arming of our ships and the aggressive assertion of American rights.

As ships piled up in home ports, American commerce threatened to come to a standstill affecting the entire national economy. The Cabinet grew seriously alarmed. Although Wilson possessed the executive authority to arm ships, he was reluctant to take the step that would inevitably start the shooting. He preferred to ask Congress for authorization, thus touching off the great debate and filibuster on the Armed Ship Bill. In the midst of it came the revelation of the telegram from German Foreign Minister Arthur Zimmermann inviting Mexico into alliance as a belligerent. As a scheme to keep U.S. forces occupied on their own border, it offered to help Mexico regain her lost territories of Texas, Arizona, and New Mexico. Intercepted and decoded by British naval intelligence and made available to this country, the telegram was released to the press on March 1 in the hope of influencing "the little band of willful men" in the Senate. It failed of that purpose, but aroused the American public more than anything since the outbreak of war. As a proposed assault on U.S. territory, it convinced Americans of German hostility to this country.

On March 9 Congress adjourned without passing the bill. The President issued the order for arming ships anyway and waited for the "overt act." It came on March 18 in the torpedoing without warning of three American merchant ships with heavy loss of life. Conveniently at this moment the overthrow of the Czar by the preliminary revolution in Russia purified the Allied cause, and the advent of the great new convert to democracy under the Kerensky regime brought a glow of enthusiasm to liberal hearts. At the same time the relentlessly mounting toll of the submarine was making a graveyard of the Atlantic and raising a serious prospect of the Allies' defeat.

For two more weeks the President hesitated in his agony, afflicted by his sense, as he had said earlier that month, that "matters outside our life as a nation and over which we had no control . . . despite our wish to keep free of them" were drawing the country into a war it did not want. "If any nation now neutral should be drawn in," he had said in November, "it would know only that it was drawn in by some force it could not resist."

This is as just a statement of the truth as any. We were not artificially maneuvered to a fate that might have been otherwise; what engulfed us were the realities of world conflict. In the latest of a long train of scholars' examinations, Ernest May of Harvard in his *The World War and American Isolation, 1914–17*, published in 1959, concluded, "Close analysis cannot find the point at which he [Wilson] might have turned back and taken another road."

On April 2 Wilson went to Congress to ask for its formal acceptance of "the status of belligerent that has been thrust upon it." He put the blame specifically on submarine warfare: "a war against all nations." He said "neutrality is no longer feasible or desirable" when the peace of the world and freedom of its people are menaced "by the existence of autocratic governments backed by force which is controlled wholly by their will, not by the will of the people."

The validity of this proposition was somewhat weakened by the fact that he had believed neutrality feasible and eminently desirable in coexistence with these same nations for nearly three years. "A steadfast peace," he now discovered, "can never be maintained except by a partnership of democratic nations." Citing the Zimmermann telegram as evidence of hostile purpose, he said there could be no assured security for the democracies in the presence of Prussian autocracy, "this natural foe of liberty." And so to the final peroration: "The world must be made safe for democracy . . . the right is more precious than peace."

Nothing that Wilson said about the danger to democracy could not have been said all along. For that cause we could have gone to war six months or a year or two years earlier, with incalculable effect on history. Except for the proof of hostility in the resumed submarine campaign and the Zimmermann telegram, our cause would have been as valid, but we would then have been fighting a preventive war—to prevent a victory by German militarism with its potential danger to our way of life—not a war of no choice. Instead, we waited for the overt acts of hostility which brought the war to us.

The experience was repeated in World War II. Prior to Pearl Harbor the threat of Nazism to democracy and the evidence of Japanese hostility to us was sufficiently plain, on a policy level, to make a case for preventive war. But it was not that plain to the American people, and we did not fight until we were attacked.

In our wars since then the assumption of responsibility for the direction, even the policing, of world affairs has been almost too eager —as eager as it was formerly reluctant. In what our leaders believe to be a far-sighted apprehension of future danger, and before our own shores or tangible interests have been touched, we launch ourselves on military adventure half a world away with the result that the country, as distinct from the government, does not feel itself fighting in self-defense. Korea was thoroughly unpopular and Vietnam— where we have gone a step further into a purely preventive war, to contain Chinese communism—even more so. In the circumstances the instinct of the country is uneasy, consciences troubled, and counsels divided.

Two kinds of war, acquisitive and preventive, make hard explaining and the last more so than the first. Although the first might be considered less moral, so far in human experience abstract morality has not notably determined the conduct of states and a good, justifiable reason like need, or irredentism, or "manifest destiny," can always be found for taking territory. Besides, acquisitive wars tend to be short, sharp, and successful and success never needs explaining. But it is never possible to prove a preventive war to have been necessary, for no one can ever tell what would have happened without it. Given the gap in modern power and organized resources between China and ourselves, our exaggerated fear of Chinese communism, both as threat to us and in its appeal to the rest of Asia, seems unwarranted by a "clear and present danger." In the grip of a new illusion we have not waited, as in World Wars I and II, for the enemy's shot to be aimed at us.

In April 1917 the illusion of isolation was destroyed. America came to the end of innocence, and of the exuberant freedom of bachelor independence. That the responsibilities of world power have not made us happier is no surprise. To help ourselves manage them, we have replaced the illusion of isolation with a new illusion of omnipotence. That screen, too, must fall.

Where once we saw ourselves self-contained and free to stand apart, we now see ourselves as if endowed with some mission to organize the world in our image. Militarily we could knock out Hanoi, and doubtless Peking, too, tomorrow, but we cannot raise a clean new democracy on nuclear ashes. Whatever our material or political power, it is not enough for omnipotence. We cannot mold the non-Western world to our desires nor require its acceptance of our concepts of political freedom and representative government. It is too late in history to export to the nations of Asia and Africa with un-schooled and undernourished populations in the hundreds of millions the democracy that evolved in the West over a thousand years of slow, small-scale experience from the Saxon village moot to the Bill of Rights. They have not had time to learn it and history is not going to give them time. Meanwhile we live on the same globe. The better part of valor is to spend it learning to live with differences, however hostile, unless and until we can find another planet.

Israel's Swift Sword

A people considered for centuries non-fighters carried out in June against long odds the most nearly perfect military operation in modern history. Surrounded on three sides, facing vast superiority in numbers and amount of armament, fighting alone against enemies supported and equipped by a major power, and having lost the advantage of surprise, they accomplished the rarest of military feats, the attainment of exact objectives—in this case the shattering of the enemy's forces and the securing of defensible lines—within a given time and with absence of blunder. The war, which taken as a whole was the greatest battle ever fought in this area, shook the world, leaving local and international balances in new focus, incidentally rescuing the United States from a critical position and, not the least of effects, exposing a profound failure of Russian calculations and presumably of military intelligence. That the armed forces who achieved this result drew on statehood of less than twenty years and on a population more than half immigrant raises questions about the components of effective military power. Who are the Israeli Defense Forces (IDF), and how did they do it?

The fundamental components were, of course, motivation and compelling necessity, but all the will in the world would not have sufficed without capacity. What furnished capacity primarily was that the brainpower with which this people is endowed was channeled for the first time since the Exile into the military art in defense of their own homeland.

Second, they developed by conscious choice of their General Staff

The Atlantic, September 1967.

what it calls "the Israeli answer," in tactics, weaponry, and training, to suit their own needs and people in the particular war they had to fight. Partly this was a military decision, partly it reflected political experience of disillusionment in reliance on others; basically it was temperamental, deriving from the enforced self-reliance of the early Zionist settlers from whom the higher-grade officers, largely native-born, descend.

The third component of capacity was development of a military doctrine based on absolute fulfillment of mission by all ranks under all circumstances and the fullest exploitation of every resource, particularly knowledge of the enemy and weapon capacity. A tank, plane, or gun in Israeli hands is expected to outperform its equal in other hands. The principle of exploitation is also applied to opportunities as they develop in battle, based on belief in improvisation, in action if not in plan.

Finally, the manpower of the nation, which up to the age of forty-nine constitutes the active reserve, was kept prepared through constant and rigorous exercises that were not always merely for training. A young reserve officer returning home after a brief call-up and asked by his parents what he had been doing replied succinctly, "Shooting infiltrators." What forged the Israeli armed forces was that the state had never known peace.

Three conditions at the time the state came into being determined the kind of army it would have to create: absence of peace, limitations of geography, and limitations of manpower and money. A fourth, which was an advantage, was foreknowledge of a specific enemy, familiar and contiguous.

When the war of independence of 1948 was halted by armistice without a treaty, the battered defenders, taking stock, realized that they had won a state but not peace. Across an elongated unnatural border, curving in haphazard knobs and bulges that marked positions on the day of the truce, they faced frustrated, embittered neighbors subjected to a constant propaganda of revenge. Geography was against the Israelis: They had no natural obstacles on which to base a defense, no territory to yield, and no room to retreat. Unlike larger countries, they could not afford mistakes like that of France in 1914 or rebound from an initial disaster like Dunkirk or Pearl Harbor. This fact dictated a strategy, should it become necessary, of carrying war to the enemy, and the initial strike could not be allowed to fail. Other countries can face the possibility of defeat or invasion and expect to survive, with limited or lost independence. For Israel, its people believed, defeat would mean annihilation. Once inside Israel, said General Amos Horev, Deputy Chief Scientist of the IDF, the Arabs "would have cut us to ribbons." As commander of a battalion in the fighting for Jerusalem in 1948, General Horev, who looks more like a Yale oarsman than a general officer, had had to leave his dead on the field and had come back next day to bury them. He found the bodies hacked into pieces, and with the help of another officer, matched up limbs and heads with torsos, knowing each of the dead personally, before burial. Many others knew from experience like that of the Hebron massacre of 1929 what it would mean if the Arabs were ever to gain the upper hand.

Limited manpower and money precluded a standing army adequate to the task of defense. The solution arrived at was dependence on a small professional career force which, together with each class of draftees serving their two and a half years of military duty, would constitute a standing nucleus. The rest, amounting in the June war to about eighty percent of the total, must be drawn in emergency from a national reserve in civil life. The problem was how to organize, train, and keep up to date this reserve so that it would be mobilizable in twenty-four hours and able to take the field in forty-eight. This required an "Israeli answer," since no other country had the same problem under the same conditions. The United States counts on three weeks to put the Reserve into action. An adaptation of the Swiss system was worked out by which each locality formed its own brigade —except for special volunteer units like the paratroopers or the Air Force—thus saving time in assembly. Depots for the equipment of each unit are set up, with maintenance taken care of by the draftees and regulars.

Reservists are kept to the necessary degree of readiness and fitness, with one foot in the army, by annual training periods of a month for enlisted men and five or six weeks for officers, plus shorter call-ups of up to three days every three months, depending on type of unit and the need.

The IDF *is* the nation, not a section of it. Bus drivers became tank drivers and are now back on their local routes. A supermarket manager who commanded a battalion in Sinai and captured an Egyptian general has returned to his groceries. Even one divisional commander was a reservist—General Avram Yoffe, who is Parks Commissioner in civil life. The *kibbutzim*, representing six to seven percent of the population, with their long commitment to the land and strong ideological tradition, provided fifty percent of the officers and twenty-five percent of casualties. Virtually every family had a connection with someone in the war. "My niece's husband who captured Government House," or "Jaacov's brother on the PT boat," is part of every conversation.

The surprise was the performance of the "espresso" generation in their twenties, mistrusted by their elders, who considered that they had discarded the old ideals and sat around in the cafés over espresso, long on apathy and short on dedication. In the test it was these young men who carried the bulk of the combat with a fierce commitment that was as important to the nation as the victory itself.

Regional organization of units gave added incentive in battle, as in the Northern Command, when men fighting the Syrians were defending or avenging their own frequently shelled villages. Wherever they came from, said one officer, "whether from the Galilee, Tel Aviv, or the Negev, each man fought as if everything depended on *him*." In the general mobilization for the crisis, units often found themselves with twenty percent surplus. Men over-age or not called for some other reason appeared anyway, including a father in one brigade who joined his son, and were accepted as familiar faces by the company commander without too much question. He does not care who is surplus, General Chaim Barlev, Deputy Chief of Staff, explained: "Only the computer knows later."

Units trained for years in terms of a particular terrain. All the relevant information that could be obtained before war was assembled and learned. The IDF allotted a higher percentage of ammunition—up to fifty percent of total training ammunition—to actual tactical problems with fire rather than to range marksmanship as in other countries.

The IDF does not believe in officers' starting as officers, but selects candidates for officer training from the draftees who show promise, after they have learned how it feels to serve as a private. Candidates must survive rigorous testing and pass through NCO school and service first. Reserve officers of company level and up are required to take three-months courses every two or three years or else give up their commissions.

Because of stringent budgets, officers' training in Israel is more condensed than in any other country, lasting no more than six months for the ground forces. When they leave, according to General Uzi Narkis, chief of the Central Command, "they feel the gap between what they have learned and what they ought to know and so they try to learn more on their own." A small, compact, bright-eyed, serious man who established his headquarters in the Old City of Jerusalem after hostilities and drives there in his car unescorted, he talked sitting with one leg tucked under him, sipping the bottled orange drink on which the IDF fought the war. The Jews' intellectual curiosity, he said, was an important military asset. "They want to know *why*: why this hill, not the other, why this way rather than that. They are skeptical and critical. Israelis are critical of everything, all the time, of the government, the army, of themselves. It is important for an officer to be self-critical—and obstinate. He must be obstinate about sticking to his mission until it is carried out." The three essentials for an officer, he said, are a spirit of inquiry, execution of mission, and orientation—to the terrain and the task. "And of course leadership and audacity, that is understood." An officer is one who leads, and to lead he has to be ahead, "ahead too of what occurs." Evidence that officers led their units during the six days of June was a casualty rate of thirty percent compared with less than ten percent for the whole.

The officer class is young; youth is a fetish of the IDF. Yigael Yadin, now professor of archeology and director of the historic Massada dig, was thirty-three as Chief of Operations in the war of 1948. The present Chief of Staff, General Itzhaak Rabin, now forty-six, was appointed at forty-three, and his staff on average is probably the youngest in the world. This is deliberate policy reflecting the military leaders' tense consciousness that on them may depend at any moment the country's continued existence. They are determined to maintain the IDF primed to the last minute, never satisfied, constantly improving.

For the General Staff and virtually all higher-grade officers now over the age of forty, as well as many of the enlisted men, this is their fourth war. They fought in World War II as part of the British Army, in their own war of independence against the Arabs in 1948, and in the Sinai campaign against Egypt in 1956. In 1941 when Palestine seemed in danger of invasion by Rommel's forces in North Africa, its young Jewish citizens joined either the British Army or the Palmach, the professional nucleus of the Haganah, whose members were intensively trained for resistance to the expected invasion. It was then that their attention was first turned to the Sinai peninsula, for that would have been Rommel's route. After 1945 the Palmach gained another kind of military experience in the illegal struggle to bring in the refugees. Its seagoing and coastal operations in that effort provided the early experience of Israel's Navy. Facing the coming showdown with the Arabs upon end of the Mandate, the Palmach began that systematic study of the enemy which was to give the IDF of 1967 the most thorough and accurate information ever provided by any Intelligence to Operations.

The present Chief of Staff, the Deputy Chief, the Chiefs of Intelligence, of Operations, of the Air Force, and Armored Corps, as well as the three area commanders, are all veterans either of the British Army or the Palmach, and all but three are Palestine-born.

Most of the high command have studied briefly at the command and staff colleges in France, Britain, and the United States, but this is nothing they boast of; it has to be pried out of them. One theme they notably and unanimously maintain is refusal to acknowledge any debt to foreign methods or doctrines and insistence on their independent development. There are no foreign experts or advisers in the IDF.

The Israelis want to leave no doubt that they have grounded their armed forces on their own experience from the Palmach on. This effort too has been deliberate because, new to military endeavor and small in size, they have had to resist any temptation to follow some military father figure represented by one or another of the major powers. A deeper reason is the sense of uniqueness that has characterized the Jews since Abraham made his covenant with God. Recognizing both tendencies, General Ezer Weizmann, Chief of Operations of the IDF, said, "We had to guard against the extremes of being either too arrogant or too humble, saying, 'Oh, we are so tiny, tell us what to do.'" What influenced him at the *Ecole de l'Etat Major*, said General Aharon Yariv, Chief of Intelligence, was *la méthode*, a way of thinking and analyzing a problem, not the problem itself. He and his colleagues, when setting up their own General Staff school, "copied nothing." Doctrine and methods had to be of practical value for local circumstances, not just repetitions of accepted principle, however classic.

These officers have in common a self-assurance so confident that it can afford to be quiet, if not exactly modest. There is no reluctance whatever to acknowledge, in the most charming and friendly way, that "we're *good*." General Rabin, a subdued, thoughtful, intensely self-contained man and a chain smoker, conveying an impression of inner tension rigidly suppressed, is almost shy in company, but when talking on his subject, becomes magisterial. In all the staff and command officers an evident knowledge of their subject finds expression in readiness, even eagerness, to talk of it. They spill over with ideas. Because of the challenge and the need, the military profession in Israel can attract the finest energy of the country.

These are the officers and men who sprang into battle on June 5; who fought their way across Sinai almost without stopping for seventy-two hours except for refueling and one or two hours' sleep; who in the case of one company of paratroopers fought on all three fronts, Sinai, Jerusalem, and Syria; who in the case of another unit continued to advance after all its officers one after the other were put out of action; who in the last two days plunged and scrambled up the Syrian heights against a position that even now, to anyone seeing its gun emplacements, lines of fire, cement bunkers, barbed wire, and stone-lined trenches, seems impossible to have been taken by human assault.

The impetus and force that carried the Israelis forward through the six days cannot be understood separately from the period of crisis that preceded. The "tension," as they call it, was the worst time, everyone agrees. The people at large, not sharing the high command's exact knowledge of its own capacity, felt the enemy closing in. With Egyptian armor massing, the radios of Cairo, Damascus, and Amman bellowing annihilation, they saw the specter of genocide again. They knew they would have to fight alone if they fought at all. One by one the nations had dropped away from the proposed maritime armada to force the Gulf of Aqaba. The experience was familiar. Britain had closed the doors of Palestine to Jews seeking escape from Hitler. The U.N. after voting partition had left them to Arab attack, embargoing arms. The assurances of 1956 had not been honored. World indifference, they felt, was now repeating itself, leaving them to another "final solution." The Nazi program to wipe out the Jews is never out of mind in Israel, and they lived with the knowledge that the Arabs who have adapted it to their purposes were now gathering for the attempt.

Alongside the fear and depression of some, a more resolute mood possessed others, a feeling that they had had enough of Arab belligerence, threats, sabotage, terrorists, and diversion of water, that *this* time they must make a thorough job of it. They had reached, in General Rabin's words, "an accumulated frustration, because everybody felt that we had tried every way to avoid war but that now it was forced on us."

For the high command the period of waiting was "agony," for with each day that it was prolonged their war casualties would be that much greater. As compared with 1956, so they believed, they would be entering war at a greater disadvantage: This time the bulk of Egyptian force was already east of the Canal zone, with an enormous quantity of modern weapons and ten years of Soviet training they had lacked before. Israel would be advancing against them alone with no allies to pin down enemy planes; in addition it would be fighting on two, possibly three fronts instead of only in Sinai. Yet the alternative —acceptance of the blockade—would have been intolerable: "We would have been buried alive," as one officer said. The decision had to be taken, for the choice, as summed up by the same man, was clear: "Not to be strong was to be smashed like a worm." Held in restless waiting for three weeks, the IDF shot forward as if released by a spring.

Its spearhead was the Air Force, which established the conditions of victory—Air Chief General Mordecai Hod prefers to say "won the war," but that seems unfair to the ground forces—in eighty minutes. "We planned and trained eighteen years for those eighty minutes," he says, sparkling with pride. As commander of a performance of spectacular brilliance and sensational success, he cannot hold in his delight. A smile quivers in his eyes and on his mouth as he talks, and breaks easily into a grin. He is brimming with happiness. Before succeeding to the command, Hod was for five years deputy commander under his no less exuberant predecessor, Ezer Weizmann, and they are much alike in style. Weizmann, nephew of Israel's first President, was born in Tel Aviv and Hod in Israel's oldest *kibbutz*, Degania A in the Galilee. At forty, he still flies every week with one of his squadrons, feeling that he must be able to do himself whatever he demands of them. It gives confidence in their orders to the fighter pilots, who start training at eighteen and whose average age is twenty-two to twenty-three.

The Air Force convinced its colleagues that though Israel might stand off the enemy, it could not *win* without air superiority. To create the perfect and infallible instrument for this purpose was the goal of Hod and Weizmann. Appointed to command the Air Force at thirty-four in 1958, Weizmann describes the following eight years until shifted to his present post as Chief of Operations as "the happiest of my life." He was working on the frontiers of the jet age with knowledge of a vital task on which his country's life depended.

Tall, slender, and voluble, with a small mustache and English-accented speech, Weizmann moves restlessly, flinging himself back in his chair, twisting his long legs over the arm, leaning forward to make a point, or striding up and down while rapid sentences tumble over each other in a losing race to keep up with his thoughts. He has a gift of distilled phrase. Speaking of the meaning of Jerusalem to a Jewish state, "I could not raise my children on the history of Tel Aviv." Or on the incompatibility of national character as a factor in Russia's imperfect success in training the Arabs, "What Ivan has in common with Muhamed, kill me if I know." Because of the extraordinary record of the Air Force, he says, foreigners think it had some electronic, super-sophisticated secret weapon, "something that whistles and sings the Hatikvah," but the answer was simpler than that: perfect command of the machine as redesigned and adapted to suit both the short distances of air war in the Middle East and Israel's narrow means. In negotiating with the French, for instance, for purchase of Mirages in 1958–9, the Israelis insisted on the plane's having two cannon built into it although it was designed to carry only missiles. The French argued that with new sophisticated developments only missiles were needed in air-to-air combat, but the Israelis had a dual purpose in mind. They wanted to use the planes not only to intercept bombers and fight Mig 21s, which carried missiles plus one cannon, but also to destroy planes on the ground, the essence of their strategy. Weizmann stuck to his guns and got them. "I wouldn't have bought the planes without them."

"We were fanatics in the Air Force," he says. "We knew exactly what we wanted. We meant to rely on our own ideas and not be prisoners of computers." This was the secret of their ultimate supreme confidence that "we could clobber the enemy," even though the enemy represented the combined air forces of Egypt, Syria, Jordan, and Iraq. Why? "Because the military world has become a victim of its own sophistication in weaponry, bewildered by the technology of the atom age. It has forgotten that brains, nerve, heart, and imagination are all beyond the capacity of the computer. No computer can go 'beyond the call of duty,' but that is what medals are given for."

The Air Force planned its weapons and trained its fliers in terms of an exact objective and the capacity of the enemy. On this problem Israel's Intelligence forces went to work, collecting, piecing together, building up over months and years, by photo reconnaissance and other means, despite the disadvantage of having no military attachés or other representatives in the Arab countries, a complete picture of the enemy. "We knew everything about the Egyptian Air Force," said Hod, "how they work, what was their training, where, when, and how," including exactly how long it took them to take to the air after an alert—up to twenty-five minutes on certain bases, in comparison to an Israeli figure which, though he would not disclose it, elicited from Hod his broadest smile.

No commander, he said, has ever been provided with better intelligence. So precise was his planning that he was able to take out the nearer Egyptian fighter bases before the more distant bombers and still reach the latter at the exact moment they were taxiing for the take-off.

The work of the Intelligence Corps is the ground on which the IDF stands, and its chief, General Yariv, a spare, alert man in rolled-up sleeves and eyeglasses, is regarded by many as the key figure of the armed forces. Born in Latvia, he came to Palestine at fourteen, "young enough to be accepted by the Sabras, old enough to know the outside world." He speaks six languages and is forty-six, but looks ten years younger. To brief a roomful of 150 correspondents, covering the field from Kuwait to the Canal, discoursing on everything from weapons to politics, holding his auditors absorbed for over an hour while telling them nothing security would not permit them to know, fielding questions for another hour, and ending to spontaneous applause, immediately to be converged upon by a crowd eager for more—this was a bravura performance presented with the logic of a teacher and the instincts of an actor.

Israel's Staff is exceedingly security-conscious, and nothing is to be learned of its intelligence methods. All that Yariv will say is that whatever means exist, "you can be sure we used all of them." Meanwhile he has created a legend that has crossed the border. The Arab caretaker of an American institute in the Old City assured me that a knife-grinder of Bethany, living for seven years on a few piasters a day and posing as a kind of village jester dressed all in green, who told funny stories while turning his wheel outside the church door, was in reality an Intelligence agent and high officer of the Israeli Army. From this fairy tale he drew the not inappropriate moral, "It shows what they can do, and we have to learn."

In action the Israeli soldier demonstrated the basic precepts on which the IDF was formed: the ability of the individual commander to see what in a situation could be exploited, and the flexibility to take advantage of the opportunity without referring to higher authority or sending for additional help—"to see and to solve," as General Rabin puts it. Next, physical leadership by officers and in all ranks the spirit to carry out a given mission no matter what. In the desert a battalion, ordered to break through an Egyptian fortified position protected by a field solid with mines, failed and fell back, was ordered forward again, and with advance guards on hands and knees probing for the mines with steel wires, cleared a path and took the position. In the desperate rush to take the Syrian heights before cease-fire, men of one company flung their bodies on a barrier of barbed wire to let their fellows advance. In the unexpected battle for the heights outside Jerusalem when an artillery commander, lacking the necessary equipment, found himself unable to clear space for a gun emplacement, two reservists of his company who were residents of the city in the construction business offered to bring their own bulldozers and do the job, which they successfully accomplished. In Jerusalem, too, Colonel Motte Gur, commander of the paratroopers, personally led his troops in a charge through St. Stephen's Gate against a barrier of an overturned Jordanian bus roaring in flames.

In initiative, persistence, and refusal of self-deception the Israeli is the opposite of the Arab. The IDF, it must be remembered, does not exist in a vacuum; it is the obverse of its opponent, and any analysis of its performance must take the opponent into account. Where the Jew questions, the Arab dreams. To quote General Narkis, "The Arabs build castles in the air, and then become prisoners of their castles." Where the Jew fights facts, the Arabs accept: It is the will of Allah.

Essentially the war was a conflict of societies whose terms can be seen any day on a road between Syria and Israel, literally brown on one side and green on the other. The Jews who made the state belong to the activist West, and through the Zionist experience of return, of colonizing and reviving the neglected land, of making it flourish and capable of supporting a modern nation, they have undergone a mental and emotional revolution. They have become masters of their fate instead of sufferers. Egypt and Syria, despite all the verbal socialism, have made no revolution, none that has reached down into the lives of the people. The Syrian peasant in a hovel on a miserable patch of ground, the Egyptian fellaheen of the delta with seven diseases per capita have no society so precious as to fight and die for.

Militarily the victory of two and a half million against fifty million was one of professionalism. The Egyptian officers, according to the Israelis, are not professionals at their job. They have no conception of precision, thoroughness of preparation, the obligations of leadership, or of the Israelis' favorite tenet, "execution of mission." When over a thousand years ago Arab conquerors swept triumphantly across North Africa, they were fighting with their own weapons in their own tradition. Today, lacking the Israelis' capacity to create their own armed forces, they are trying to operate in others' terms. An Egyptian manual picked up in the desert still illustrates drill with drawings of flat-faced smiling Occidentals obviously taken from some British manual circa 1930. Jordan's army is a British creation. Syrian Artillery listened to instructions in Russian. Egyptians were more dazed than aided by their Russian equipment. They fired not one—or possibly only one—missile from the twenty-odd SAM sites provided for them by the Russians. Their fighter pilots flew Migs, but could not successfully fight in them. Their rocket crews lacked the accuracy to fire surface-to-surface missiles lest, aiming at Tel Aviv, they might leave Beirut in ruins. On the whole, as Nasser suspected, they are not yet fully capable of modern warfare. Nevertheless their numbers, combined with Russian alliance, remain overwhelming and dangerous, and the Israeli command knows it can never succumb to the mood that says, "The Arabs have surrounded us again, the poor bastards."

Where the Israelis depend on mobility and penetration, the Arabs fight best from fortified positions. Scores of their Soviet heavy tanks were dug in for use as stationary artillery. They were captives of their wealth in manpower and armament. The Soviet-designed system, based on bands of entrenched positions and deep bunkers backed up to a depth of several kilometers, required enormous manpower to construct. "That's for the rich," say the Israelis. For all the Arabs' deep resentment of the intruders in their world, and for all their pre-war threats and engineered orgies of hate, their cause against Israel is not for them a matter of life or death, and once they lost air cover they could neither advance nor hold their ground.

The Russians misjudged Arab capabilities—and Israel's as well—perhaps because they are materialists, disinclined to give weight to imponderables. They ask scornfully, but doubtless in honest bewilderment, "How many divisions has the Pope?" The iron mass of armament they bestowed upon their clients, Migs, tanks, missile sites, rockets, anti-aircraft guns, half-tracks, tons and tons of other arms and ammunition, must have seemed to them certain to be decisive. They may have been misled too by customarily thinking of the Jews with contempt as victimized second-class citizens. They failed to recognize that the Israelis indeed possessed a secret weapon—a homeland.

A final component of the IDF's capacity was the civil population —its other self. The outpouring of help, solicitude, and love in the form of letter-writing, home-baked cakes, sunburn cream, and other ministrations was phenomenal. The Israeli Air Force may have at this moment the finest combat fliers in the world, and the Israeli soldier may be the toughest fighter, but the campaign had its Jewish-mother aspect nevertheless. In Jerusalem a volunteer women's organization came into being during the "tension," starting from one soldier's call home for mosquito repellent for his company. A campaign of collections from pharmacies, drug companies, and private homes, assembled and distributed by volunteers in their own cars, jumping Army bureaucracy, succeeded in getting eight thousand units to the soldiers within five hours.

From that moment there was no stopping them. Gripped by the national danger and a sense of the country facing its ultimate test of existence, everyone wanted to give something. Within three days the Jerusalem women's group had 450 volunteers registered and card-indexed according to the kind of contribution each was prepared to make. Some served as baby-sitters where a wife was filling an absent husband's job, some as messengers to take news of casualties to families. Some drove out along the roads to give lifts to soldiers trying to reach home on a twelve-hour leave during the "tension" or to bring them to homes which had offered bathtubs or showers for their use. A mere mention of home-baked cakes brought in eight hundred in one day, and a mention of wine, five hundred bottles.

Schools organized a program to send a letter from each pupil enclosed with small gifts in a parcel from each family. After the war an armored-corps corporal confessed that on the third day in the desert under fire, with the heat and deaths and burning metal, he was finished, shattered, unable to move, not caring whether he lived. One of these parcels was dropped on his bunk. He thought, "Some silly crap," but caught sight of the letter and read it: "Dear Soldier, I am sending you this chewing gum. I am not afraid of bombs because I know you are out there protecting me and will not let anyone kill me." He rose at once, the corporal said; "I felt like a lion."

These lions fought with tears. A recurrent mention in the post-war talk is of weeping. "I was fighting and crying," a reserve officer of field rank told me, "because I was shooting and killing." The wife of a commander in the battle for the Old City, whose troops suffered excessive casualties because use of artillery was eschewed, told how he came home unwashed, unharmed, and apparently unchanged, and only after picking up his sleeping child, broke down and silently wept. A soldier in the North, suddenly confronted by a Syrian emerging from a trench six feet away, shot and killed him and then noticed a wedding ring on the dead man's hand. The thought flooded his mind, "He has a wife and children," and he felt the tears rise. Not everyone reacted that way. One wife said that while her husband brooded speechless for days after he returned, his brother reported killing as many Arabs as he could and was perfectly pleased with himself. Another who saw his tank crew blown up, leaving him the only survivor, thereafter turned his guns on the Egyptians and blasted his way through with savage satisfaction.

Afterward the amazing victory brought no parades or cheers or the usual celebrations of triumph. The emphasis was on the dead. Jubilation was missing. The old grieved and the young were somber, conscious of contemporaries maimed or killed. Memorial services and black-bordered announcements in the newspapers were almost a daily occurrence. Israel's concentration on grief would have seemed exaggerated in another country, but the Jews have known many killed over the centuries and the 700 lost in this war could ill be spared. On a per-capita basis, a comparable loss to the United States would have been 60,000. The race against the stopwatch of the impending U.N. cease-fire required taking military risks which added to the casualties. To Israel as a nation, desperately concerned over its future as a Jewish state in a sea of Arabs, a Jewish life is not expendable. Each loss is a tragedy. But the feeling goes deeper than the loss to the state. It comes from an old, inherited high value placed on human life.

No aspect of the IDF is more striking than its concern for casualties. Every man wounded or dead is brought back regardless of cost, even that of mounting an offensive to recover the missing. In most cases the wounded were in hospitals within an hour, transported directly from the place they fell by helicopter, and the knowledge of this was a strong morale factor. A commanding officer or civilian employer attends the funeral of anyone lost from his outfit and pays the family a visit of condolence. The value of one man was deliberately dramatized when General Hod went to occupied Syria to attend the exchange of 550 Syrian POWs for one Israeli flier and the bodies of two dead.

Yet it is not only for lives that Israel grieves; there is something more. Its people, so long and so often the victims of violence, have had to become, against their ethic, against the hope that brought them back to Zion, users of violence. They had to win the right to nationhood, like the United States, by force of arms, and now by the same means have reconfirmed it. Notwithstanding the pride of the IDF—and even happiness of the Air Force—in a job well done, many people in Israel are profoundly troubled by their new role and their own success in it. From Auschwitz to Sinai and the recovery of Jerusalem has been barely a generation, and the transformation is almost too sudden. In less than a lifetime the Jews have come from persecution to rule over others.

General Rabin, the quiet, thoughtful man who led the IDF in this attainment, was the first to recognize its burden. In his speech on Mount Scopus after the victory, he said, "The Jewish people are not accustomed to conquest, and we receive it with mixed feelings." What they will make of it and what conquest will make of them is the question that remains.

If Mao Had Come to Washington

One of the great "ifs" and harsh ironies of history hangs on the fact that in January 1945, four and a half years before they achieved national power in China, Mao Tse-tung and Chou En-lai, in an effort to establish a working relationship with the United States, offered to come to Washington to talk in person with President Roosevelt. What became of the offer has been a mystery until, with the declassification of new material, we now know for the first time that the United States made no response to the overture. Twenty-seven years, two wars, and x million lives later, after immeasurable harm wrought by the mutual suspicion and phobia of two great powers not on speaking terms, an American President, reversing the unmade journey of 1945, has traveled to Peking to treat with the same two Chinese leaders. Might the interim have been otherwise?

The original proposal, transmitted on January 9 by Major Ray Cromley, acting chief of the American Military Observers Mission then in Yenan, to the headquarters of General Wedemeyer in Chungking, stated that Mao and Chou wanted their request to be sent to the "highest United States officials." The text (published here for the first time) was as follows:

> Yenan Government wants [to] dispatch to America an unofficial rpt unofficial group to interpret and explain to American civilians and officials interested the present situation and problems of China. Next is

Foreign Affairs, October 1972.

strictly off record suggestion by same: Mao and Chou will be immediately available either singly or together for exploratory conference at Washington should President Roosevelt express desire to receive them at White House as leaders of a primary Chinese party.

Chou requested air travel to the United States if the invitation from Roosevelt were forthcoming. In case it was not, Mao and Chou wanted their request to remain secret in order to protect their relationship with Chiang Kai-shek, which was then in the throes of negotiation.

The message, received in Chungking on January 10, was not forwarded, except as secondary reference in another context, either to the President, the State Department, or the War Department. It was held up in Chungking by Ambassador Patrick J. Hurley with the arm-twisted concurrence of General Wedemeyer.

Before examining the circumstances and reasons for this procedure, let us imagine instead that, following a more normal process, the message had been duly forwarded to the "highest officials" and had received an affirmative response, which is 99 44/100 percent unlikely but not absolutely impossible. If Mao and Chou had then gone to Washington, if they had succeeded in persuading Roosevelt of the real and growing strength of their subgovernment relative to that of the decadent Central Government, and if they had gained what they came for—some supply of arms, a cessation of America's unqualified commitment to Chiang Kai-shek, and firm American pressure on Chiang to admit the Communists on acceptable terms to a coalition government (a base from which they expected to expand)—what then would have been the consequences?

With prestige and power enhanced by an American connection, the Communists' rise and the Kuomintang's demise, both by then inevitable, would have been accelerated. Three years of civil war in a country desperately weary of war and misgovernment might have been, if not entirely averted, certainly curtailed. The United States, guiltless of prolonging the civil war by consistently aiding the certain loser, would not then have aroused the profound antagonism of the ultimate winner. This antagonism would not then have been expressed in the arrest, beating, and in some cases imprisonment and deportation of American consular officials, the seizure of our consulate in Mukden, and other harassments, and these acts in turn might not then have decided us in anger against recognition of the Communist government. If, in the absence of ill-feeling, we had established relations on some level with the People's Republic, permitting communication in a crisis, and if the Chinese had not been moved by hate and suspicion of us to make common cause with the Soviet Union, it is conceivable that there might have been no Korean War with all its evil consequences. From that war rose the twin specters of an expansionist Chinese communism and an indivisible Sino-Soviet partnership. Without those two concepts to addle statesmen and nourish demagogues, our history, our present, and our future would have been different. We might not have come to Vietnam.

Although every link in this chain is an "if," together they tell us something about the conduct and the quirks of American foreign policy. What we have to ask is whether the quirks were accidents only, or was the bent built in? Was there a real alternative, or was the outcome ineluctable? Looking back to find the answer, one perceives the ghost of the present, and from the perspective of a quarter-century's distance its outline is more clearly visible than among the too-near trees of the Pentagon Papers.

In the circumstances of 1945 there are three main points to remember: First, the Japanese were as yet undefeated; second, American policy was concentrated urgently and almost obsessively on the need to bring Nationalists and Communists into some form of coalition; third, the American Military Observers Mission of nine, later enlarged to eighteen, members (known as the Dixie Mission), was already in contact with the Communists, having been functioning in Yenan since July 1944. Its purpose was to organize an intelligence network using Communist men and facilities in a strategic area vital to future operations, and generally to assess Communist capabilities and aims. These had become acutely important with the approach of an American landing in China (at that time still contemplated as part of the final assault) and with the approach, too, of Russian entry against Japan.

Coalition was the central factor in American plans because only in this way would it be possible, while still supporting the legal government, to utilize Communist forces and territory against the Japanese entrenched in the north. A patched-up unity was the more imperative from our point of view because of the need to avert civil war between the Chinese parties. This above all else was the thing we most feared because it could defeat our major objective, a stable, united China after the war—and because civil chaos would tempt outsiders. If the conflict erupted before the Japanese had been defeated and repatriated, they might take advantage of it to dig themselves into the mainland. And then there was the looming shadow of the Soviet Union. In the absence of coalition, we feared the Russians might use their influence, when they entered the war, to stir up the Communists and increase the possibility of a disunited China afterward. As early as May 1941, it may be worth noting, an unpublished policy study of the Council on Foreign Relations on the interrelation of the Chinese Communists, Japan, and the Soviet Union stated: "It is vital that there be no civil war in China."

During November and December 1944 negotiations for coalition were pursued by Ambassador Hurley as go-between, with optimism, enthusiasm, and a minimum of acquaintance with the causes, nature, and history of the problem. On November 10 he had succeeded in hammering out with the Communists a Five-Point Plan for their participation in a coalition government. Its terms would have allowed them relative freedom of political action while acknowledging Chiang's leadership and joint authority over their armed forces. Because Mao and his colleagues saw coalition as an avenue to American aid and, in the long run, to national power, they were prepared to pay this temporary price. To Hurley, who thought the Communists were a kind of Chinese populist Farmer-Labor party whose aim was a democratic share in national government, the terms seemed so workable and such a triumph of his own diplomacy that he signed the document along with Mao.

On November 16, to his dismay, Chiang Kai-shek rejected the plan *in toto* on the ground, as he told Hurley, that to admit the Communists to government on the terms Hurley had signed would eventually result in their taking control of it. Hurley, who identified the Generalissimo's tenure with American interest—and with his own—was ready at once to adapt coalition to the Generalissimo's terms. That these did not reflect the realities in China was not apparent to the Ambassador, although it was to his staff, who had been observing conditions under the Kuomintang for years and now had the opportunity to visit and investigate the Communist zone. Their assessment pointed to a different American interest, and this became the critical issue: Was the American objective preservation of the Generalissimo, or was it a wider option that would not involve us in the fate of a "steadily decaying regime"?

Hurley and Wedemeyer were convinced converts of the first thesis. It was not easy at that time to envisage China without Chiang Kai-shek. His towering reputation as national leader made it an article of faith to most outsiders that no one else could hold China together and that his fall would carry chaos in its wake. It was easy for Hurley and

Wedemeyer to believe in him: The trappings of power are very persuasive. Both the new ambassador and the new commander were ambitious to show how they could succeed where General Stilwell had failed, and both saw the obvious path to success as keeping in step with the Generalissimo.

Pressed by Hurley into making a counter-offer to the Communists, Chiang proposed a plan of coalition which would bring the Communist armed forces under Nationalist control and in return legalize the Communists as a party. Hurley promptly espoused the Generalissimo's plan although it nullified the terms he had negotiated with Mao, and exerted his most strenuous efforts, assisted by Wedemeyer, to persuade the Communists to accept it. They naturally refused an arrangement which would have meant submission, not coalition. Concluding that negotiations through a mediator who had committed himself to the other side were useless, they broke off the talks, and from that time on ceased to trust Hurley. When Wedemeyer argued that if they came to terms with the Generalissimo the United States could send them arms and supplies, they were not persuaded because they knew Chiang would control the distribution. When Hurley offered to revisit Yenan to resume the talks, he was turned down, and when Colonel David D. Barrett, chief of the Dixie Mission, was asked to add his persuasion, he was told by Mao and Chou that they still hoped for and needed American arms but not on Chiang's terms. They said the United States was propping up a "rotten shell" in Chiang Kaishek, who, in spite of all the United States might do, was "doomed to failure." Barrett left the interview feeling he had talked to two leaders who were "absolutely sure of the strength of their position."

Negotiations were thus deadlocked, leaving the Communists, who had made a serious effort from which they had hoped to gain much, in need of a new approach. Haphazardly at this point certain exploratory and apparently unconcerted overtures from American military sources were made to them which left them encouraged but confused. The proposals were brought on December 15 by Colonel Barrett, and simultaneously but separately by Colonel Willis H. Bird, deputy chief of OSS in China. Both projects concerned possible airborne landings of American technical units to operate jointly with Communist forces. Colonel Bird's plan, which was the more grandiose, involved the "complete cooperation" of all Communist armed forces "when strategic use required" by the American command. Whether this plan was intended to bypass the Generalissimo or whether Colonel Bird had ever considered this aspect of the problem is not mentioned in his rather jaunty report, which does, however, make the claim that "Theater Command already agreed on principle of support to fullest extent of Communists. . . ."

Colonel Barrett brought two proposals authorized by Wedemeyer's chief of staff, General Robert B. McClure. McClure had cleared the first one, limited to 4,000 to 5,000 American technical troops, with General Chen Cheng, the Generalissimo's chief of staff, and secured the kind of ambiguous reply which a Chinese uses to disguise "No" and an American takes to mean "Maybe." The second, more startling proposal on December 27 carried McClure's verbal assurance to Barrett that it had been cleared with Ambassador Hurley. It projected, after victory in Europe, a beachhead on Shantung and the landing of an entire U.S. paratroop division of some 28,000 men for whom the Communists were asked if they could take care of supplies, other than arms and ammunition, until U.S. Army supply procedures could begin to function. They said they could, although Barrett could not help wondering whether, behind Chinese composure, they might not have been slightly dazed by the responsibility and its implications.

Faced by such prospects, uncertain how far they were authorized at the summit, the Communists understandably felt a need for clarification by direct contact in Washington, bypassing Hurley. More than clarification, what they wanted was recognition. The offer to make the distant journey—which would have been Mao's first outside China—was a measure of their seriousness. Today, after twenty-five years of Mao's vicious denunciations of the United States as the fixed—and doomed—enemy of the Socialist camp (matched by vintage Dulles, early Nixon, and others from our side), the obvious question is: Were the Chinese Communists ideologically still sufficiently flexible in 1945 really to desire an association with the United States?

Before everything else the Chinese Communists were pragmatic. Ideological purity having proved nearly fatal in the 1920s, they had learned to adapt political action to present fact, and were ready to deal, for survival or advantage, with whatever ideological opponent the situation required. If they could deal with Chiang Kai-shek, as they had in 1936 and were prepared to again, why not the United States? What they hoped to gain can be reconstructed from the frank conversations held by Mao and Chou with John S. Service, political officer of the Dixie Mission, who reported them at length.

Primarily they wanted to convince President Roosevelt that they, not the Kuomintang, represented the future of China. They knew that time was working in their favor, that the mandate of heaven was slowly and irresistibly shifting. If they could somehow make this plain at the policy-making level in Washington, then the United States might be persuaded to mitigate its support of Chiang and thus hasten the shift. Second, they wanted access, as a partner in a coalition government, to American arms and other munitions on the model of Tito, their Communist counterpart in Europe. On the basis of usefulness against the enemy, they considered they had no less a claim. Armament was their most serious deficiency; they had gained control of North China beyond and behind Japanese lines by an astonishing organization but without enough weapons to risk a real battle. In Washington they hoped to persuade the President of the validity of their claim. They felt the United States was blind to the real state of the Kuomintang's decline and their own rise, and that if they could reach Roosevelt they could make this clear.

Roosevelt's aura as a man with sympathy for the oppressed had penetrated the remotest corners of the world. In *Christ Stopped at Eboli* Carlo Levi tells how, on entering a hovel in a miserable village in God-forsaken Calabria, he was confronted on the wall by a crucifix, a picture of the family's absent son, and a picture of Roosevelt. While it is doubtful if, apart from propaganda posters of the four Allied chiefs, the American President appeared on any private walls of Yenan, he was present in the minds of the leaders. On Roosevelt's re-election in 1944, Mao sent him a message of congratulation and received a reply in which Roosevelt said he looked forward to "vigorous cooperation with all the Chinese forces" against the common enemy, Japan. If not definitive, this was at least an opening.

The American observers in Yenan found their hosts intensely curious about the United States, anxious to learn what they could of means and techniques, especially military, developed by the Americans. Mao, according to Major Cromley, "would grab intellectually anything about the United States that anyone could tell him." He and his colleagues had been impressed by the steady advance of American forces in the extraordinarily difficult campaign across the Pacific, and they realized it was this that would be the main force in the defeat of the Japanese homeland. In the real world in which they now had to make their way, the United States with its money, its resources, and its current presence in Asia was the country they had to deal with—for the interim.

"We can risk no conflict," Mao told Service, "with the United States." They were not concerned about adulteration by a rival ideology because they were confident of the ultimate victory of their own. They wanted American recognition of what they had accomplished and were capable of accomplishing, and thus recognition as a major party, not an outlaw. They wanted to acquire belligerent status as a party to the coming Allied victory so that they could not be ignored in the arrangements for post-war China, nor in the organization of the United Nations. And certainly they had in mind that an American connection would help them to meet that none-too-welcome day when the heavy tramp of the Soviet Union should enter Manchuria. In short, they wanted to find out at the source whether, if Chiang continued to refuse coalition, there was "any chance," as Mao asked Service, "of American support of the Chinese Communist Party." They wanted to know where they stood.

The governing factor was that in their own minds they fully expected to succeed to the sovereignty of China. Here lay the problem which in the Communists' relation to the United States eventually became the shipwreck rock. The Communist view of it was made explicit by Mao as early as August 1944: "For America to give arms only to the Kuomintang will in its effect be interference because it will enable the Kuomintang to oppose the will of the people of China." While this may have been a subjective judgment of the will of the people, it was more realistic than otherwise, and recognized as such by American observers whose duty was to assess the evidence. As "the only group in China possessing a program with positive appeal to the people," reported John P. Davies, second secretary of the Embassy, who was attached as political officer to the Theater Command, the Communists were the first group in modern Chinese history to have "positive and widespread popular support. . . . China's destiny is not Chiang's but theirs." He thought this was a consideration that the United States in seeking to determine policy should keep in mind.

The tenor of advice by our career officers both in China and the State Department at this time was that unqualified support of Chiang Kai-shek was not the best means of achieving unity in China. By encouraging in Chiang a false sense of his own strength, it made him intransigent to compromise and therefore more likely to precipitate civil war than prevent it. The staff in China felt that we should retain our freedom to establish contact with the Communists, who were certain to retain North China and very likely inherit Manchuria after the war, because only through U.S. contact and economic aid could we keep them out of the coming Soviet embrace. The plea of officers in the field for greater "flexibility of approach" grew almost impassioned. Sustaining Chiang should not become, as one said, "an end in itself." The China Affairs and Far East Divisions of the Department tried to convey the voice of the field upward to the policy-making level, even to the point of suggesting that if Chiang himself did not take remedial action, re-examination of U.S. policy would not only be justified but "very likely imperative."

The difficulty was the not unusual one in the conduct of American foreign policy, that the voice of the field was not reaching, or certainly not influencing, the ear at the policy-making level—in this case the President. Out of an old prejudice against career diplomats, justifiable almost anywhere but in China, Roosevelt always felt he would be better informed by a personal envoy—in this case Ambassador Hurley.

The personality of Hurley is a major quirk in this history. One would like to think that historical factors were more rooted in natural law, less haphazard in scope, than the chance character of a minor individual who was neither heroic nor demonic. But history is not law-abiding or orderly and will often respond to a breeze as carelessly as a leaf upon a lake.

It happened that Hurley was a man whose conceit, ambition, and very vulnerable ego were wrapped up in his mission to the point of frenzy. From birth in a miner's cabin in Oklahoma he had risen through a Horatio Alger boyhood to the practice of law and a lucrative representation of the oil interests of the Choctaw Indians. A later client was Sinclair Oil. He made a fortune of $15 million, served overseas in World War I, became Hoover's Secretary of War, and coated the rough ebullience of a frontier background with the glossy Republicanism of Andrew Mellon. Tall, handsome, and impressive, he dressed with the care of a Beau Brummel and, when ordered to wear civilian clothes as Ambassador, could only be induced to shed a general's uniform and medals on the direct intervention of the President. Vanity was Hurley's security.

His initial assignment to China as special envoy to facilitate the appointment of General Stilwell as commander-in-chief of China's armed forces had ended in a notable reverse. Instead of Hurley's cajoling Chiang, Chiang had cajoled Hurley into supporting his demand for Stilwell's recall. Hurley therefore felt a double need to make a success of coalition. He had wrecked his chances as mediator, however, by allying himself with the Generalissimo for the sake of the Ambassadorship. Hurley was just what Chiang had always wanted in an envoy—a man with direct access to the President and no experience of China, who was easy to manipulate through his vanity. When Ambassador Gauss resigned at the time of Stilwell's departure, Chiang was only too pleased to ask for Hurley as successor. In a personal message to Roosevelt (sent via T. V. Soong to Hopkins, avoiding the State Department) he solicited a "more permanent" mission for Hurley, who "has my complete confidence" in dealing with the Communists, and would thus be able to make a contribution to the war effort by solving the problem of coalition. Roosevelt was lured; he believed in the efficacy of harmony. If nothing else had worked in China, maybe a person pleasing to Chiang Kai-shek might. Hurley received the appointment and owed it to Chiang.

As a result, he at once convinced himself that his mission and the policy of the United States ("my policy," as he sometimes called it) were to "prevent the collapse of the National Government" and "to sustain Chiang Kai-shek as President of the Republic and Generalissimo of the Armies." No such instructions appear in the documents, and despite Hurley's later claims, they could hardly have been oral since he was in China when he was appointed. It should be added, however, that when he stated this understanding of his mission in a rare communication to the State Department, no one disabused him. This was partly because the Department had no rein on Hurley, who generally bypassed it, and partly because it was unable to decide, except in noble generalizations, exactly what our China policy was. And no one knew for sure what it was in the President's mind.

Before he ever reached China, Hurley's estimate of the situation was shaped by the premise, which he accepted without question because it was told to him personally by Molotov, that the Soviet Union was not interested in the Chinese Communists, who were not really Communists at all. He thereafter underestimated them, said their strength and popular support were greatly exaggerated, and insisted that as soon as they were convinced that the Soviet Union would not support them, they would settle with the National Government and be content with minority status. Coalition would be easy. "There is very little difference, if any," he reported, between the "avowed principles" of the Kuomintang and the Communists; both "are striving for democratic principles." This may well be the least sophisticated statement ever made by an American ambassador. It reflects the characteristic American refusal to recognize the existence of fundamental divergence; hence the American assumption that there is nothing that cannot be negotiated.

Hurley accepted no guidance from his staff. Because he was over his head in the ancient and entangled circumstances which he proposed to settle, he fiercely resented and rejected the counsel of anyone more knowledgeable about China than himself. When the coalition blew up in his face and he found Chinese affairs resisting his finesse, depriving him of the diplomatic success he had counted on, he could find an explanation only in a paranoid belief that he was the victim of a plot by disloyal subordinates. He did not consider there might be a Chinese reason.

On the premise that his mission was to sustain Chiang Kai-shek, Hurley of course blocked the bid of Mao and Chou to go to Washington, the more so as it was intended to bypass himself. Although their message had been addressed to Wedemeyer for just that reason, it reached Hurley because Wedemeyer was absent in Burma at the time and he and Hurley had an agreement to share all incoming information. A second message from Yenan the next day, addressed to Wedemeyer on an "eyes alone" basis, quoted Chou En-lai as specifically stating that "General Hurley must not get this information as I don't trust his discretion." This, too, reached Hurley with effect that can be imagined. At the same time he learned through information passed by Nationalist agents in Yenan of Bird's and Barrett's military proposals to the Communists. A terrible bell rang in his mind: Here was the reason why the Communists had walked out on coalition. They had received a direct offer and were already secretly proposing to go to Washington over his head!

Barrett's proposals had, of course, emanated from Theater Command, but Hurley ignored that out of his need to find some conspiratorial reason for the breakdown of coalition. Wrathfully claiming that Bird and Barrett had acted without authority, he informed the President on January 14 that their action had become known to him only when it "was made apparent by the Communists applying to Wedemeyer to secure secret passage for Mao Tse-tung and Chou En-lai to Washington for a conference with you."

Only in this context (repeated in a second telegram of February 7) was Roosevelt informed of the Communist request. It appeared as no more than a by-product of unwarranted action by American officers undermining Hurley's efforts for coalition.* The plan for military cooperation with Yenan, Hurley said, would constitute "recognition of the Communist Party as an armed belligerent" and lead to "destruction of the National Government . . . chaos and civil war, and a defeat of America's policy in China." In the meantime, he assured Roosevelt, by discovering and frustrating the Communists' maneuver, he had now prevailed upon Chou En-lai to return to Chungking to resume negotiations.

What of the receiving end? The Communist request reached Roosevelt in terms already condemned by his Ambassador. It reached him, moreover, when he was plunged into preparations for the Yalta conference and overwhelmed by the dismaying problems of approaching victory. (Hurley's second, fuller telegram arrived after the President had already left Washington for Yalta.) War crimes, the post-war treatment of Germany, the Soviet claim to sixteen seats in the United Nations, the Polish border, the arrest of Badoglio, trouble in Yugoslavia and Greece, the fall of the Iranian government, not to mention the necessity, according to Secretary Stettinius, of a "private talk with Mr. Churchill on British meat purchases in Argentina"—all these in the thirteenth year of a crisis-filled Presidency did not leave Roosevelt eager to precipitate a new crisis with the unmanageable Chiang Kai-shek.

Bewildered by the intractability of China, disenchanted with the Generalissimo but fearful of the troubles that would rush in if the United States relaxed support, Roosevelt was inclined to look for a solution in the coming conference with Russia. His hope was to secure Stalin's agreement to support the Nationalist government, thus giving the Chinese Communists no choice but unity. He succeeded in ob-

---

* Hurley's accusations, passed on by the White House to General Marshall and by him in a peremptory query to Wedemeyer, caused a furious quarrel between Wedemeyer and Hurley, followed by an enforced agreement between them on an explanation for Marshall that would leave Wedemeyer's command blameless while not disputing Hurley. This was accomplished in a convoluted masterpiece covering everybody except Colonel Barrett, who had neglected the soldier's elementary precaution of obtaining his orders in writing. At Hurley's insistence, unopposed by Wedemeyer, Barrett's nomination for promotion to brigadier general, which had already gone forward, was withdrawn. His was the first in a line of honorable careers damaged to fill the need for scapegoats in China.

taining the desired agreement at Yalta, and returned to be confronted by a choice in our China policy. Tired, ill, and in the last month of life, he made a decision that closed this episode.

Coalition having reached another deadlock, Hurley and Wedemeyer arrived in Washington in March 1945 for consultation. Choosing their presence there as the opportunity to bring to a head the issue in American policy, all the political officers of the Embassy in Chungking, led by the chargé d'affairs, George Atcheson, joined in an unprecedented action. With the concurrence and "strong approval" of Wedemeyer's chief of staff, they addressed a long telegram to the Department, in effect condemning the Ambassador's policy. It pointed out that the Communists represented a force in China that was on the rise, that it was "dangerous to American interests from the long-range point of view" to be precluded from dealing with them, that with the approach of a landing in China the time was short before we would have to decide whether to cooperate with them or not. They recommended therefore "that the President inform the Generalissimo in definite terms that military necessity requires that we supply and cooperate with the Communists," and that such decision "will not be delayed or contingent upon" coalition.

After precipitating the explosive reaction of Hurley, who could see only an "act of disloyalty" to himself, the telegram was submitted to the President with the Department's recommendation that it provided an opportunity to re-examine the whole situation and "in particular" the possibility of "giving war supplies to the Chinese Communists as well as to Chiang Kai-shek." The President discussed it in two conversations with Hurley on March 8 and 24, with no officer of the State Department recorded as present on either occasion. Hurley evidently argued convincingly that the Russian agreement secured by the President at Yalta would sufficiently weaken the Communists so that he could promise unity in China by "the end of April," as he had already told the Department. Roosevelt, clinging to the goal he had started with and ever the optimist, decided in favor of Hurley's policy of dealing exclusively with the Generalissimo and of making no connection with the Communists without his consent. In effect, this rejected the recommendation of the Embassy staff and left the conduct of American policy to the tyro Ambassador. Thus confirmed, Hurley was able to insist on his requirement that Atcheson and his colleagues involved in the Embassy telegram, five out of six of them Chinese-speaking and representing nine decades of Chinese experience, should be transferred out of China. This was duly accomplished on Hurley's return.*

In making his choice the President undoubtedly believed or was persuaded by Hurley that it would compel the Communists to accept Chiang's terms for coalition. But it was only possible to believe this by rejecting the Embassy's appraisal of the seriousness and the dynamism of the Communist challenge. The choice was the last important decision of Roosevelt's life. A few days later he left for Warm Springs, where he died.

In March when the President made this decision, Mao and Chou in conversations with Service were still emphasizing and amplifying their desire for cooperation and friendship with the United States. The rebuff suffered by the lack of any reply to their offer to go to Washington was never mentioned (doubtless because they wished to keep it secret) and in fact none of the political officers attached to the Dixie Mission knew anything about it. Supported by Chu Teh, Liu Shao-ch'i, and other leaders of the Party, Mao and Chou returned repeatedly to the theme that China and the United States complemented each other economically—in China's need for post-war economic development and America's ability to assist and participate in it. Trying to assess how far this represented genuine conviction, Service concluded that Mao was certainly sincere in hoping to avoid an exclusive dependence on the Soviet Union.

The banishment shortly afterward of Service and the others concerned in the Atcheson telegram was a signal to the Communists of the American choice. In reaction their first overt signs of hostility

---

* Morale at the Embassy having sunk low under the effect of Hurley's rages and vendettas, the officers on duty in Chungking, whose careers were vulnerable to unfavorable action by the chief of mission, were anxious to be transferred or, in the case of two who were on leave in the United States, not to return. Atcheson, as Hurley's ranking subordinate, though too senior to be adversely affected, could not remain under the Ambassador's violent objection, and was transferred to General MacArthur's command as political adviser. Hurley personally obtained the removal of Service, whom he correctly guessed to be the principal drafter of the telegram, by direct request to Secretary of War Henry L. Stimson (Service being attached to the Military Command). In the case of Raymond Ludden, a political officer who had also served with the Dixie Mission and after a four-month tour of Communist territory had reported the likelihood of their coming to power, Hurley obtained a statement from Wedemeyer that he "no longer required Ludden's services." Fulton Freeman, third secretary of the Embassy, Japan Language Officer Yuni, and Arthur Ringwalt, former consul in Kweilin recently transferred to Chungking, who suffered the longest under Hurley's vindictiveness, were all variously reassigned. With the exception of Atcheson, who died shortly thereafter, the careers of all these men were slowed or otherwise damaged to greater or less degree by this episode. (Information supplied to the author by John S. Service.)

appeared in the form of articles by Mao in the Communist press. Confined so far to attacks on the "Hurley policy," these seemed still to retain hope of a change by Roosevelt's successor. In his speech to the Seventh Party Congress in June, Mao seemed to be half warning, half pleading. If the pro-Chiang choice by "a group of people in the U.S. government" were to prevail, he said, it would drag the American government "into the deep stinking cesspool of Chinese reaction" and "place a crushing burden on the government and people of the United States and plunge them into endless woes and troubles."

After V-J Day American forces enabled the Nationalists, who had neither the means nor the plans ready for the occasion, to take the Japanese surrender on the mainland and regain the occupied cities. The United States moved its marine forces into the important northern cities and ports (Tientsin, Tsingtao, Peking, Chingwangtao) to deny these centers and the railroads in the area to the Communists until Chiang's troops, ferried by American ship and planes, could get there. This constituted clear intervention to the Communists since their own forces would otherwise have reoccupied the north. Though justified by us under the pressing necessity of disarming the Japanese, our action was a logical development of the decision to sustain Chiang, and was taken as such by the Communists. Confirmed, as they saw it, by the United Nations Relief and Rehabilitation Administration's discrimination against Communist areas and by American toleration of Japanese troops serving with the Nationalists, they took the turn toward antagonism which in the course of the next four years was to become definitive.

Through 1945 efforts for coalition, mediated by Hurley, continued —largely because neither side wished to appear to have chosen the course of civil war—but they were empty of intent. Failing to move either side any closer to the unity he had so often and so confidently promised, Hurley grew increasingly erratic and disturbed and suddenly resigned in November 1945 with a famous blast, the first salvo of McCarthyism. His mission had been thwarted, he claimed, by a section of the State Department which was "endeavoring to support Communism generally as well as specifically in China." He could not admit, and perhaps never understood, that his own estimate of the situation had been inadequate and the current of Chinese affairs simply too strong for him.

Beyond Hurley, responsibility lay with the President. Hindsight makes his rejection of the Embassy's advice appear short-sighted, but every historical act is entitled to be examined in the light of the circumstances that surrounded it. Without doubt the primary factor influencing him was the Russian agreement obtained at Yalta. Both Roosevelt and Hurley believed that the Soviet Union held the key and that its still secret pledge to enter a treaty of alliance with Chiang Kai-shek (subsequently fulfilled in August) would in its effect on both sides in China serve to block the danger of civil war.

This belief was made possible only by underestimating the Communists as a *Chinese* phenomenon with roots reaching down into a hundred years of unmet needs and strength drawn from the native necessity of revolution. Back in 1930 Ambassador Nelson Johnson, a man of no unusual powers but able to observe the obvious, reported that communism was not the cause of chaos in China but rather the effect of "certain fundamental conditions." One such small voice, however, was overwhelmed as time went on by the conventional wisdom which held, first, that the Chinese would never accept communism because it was incompatible with the structure of Chinese society, and, second, according to the Molotov dictum which much impressed Roosevelt, that the Chinese Communists were not Communists at all. On these premises it was easy to persuade oneself that the Communists were not the coming rulers of China but a party of rebellious "outs" who could eventually be reabsorbed. When Hurley and Wedemeyer during this visit, along with Commodore M. E. Miles (chief of Naval Intelligence in China), conferred with the Joint Chiefs, "they were all of the opinion," as reported by Admiral Leahy, "that the rebellion in China could be put down by comparatively small assistance to Chiang's central government."

A second factor was that no proponent of another view, no one within the government who could effectively counter Hurley's version, had regular access to Roosevelt. This left a terrible gap. The President, again according to Leahy, who lived in the White House, "had much confidence in Hurley's reliability in accurately carrying out the duties assigned to him in the foreign field." Moreover, if Leahy can be used as a mirror, the White House bought the thesis that Hurley was undermined in his efforts by a group of jealous career diplomats who had "ganged up on the new Ambassador appointed from outside the regular foreign service."

Here is a beam of light on the most puzzling aspect of our China policy: why the information and opinions provided by experienced observers maintained in the field for the express purpose of keeping our government informed were so consistently and regularly ignored. The answer lies in the deep-seated American distrust that still prevailed of diplomacy and diplomats, the sentiment that disallowed knee-breeches for Americans. Diplomacy means all the wicked devices of the Old World, spheres of influence, balances of power, secret treaties, triple alliances, and, during the inter-war period, appeasement of fascism. Roosevelt reflected the sentiment in his attitude toward the career Foreign Service, which he considered a group of striped-pants snobs drawn from the ranks of entrenched wealth (as many of them were), unrepresentative of America, and probably functioning as tools of the British.

There was enough truth in this picture to make it persist despite passage of the Rogers Act in 1924 formalizing the Foreign Service as a career based on entry by examination and promotion by merit. The Act itself had been the result of wide criticism of cliques in the State Department, leading to a congressional investigation.

Ironically, the snob reputation had not on the whole been valid for China, which, not being considered a particularly desirable post by socialites who preferred the Quai d'Orsay and the Court of St. James's, had been filled by academics, missionaries' sons, and hardworking men promoted from the consular service, like Johnson and Gauss, the two ambassadors preceding Hurley. By a double irony, just such men would not have found themselves on easy terms with the White House.

Hurley started his mission with his mind equally set against the Foreign Service. When he came to blame it for his troubles, he accused it alternately of conspiring to support communism and of sucking the United States into a power bloc "on the side of colonial imperialism." In this odd coupling he was not unique. Robert Sherwood, when conferring with General MacArthur's staff in Manila, found a persecution complex at work which seemed to conceive of the War Department, the Joint Chiefs, and even the White House as under the domination of "Communists and British Imperialists."

Finally, the weight of domestic opinion on Roosevelt must be taken into account. If the hold of Chiang Kai-shek as the archetype anti-Communist on American public opinion was such that his cause perverted American politics for a decade after the war, and if it has taken us twenty-seven years to untie the silver cord and even yet have not cut it loose, it can hardly have been easy for Roosevelt to untie it in 1945. Fear of communism lay very close beneath the skin, so close that in his final speech of the campaign of 1944 Governor Dewey, the Republican candidate, charged that Communists as a small disciplined minority, acting through Sidney Hillman, had seized control of the American Labor movement and "now . . . are seizing control of the

New Deal through which they aim to control the Government of the United States." Roosevelt, said this disciplined and respectable lawyer, had auctioned control of the Democratic Party to the "highest bidder"—i.e., Hillman and Earl Browder—in order to perpetuate himself in office. Through him communism would destroy liberties, religion, and private property.

If a man like Dewey could resort to the tactics of the enormous lie and to a charge as reckless as any in the history of political campaigning, Roosevelt was politician enough to know how little would be needed to revive it. The autocrat of the *Time-Life* empire, Henry R. Luce, was rabid on this subject, especially with reference to China; his publications were the trumpet of Chiang's cause. Summoned to battle by Chiang's partisans, some of them sincere and passionate advocates like the former medical missionary Congressman Walter Judd, any of the myriad enemies of the administration could create serious trouble. Roosevelt was concentrating now on the coming conference in San Francisco to organize the United Nations and on his hopes of a four-power alliance after the war to keep world peace. It was a time at all costs to avoid friction. Since China was in any case secondary to Europe—a disability it suffered from all through the war—it did not seem worth the risk that the Atcheson telegram asked him to take.

Thus passed the opportunity Mao and Chou had asked for. The factors operating against it suggest there never was an "if." And yet there remains one strange contradictory sliver of evidence. Edgar Snow, the kind of outsider from whom Roosevelt liked to get his facts, reported a conversation with the President in March 1945 at the very time of the Hurley-Wedemeyer visit. Roosevelt was "baffled yet acutely fascinated," Snow said, by the complexity of what was happening in China and complained that nobody explained it satisfactorily, Snow included. "He understood that our wartime aid was actually a form of intervention in China"; he "recognized the growing strength of the Chinese Communists as the effective government of the guerrilla area"; he asked "whether they were real Communists and whether the Russians were bossing them," and asked further, "what, concretely, the Eighth Route Army could do with our aid in North China. He then said that we were going to land supplies and liaison officers on the North China coast as we drew closer to Japan." Snow questioned whether, so long as we recognized Chiang Kai-shek as the sole government, all supplies would have to go through him. " 'We can't support two governments in China, can we?' " he asked.

" 'Well, I've been working with two governments there.' The President threw back his head decisively. 'I intend to go on doing so until I can get them together.' "

This is a puzzle. It seems irreconcilable with the decision to uphold Hurley, unless Roosevelt was so convinced that Hurley would indeed achieve coalition "by the end of April" that what he had in mind was sending the Communists arms and aid *after* they had become part of the national Government.

Of the major quirk in the case one has to ask whether there might have been a different result if the ambassador had been a different man. A different man could still not have achieved coalition because no one on earth could have arranged terms that both parties could accept. A different man might have facilitated rather than blocked the visit of Mao and Chou to Washington, but if he had been a different man in whom they had confidence, they would not have asked to go. There remains only the remote chance that an ambassador who both listened to his staff *and* had the ear of the President might have turned the President toward a wider option than the blank check to the Generalissimo.

Otherwise it would seem from the record that our course was destined not by our stars but by ourselves and our inclinations; that the President, the public, and the conduct of foreign policy combined to work toward an inescapable and, from our point of view, a negative end.

Is any principle contained in this dusty answer? Perhaps only that every revolutionary change exacts a price in loss as well as gain, and that history will continue to present us with problems for which there is no good and achievable solution. To insist that there is one and commit ourselves to it invites the fate set apart for hubris. We reached in China exactly the opposite of what had been our object. Civil war, the one absolute we tried to prevent, duly came about. Though we defeated Japan, the goal that would have made sense of the victory, a strong united China on our side after the war, escaped us. The entire effort predicated on the validity of the Nationalist government was wasted.

What should have been our aim in China was not to mediate or settle China's internal problem, which was utterly beyond our scope, but to preserve viable and as far as possible amicable relations with the government of China, whatever it turned out to be. We were not compelled to make an either/or decision; we could have adopted the

British attitude, described by Sir John Keswick as one of "slightly perplexed resignation." Or, as a Brookings Institution study concluded in 1956, the United States "could have considered its China policy at a dead stop and ended all further effort to direct the outcome of events."

Yet we repeat the pattern. An architect of our involvement in Vietnam, Mr. Walt Rostow, insists that a fundamental premise of American policy is the establishment of a stable balance of power in Asia. This is not a condition the West can establish. Stability in Asia is no more achievable by us than was unity in China in 1945.

Basic to the conduct of foreign policy is the problem basic to all policy: how to apply wisdom to government. If wisdom in government eludes us, perhaps courage could substitute—the moral courage to terminate mistakes.

The author wishes to acknowledge with thanks the assistance of Mr. Ray Cromley and Mr. John S. Service, and of Mr. William Cunliffe of the Military Records Division, National Archives, who found and secured declassification of the relevant documents.

The Assimilationist Dilemma: Ambassador Morgenthau's Story

The incident that suggested Henry Morgenthau, Sr., as a focus of the modern Jewish dilemma is one of history's classic ironies: that by his alert dispatch of assistance to the Jewish colony of Palestine in August 1914—when serving as U.S. Ambassador to Turkey—he saved it from starvation and probable extinction, thus preserving it for the ultimate statehood which he came to believe was a "stupendous fallacy" and "blackest error." Measured in material terms, the aid was minuscule, and the incident remains virtually unknown except to a few investigators; but it was of decisive and immense historical importance.

The circumstances were these: The Jewish settlement in Palestine, numbering about 100,000, consisted, on the one hand, of pious and impoverished believers who had trickled in over the centuries to die in Jerusalem, together with some families who had never left the homeland, and, on the other hand, of the later wave of conscious Zionists who had immigrated since the 1880s and were endeavoring to establish themselves on land sold to them as worthless by Turkish and Arab landlords. Almost all were dependent either on remittances from abroad or, in the case of the new colonists, on the export of agricultural products to the West and some subsidy from the Diaspora. They would be cut off from these contacts if Turkey joined the Central Powers—which, Morgenthau foresaw, contrary to Allied expecta-

Address, American Historical Association, December 1976. *Commentary*, May 1977.

tions, was bound to occur. From his close, and at that time friendly, relations with the Turkish leaders—who were so taken with this unorthodox Ambassador that they offered him a Turkish cabinet post— he knew the hope of Turkish neutrality was a delusion.

On August 27 he cabled to the American Jewish Committee in New York, the earliest group of its kind organized in this country for the defense of Jewish interests and of "Jewish civil and religious rights, in any part of the world." The AJC was the organ of what has been called the Jewish "establishment" of those days—that is to say, mainly the German Jews. Dedicated to assimilation in their country of residence, they were *ipso facto* opponents of the Zionist movement for a Jewish state, though not of Palestine as a center of settlement for the persecuted Jews of Eastern Europe.

Morgenthau's cable stated that "immediate assistance" to Palestine Jewry was required and suggested the sum of $50,000. Jacob Schiff of the AJC and Louis Marshall, its president, convened a meeting and raised the suggested sum within two days. Half was contributed by the AJC, $12,500 by Schiff personally, and $12,500 by the American Federation of Zionists. The funds were wired to Constantinople, converted to gold, and carried in a suitcase to Jerusalem by Morgenthau's son-in-law, Maurice Wertheim, my father, who was then visiting him.

When it came to distribution, the gold precipitated an attack of internecine quarreling among the various local organizations, until my father, who was then twenty-eight, picked up the suitcase, locked himself in an adjoining room, and told his clients he would not come out until they had reached an agreement. Under that ultimatum, they did.

The significance of the aid was perceived at the time by a man dedicated to the homeland in Palestine, Judah Magnes, first chancellor and first president of the Hebrew University, the only important American Zionist leader to transfer his home to the land of his beliefs. Speaking at a meeting of the Joint Distribution Committee at the home of Felix Warburg in March 1916, he said of Morgenthau's crucial intervention that "no word can be too strong, no expression too exaggerated" to describe the historical task thus performed.

The initial relief, of course, far from solved the problem, which, as soon as the Turks entered the war in November 1914, became grave. About half the Jewish population in Palestine, including many of the older group and most of the new colonists, were Russian by nationality and had preferred to remain stateless rather than become Ottoman subjects. They were now subject to treatment by the Turks as enemy aliens, with no recourse to protection by Russia, whose pogroms they had fled. Expulsion and even massacre became imminent threats, involving the American Ambassador in unceasing efforts to mitigate the harsh and capricious measures of the Turks while activating, with the help of many others, the aid of his own and the Allied governments.

Six thousand Jews expelled from Jaffa were carried by the U.S.S. *Tennessee*, a warship in the area, to Egypt, where the British permitted their entry. Later the U.S.S. *Vulcan* carried food supplied by Jewish relief organizations to the near-starving community of Palestine. A steady flow of funds collected by Jews in the U.S.—sufficient to give monthly allotments of a few francs each to fifty thousand Jews cut off from former sources—had to be delivered by one means or another, past erratic Turkish opposition on the one hand and Allied blockade of Syria and Palestine on the other. At first gold bullion was shipped directly from Egypt on U.S. warships, but when the Allies closed down this entry, Morgenthau resorted to sending the funds by mail from Constantinople to the American Consul in Jerusalem, who distributed it to the needy. By these measures the nucleus of the future state of Israel survived.

Another contribution to the future of Israel, as important in a different way, was the support that made possible the revival of Hebrew as a living language. Eliezer Ben Yehuda, the compiler—one might say, the creator—of the modern Hebrew dictionary, was brought to this country in 1914 under Zionist auspices to continue his work in safety during the war years. But the funds to support him and his family while he worked, as well as a house to live in and schooling for his daughters, were arranged for by my father (who had visited Ben Yehuda in Jerusalem) and were supplied largely by *his* father, Jacob Wertheim, and a committee consisting of Jacob Schiff, Felix Warburg, Julius Rosenwald, and Herbert Lehman, the magnates of the so-called gilded ghetto.

Why did they care about the revival of Hebrew? Or, in the earlier case, about the survival of the colony in Palestine? The answer to that—the unbreakable tie to the group—is the answer as well to the unique survival of the Jews for over nineteen hundred years without statehood or territory. It is also part of the assimilationist's dilemma.

Assimilation was a solution born of the Enlightenment—a dream of adaptation within a dominant Gentile society while supposedly maintaining something not quite definable called Judaism. Whether this was to be equivalent to or more than the Jewish religion depended on the individual interpreter, but in any case it tended to shrivel in partnership with assimilation. In degree and nature the whole concept of assimilation was a disturbing problem of belief tortured by doubt, and so troubling that it was not discussed in front of the children. It is likely, I suspect, to remain forever unsolved, never wholly achieved or wholly abandoned.

Meanwhile the record suffers from a certain distortion—in that the dominant voice, as in every historical record, belongs to the victors, who in this case are the Zionists. Events proved them right with regard to the revival of Israel, and the assimilationists wrong. Consequently the former appear in the record as the disciples of truth and the latter as obstructionists, blind and selfish bitter-enders, objects of scorn and sometimes of malice. The malice and falsity of Felix Frankfurter's recollections of Morgenthau, published after the subject was safely dead, are a mean-spirited example.

Yet while the Zionists supplied the impulse, the ideal, and the driving force, not to mention the settlers, the fact remains that the German-Jewish leaders in America, whether from motives of guilt or reinsurance or a sense of responsibility, or a mixture of these, gave the support without which there would have been no living settlement to incorporate statehood. The work of Louis Marshall, for one, was essential. As chief spokesman of the "establishment," he cooperated with Chaim Weizmann to create the Jewish Agency, through which non-Zionists could support the settlement in Palestine. Nathan Straus was another. His support of public-health and other projects in Palestine, estimated to have absorbed two-thirds of his fortune, is commemorated in the town named Netanya on Israel's seacoast. Ultimately it was Morgenthau's son, Henry Jr., who, on leaving Roosevelt's Cabinet, assumed the chairmanship of the United Jewish Appeal in 1947–50 and raised the funds critical for the survival of Israel in the endangered first years of statehood. He was galvanized, I have no doubt, by the failure of his ceaseless effort, as Secretary of the Treasury under Roosevelt, to make the President take some effective action to save Jews from Hitler's final solution.

Needless to say, the German program of annihilation was the experience that turned assimilationists into supporters of statehood, anti-Zionists into reluctant pro-Zionists. Nor was it Hitler alone who accomplished the change but the reaction of the Western democracies —the lack of protest, the elaborate do-nothing international conferences, the pious evasions, the passive connivance in which Hitler read his cue, the avoidance of rescue, the American refusal to loosen immigration quotas when death camps were the alternative, the refusal even of temporary shelter, the turning back of refugee ships filled with those rescued by Jewish efforts. More than nine hundred on board the *St. Louis* were turned back to Europe within sight of the lights of Miami, more than seven hundred on board the leaking *Struma* were turned back from Palestine to sink with all on board in the Black Sea. Was their fate so very different from that of Auschwitz?

The accumulation of these things slowly brought to light what had long lurked in the shadows of ancient memory: a bitter recognition that the Gentile world—with all due respect to notable and memorable exceptions—would fundamentally have felt relieved by the final solution. That the Jewish "establishment" came to believe this about the Gentiles cannot be documented because it was the great unmentionable, too painful to acknowledge, but basically this is what shattered the faith of assimilationists and brought out the funds for support of Israel.

To go back to the assimilationist's dilemma: We must be careful, as always in the practice of history, not to ascribe meanings and motives as we see them through the lens of intervening events. To a person of my grandfather's generation and background, the problem was not originally seen as a dilemma. During the first half of his life he was perfectly clear and absolutely convinced about what he wanted and what he believed he could achieve in America.

His Zion was here. What he wanted was what most immigrants wanted at a time when liberty glowed on the Western horizon: Americanization. This meant to him not the rubbing-off of identity, but Americanization as a Jew, with the same opportunity to prove himself, and the same treatment by society, as anyone else.

If he is to represent the problem, he must be fixed in terms of time, place, and circumstance. On an immigrant boy of the 1860s, America's open door to upward mobility and the nineteenth century's belief in progress were formative influences equal to, if not greater than, his Jewish heritage. This is a point that non-Jews tend to overlook. They think of a Jew as some kind of immutable entity, instead of as a product of time and place like any other human being.

Morgenthau was born in Mannheim, Germany, in 1856, the same year as Louis D. Brandeis and Woodrow Wilson, and twenty years after Andrew Carnegie, the immigrant boy's greatest success story. Brought up in early childhood in comfortable circumstances, he came to the U.S. with his family in 1865 at the age of nine, as a result of business reverses suffered by his father, Lazarus Morgenthau, a prosperous cigar manufacturer. Lazarus had risen from the German-Jewish equivalent of the American log cabin. As the son of an underpaid cantor with too many children, he had started life as an itinerant tailor, peddling self-made cravats at fairs and gradually enlarging the enterprise to a business employing others. By the time Henry, his ninth child, was born he had achieved success in the cigar business, with three factories and a thousand employees. He could provide a household with servants and the first built-in bathroom in Mannheim, educate his children, indulge the family passion for theater, opera, and concerts, and carry out the traditional philanthropies.

The ruinous effect of the American tariff on cigars plus the persuasions of a brother in America decided Lazarus Morgenthau to emigrate at the age of fifty. In New York he failed to flourish a second time. While his wife had to take in boarders, and the sons had to go out to work, he devoted what remained of his remarkable energy and inventiveness to raising funds for Jewish charities, in the course of which he invented the theater benefit. Persuading producers and theater-owners to donate a performance, he personally went the rounds of prominent Jewish homes to sell tickets at high prices. He had, however, an erratic temperament which, in the family's reduced circumstances, caused a separation from his high-minded and hard-working wife.

From these genes and environment Henry emerged—Horatio Alger with a Jewish conscience. Speedily learning English, he graduated from public high school at fourteen, entered City College for a career in law but was forced to leave before the end of his first year to help support the family by working as an errand boy at $4 a week. After clerking in a law office for four years while teaching in an adult night school at $15 a week, he put himself through Columbia Law School and was admitted to the bar at the age of twenty-one. With two friends he formed a law firm in 1879 when the average age of the partners was twenty-three.

Strongly affected by the fall in family circumstances, and intensely ambitious, he was determined to make a fortune solid enough to withstand economic caprice, to provide for his mother and assure his children the advantages he had missed. He accomplished his goal in the practice of realty law, by conceiving the corporate form of doing business in real estate and by shrewd and venturesome buying of lots at the future crosstown stops of the advancing subway system.

While he was making money, he was constantly troubled and

made restless, as shown by his notebook of moral maxims, by the demands of a political idealism and a strong social conscience, which led him to active involvement in municipal reform movements to combat the tenement system, to improve working conditions after the Triangle Shirtwaist fire, to association with Lillian Wald in social work, and most particularly to close association and friendship with a man of advanced ideas, Rabbi Stephen S. Wise. It is characteristic of Morgenthau that he was drawn to a radical figure twenty years his junior, and that when Wise refused the conditions proposed by the trustees for the pulpit of Temple Emanu-El, Morgenthau financed him in the founding of the libertarian Free Synagogue and served as its first president. The fact that Wise was already the active and outspoken secretary of the American Federation of Zionists obviously presented no dilemma.

In this respect I am struck by the fact that the two men whom I remember from my childhood as representing Jewish affairs to my assimilationist family were, paradoxically, two ardent Zionists, Stephen Wise and Judah Magnes. No doubt this was because they were both men of outstanding mind and character; but I wonder if it was not also because their primary subject—the return to Palestine —exercised a powerful appeal. Magnes' concept of a bi-national Arab-Jewish state made, I know, a strong impression on my father. I personally do not remember anything very significant about Wise, except that he was rather frightening. He wore an enormous black hat and, I think, a black cloak, and when we met him on the way to school on Central Park West near his synagogue, he used to sweep off the hat with a bow to a child of about eight and say in his booming voice, "Good morning, Miss Wert*heem*," a way in which no one else pronounced the name.

Magnes was different; there was a quality about him I cannot describe without sounding sentimental: something beautiful in his face, something that inspired a desire to follow, even to love. Although I had no individual contact with him beyond being allowed to sit at the dinner table and listen to him talk, I remember no one who made a greater impression. He talked about travels through wild areas of Palestine and a dangerous adventure in the desert—could it have been Sinai?—where he was stranded and came close to death. Beatrice Magnes, his wife, seemed to me equally admirable.

In an opposite sense from my grandfather, there was no dilemma for Magnes either, although he and Mrs. Magnes belonged to the "establishment." It is interesting that of the American Zionist leaders, both Magnes and Brandeis were second-generation Americans and Wise close to it, having come to this country from Budapest at the age of seventeen months.

To return to Morgenthau: At the age of fifty-six, moved by Woodrow Wilson's appearance on the political scene in 1912, and by a doctor's warning that a loud heart murmur left him not long to live (a prognosis happily wrong by thirty-five years), he reached the rare decision that he had made enough money and could terminate his business career to enter public service. Wilson's fight against social exclusiveness in the Princeton eating clubs made a special appeal to a Jew, who saw in him the image of a true democrat dedicated to equal opportunity for all Americans. Morgenthau pledged $5,000 a month for four months to launch Wilson's presidential campaign, undertook the chairmanship of the Democratic Finance Committee, and, with an additional personal donation of $10,000, became one of the largest individual contributors.

The reward was not, as he had hoped, a Cabinet post as Secretary of the Treasury, but a minor ambassadorship—as it then was—to Turkey, the more disappointing because it was a post set aside for Jews. Given Morgenthau's passionate desire to prove that a Jew could and would be accepted in America on equal grounds with anyone else, the offer was peculiarly painful. It was, of course, this intense faith in equal opportunity for the Jew in America, and the fear of being thought to have another loyalty, that made him and others like him resist so strongly the movement for a separate Jewish state. Again, one has to think in terms of the time. The struggle for equal position was then less advanced than it is now and anti-Semitism more emphatically operative. Jews like my grandfather, who had set their lives to overcoming it, felt that political Zionism would supply an added cause for discrimination.

Morgenthau initially rejected Wilson's offer. He changed his mind under the influence of Stephen Wise, who persuaded him of the importance of having a Jew officially in contact with Palestine. He took up his post in Constantinople less than a year before history broke over the Turkish capital, transforming it into one of the key diplomatic posts of the world. Morgenthau found himself in the role of the leading neutral ambassador, caretaker for the Allied embassies, protector and mediator for Christians, Jews, Armenians, and every person and institution caught in the chaos of the Ottoman empire. The task used all his talents—nerve, tact, imagination, humor, and, above all, a capacity for direct action in ways no trained diplomat would ever contemplate. Henry was electric, my grandmother believed; she said she felt weak when he entered the room. The spectacular activity of his tenure at Constantinople does not belong in this essay, except insofar, I think, as the praise and renown he won obscured for him the disappointment of Wilson's original offer, reinforced his optimism, ambition, and belief in American opportunity, and thus his anti-Zionism.

No dilemma entered into his aid for the Jews of Palestine. The impulse was humanitarian, redoubled by group attachment. He was to do as much, if not more, for the Armenians and later, as League of Nations Commissioner, for resettlement of the Greeks. His sense of what it means to be an oppressed people, particularly in the case of the Armenians, in whom he saw a parallel with the Jews, certainly underlay both those efforts. He remains today a national hero to the Armenians and has a street named for him in Athens, although none in Jerusalem, which is fair enough.*

Zionism did not become an acute dilemma for its opponents until about 1917, when, in anticipation of the end of the Turkish empire, Zionist agitation for a recognized homeland grew intense. In some members of the Jewish establishment the Balfour Declaration touched off almost a sense of panic. At that time Zionists were bringing pressure on President Wilson for a public commitment, and when, in March 1918, Rabbi Wise led a delegation to the White House for this purpose without informing Morgenthau, who was still president of his pulpit, the sad break came. Morgenthau resigned as president of the Free Synagogue.

In 1921 he proclaimed his opposition to Zionism in an exceedingly combative article, which he republished in full in his autobiography two years later. Zionism, he wrote, is "an Eastern European proposal ... which if it were to succeed would cost the Jews of America most of what they have gained in liberty, equality, and fraternity." Because of his opposition he saw hazards which the proponents preferred not to look at: that the Balfour Declaration was ambiguous, that the Arab inhabitants of Palestine resented the Zionist program and "intend to use every means at their command to frustrate it." Through a massive polemic of political, economic, and religious arguments, he harshly concluded that the Zionist goal "never can be attained and that it ought not to be attained."

In his eighties, in the shadow of the Holocaust, he privately ac-

* Since the appearance of this article, Mayor Teddy Kollek, the alert presiding genius of Jerusalem, has invalidated my statement.

knowledged that he had read history wrong. He died at ninety-one, a year before the re-creation of the state of Israel.

The dilemma for Henry Morgenthau was really more American than Jewish. Prior to Hitler and the ultimate disillusion, he saw no need for nationhood because he believed the future of the Jew as a free person was here, and that it was threatened by the demand for separate nationhood. In his fierce desire for proof of assimilation, he established his summer home, when he was in his seventies, in the Wasp stronghold of Bar Harbor, Maine, consorting with the snobs, to my acute embarrassment on my visits. Possibly they liked or admired him—he was a man of great charm, known as Uncle Henry to all acquaintances from FDR to the policeman on the beat—but what slights he may have endured I cannot tell. Yet he never for an instant attempted to play down his Jewish identity or remain passive in regard to his people. On the contrary, he emphasized his ties to them throughout his life, serving as founder, trustee, and officer of the Federation of Jewish Philanthropies, the American Jewish Committee, B'nai B'rith, Mount Sinai Hospital in New York, and every kind of Jewish organization.

Assimilation, for him, did not mean to cross over to Christianity; it meant to be accepted in Bar Harbor *as* a Jew: that was the whole point. He wanted to be a Jew and an American on the same level as the best. He wanted America to work in terms of his youthful ideals—and of course it did not. Perhaps the dilemma was America's, not his.

Kissinger: Self-Portrait

In the last century the historian Leopold von Ranke laid down the dictum that foreign relations were supreme among the influences that shape the history of nations. This may be arguable, but for the immediate past it is certainly maintainable. No one has been more deeply engaged at so influential a level in the conduct of foreign relations than former Secretary of State Henry A. Kissinger, or gained so much public recognition of his role. He became a cult figure, a popular celebrity, the subject of countless full-length books, studies, and analyses. Publication of his own version is thus something of a historical event.

With some relief I can report that it contains no more Metternich. Because Kissinger's doctoral dissertation and first published book, *A World Restored*, dealt with Prince Metternich, the Austrian Foreign Minister, and the resettlement of Europe after the windstorm of Napoleon, everyone writing about Kissinger since then has made a comparison between them. Kissinger, writing about himself, does not mention Metternich—rightly, for the world he has had to deal with is so different in such absolute ways that a comparison is inapplicable. The differences are important: Whatever their rivalries, the nations at the Congress of Vienna had a common outlook and a common goal— restoration of the *status quo ante*. Today nations are split between two opposing ideologies, and the globe is dominated by two antagonistic superpowers locked in quarrel. Balance of power is inoperable; the third world has emerged to upset any balance; a new risk center

New York Times Book Review, November 11, 1979.

exists in the Middle East; the industrial nations are in thrall to the oil of the undeveloped; nuclear weaponry overshadows all.

In such a world Kissinger's task as he saw it on taking office in the administration of Richard M. Nixon in January 1969 was to end the Vietnam war, manage a "global rivalry" and nuclear-arms race with the Soviet Union, reinvigorate alliance with the European democracies, and integrate the new nations into a "new world equilibrium."

How well did he succeed in his mission? He himself offers no over-all assessment—perhaps because he has allowed himself no time for reflection. To make ready for publication a text of 1,476 pages in two and a half years since leaving office is an Olympic feat leaving little room for philosophy. Kissinger has been in such a hurry to vindicate his management of complex and turbulent events that he seems not to have let a day elapse between doing and writing or removed himself in any way to gain perspective. The book is all record, no assessment. He has written too much too soon.

The plunge into writing seems to carry on a habit and a condition of his office. Its pressures did not allow time to think, to examine a problem on all sides and a course of action in all its consequences. This is undoubtedly a fault of the system rather than of character; public life, as Kissinger acknowledges, "is a continual struggle to rescue an element of choice from the pressure of circumstance." Surely that is all the more reason, once released from the pressure, to have taken time for thought.

What we have is an immensely long and superfluously detailed account of virtually every message, meeting, journey, negotiation, and conversation in the fifty months from Kissinger's appointment in November 1968 to the signing of peace with North Vietnam at the end of President Nixon's first term in January 1973. We do not need all the aide-mémoires and the daily comings and goings of Egon Bahr, Vladimir Semenov, and dozens of other secondary intermediaries to understand what was going on; indeed, the picture would be clearer if Kissinger had taken the trouble to strain out the insignificant and condense his tale as a whole. Since by training he knows better than to confuse setting down the total record with writing history, one must assume that the record—in his version—was what he wanted, and I have no doubt that specialists in strategic arms, the U.S.S.R. NATO, China, Chile, the Middle East, India and Pakistan, and Vietnam will be mining it for years.

It is enlivened (in spots) by small revelations, vivid scenes and portraits, and glimpses of the often astonishing mechanics of official life. For example, out of the blue in August 1969 a Soviet Embassy official asked a State Department official at lunch what would be the United States' reaction to a Soviet attack on Chinese nuclear facilities. Mr. Nixon's speechwriting staff had a specialist for every tone the President wished to adopt. In 1969 China had only one ambassador serving abroad—in Cairo. Through names presented privately by Kissinger to Ambassador Anatoly I. Dobrynin, the release of 550 out of 800 hardship cases of Soviet Jews was obtained over a period of time. On a presidential journey every member of the official party is given a little book listing every event and movement timed to the minute, together with charts showing where everyone is to stand. All these are surprises, at least to this reviewer.

There are sparkles amid the long stretches: the "thrill" of the first summit visit when, as the plane door opened on arrival in Brussels, "we were bathed in the arc lights of television," a red carpet and honor guard were on hand, and the King of the Belgians waited at the foot of the ramp; the papal audience, during which smoke suddenly poured from the garments of Secretary of Defense Melvin Laird (in response to Kissinger's suggestion that he dispose of his cigar, he had concealed it alive in his suit pocket). There are incisive small history lessons introducing, among others, the problems of Pakistan and of Poland. There are gems of quotation, as when Dean Acheson, asked why a meeting of senior advisers lasted so long, replied, "We are all old and we are all eloquent."

The author is less good at profundities. When he attempts them, for example in reflections on the space age, his language invariably swells into the sententious, not to say banal, and he sounds less like himself than Gerald R. Ford. On the "agony of Vietnam" he sees his role as "helping my adopted country heal its wounds, preserve its faith and . . . rededicate itself to the great tasks of construction awaiting it." Or, on the end of the war, he hopes Americans will "close ranks" and the peoples of Indochina "perhaps attain at long last the future of tranquility, security and progress . . . worthy of their sacrifices." Coming from the sardonic gentleman who once, on being thanked by an effusive well-wisher for "saving the world," is reputed to have replied, "You're welcome," this is pure hype on a level with campaign rhetoric, as if he were running for office. Perhaps he is.

Perhaps that explains his hurry to bring out the book, in good time to make its impression before November 1980. Could it be that this tremendous tome is a campaign document designed to exhibit the author as the most knowledgeable, experienced and expert, the ineluctable, the only possible Secretary of State under the next Republican President? I cannot believe that his eye is on Capitol Hill. The Senate has no scope for the summiteer, for shuttle diplomacy, for the commuter from Tel Aviv to Peking to Moscow to Bonn, the guest at Chequers and the Elysée. I imagine it is to this life of the Air Force One jet set that he wants to return.

That would explain why—for the sake of dignity—Kissinger as a personality, the phenomenon of Super-K, the swinger, the media's delight, is missing from this book. Beyond some rather stilted references to "my warped sense of humor," no hint comes through, yet the attention showered upon him must be a factor in the record. "Power is an aphrodisiac," Kissinger himself has said (though not in this book), and although popularity is a different thing, it reinforces power. Kissinger's explanation of his popularity with the press is that because its members disliked President Nixon they tended to give credit for favorable developments to "more admired associates . . . and I became the beneficiary of this state of affairs." Clearly more than that was at work; a distinct personality made itself felt. Kissinger was refreshing and the press succumbed to the wit and charm he knew how to exercise, although they find virtually no expression here.

How did the sudden blossoming of this pudgy professor into the rose of the Nixon administration affect American foreign policy? I would speculate that it enhanced his belief, already embedded intellectually, in his own powers of manipulation and hence in over-reliance on personal negotiation. It may have nurtured fantasies of omnipotence. Although his text is impersonal, that is not from modesty. The illustrations tell a different story. Out of sixty-five photographs, Kissinger himself appears in sixty-three, twenty-eight of them in the company of Mr. Nixon, as if to assure posterity of his close and constant access to the President. It seems that he even needed to reassure himself. Apropos of the low protocol rank of his office, which seated him far below the salt at official dinners, "I spent much time calculating the distance separating me from the Presidential person and the odds on my reaching my car before the Presidential limousine pulled out." Who can envy the life of officialdom weighed down by these concerns?

If there is a key to Kissinger's concept of a minister for foreign affairs, it lies in this sentence: "My approach was strategic and geopolitical; I attempted to relate events to each other, to create incentives and pressures in one part of the world to influence events in another." Here is the activist, the great manipulator, convinced that he can pull the strings that will make the nations, like puppets, play out his scenario. No matter how often they evade or refuse, he pursues his objective with unswerving persistence and intensity. "Geopolitical" is his favorite word, applied to every problem in every region—and it is, in this outsider's opinion, the explanation of American mistakes. Our approach is too geopolitical and not sufficiently local. If we had paid more attention to the history of Vietnamese nationalism or to the internal stresses in Iran, we could not (one hopes) have invested our policy and support in regimes lacking a valid mandate from their own people. "Geopolitical," as Kissinger uses it, is just another word for cold war. It means combating the machinations of communism wherever they are exercised on the globe. The contest with communism is indeed serious, but, as we should have learned by now, the opponent is divided and disparate, not solid, and the combat will be lost if we are not more sophisticated about conducting it in local terms.

Kissinger's activism was risky because it set in motion reactions and consequences that could not be controlled or even at times foreseen, as happened in Cambodia and Chile. He had been warned that it would be a mistake to try to solve the problem of North Vietnamese presence in Cambodia by force and that it would be wiser, as a State Department official put it, "to wait on events, saying little." Had this counsel been followed, Cambodia would have been spared untold agony and Kissinger a stain that will not wash away.

Because the North Vietnamese were unquestionably the first to violate the neutrality of Cambodia—as the Germans were of Belgium in 1914—the current controversy about American violation is a false issue. American guilt lay in extending the war to a non-participating land and people and in requiring our Air Force deliberately to falsify the record. Kissinger's strained defense—on the ground that it was necessary to keep silent in order not to force the necessity of a protest on Prince Norodom Sihanouk or provoke North Vietnam to retaliate —is not impressive. Keeping silent is one thing; extreme precautions of secrecy (which Kissinger omits to mention), to the point of transgressing our own military code, are quite another.

Equally, the justification on the ground that American soldiers were being killed by North Vietnamese based in Cambodia seems inappropriately indignant. Kissinger fulminates about an "unprovoked offensive killing 400 Americans a week" and the "outrage of a dishonorable and bloody offensive." Is an offensive supposed to be bloodless? Is there something peculiarly shocking about killing enemy soldiers in war? When it comes to "dishonorable," I cannot follow Kissinger's thinking at all.

He talks a lot about honor in these pages. "American honor" and "American innocence" are terms that recur as often as "realities" and "*realpolitik*," with which they consort oddly. The United States is said to have entered Vietnam "in innocence, convinced that the cruel civil war represented the cutting edge of some global design." One fails to comprehend why containment of communism is described as innocence. Elsewhere he says we entered the war out of "naïve idealism," which sounds strange coming from Henry Kissinger, the unsentimental dealer in hard realities. Why is he trying in this book to make himself appear something he is not, to wear a Roman toga, as it were, over a coat of mail? Perhaps, with an eye on office, it is to legitimize himself with those on the right.

The vicious tyranny that has descended upon Chile, with the assistance of the United States, belongs to the period after this book closes in January 1973 and presumably will be dealt with in Kissinger's next volume. Here he includes a chapter on the decision by the so-called 40 Committee, of which he was chairman, to authorize expenditures by the Central Intelligence Agency to influence the Chilean elections of 1970. Here we come to an outright instance of American illegality in a cold-war cause, even if in the first instance it was ineffectual.

With copper and ITT in the background, Kissinger eschews reference to American innocence and concentrates instead on making a fervent case of the danger represented by Salvador Allende, who is credited with the "patent intention" to accomplish the transition to communism. His predicted electoral victory (by a plurality but miniority vote) would establish another Castro in the Western hemisphere. He "would soon be inciting anti-American policies, attacking hemisphere solidarity, making common cause with Cuba, and sooner or later establishing close relations with the Soviet Union," with profound effect "against fundamental American national interests."

If such was the case—and Kissinger can be very persuasive—a legitimate question arises. In the national interest, was it not an American duty to do what it could to fend off a second communist state in Latin America? The answer, in this case, must be no, for, whatever the threat, Allende's approaching presidency was to be accomplished by constitutional means. For the United States to interfere in the domestic affairs of a neighboring state in an attempt to thwart their legitimate operation is intolerable. We have come a long way from the election of 1888, when the British Ambassador to the United States advised a correspondent in a private letter to vote for Grover Cleveland and, on this being leaked to the press, the Ambassador's recall was demanded for interference in American politics. I do not believe that international relations can be guided by morality, but I believe in obeying as far as possible the rules we have worked out for the social order, otherwise society slides back into anarchy—which is as dangerous for the right wing as for the left.

In Nixon circles Kissinger was an ambivalent figure, suspect on the right for friendship with Nelson A. Rockefeller, a Harvard background, entree in Georgetown, and flexibility on Russia. Yet, as agent of a President farther to the right than any since McKinley, he accomplished progress in important areas: in China, in the Middle East, even in détente with Russia and in the Stygian labyrinths of strategic-arms limitation.

One thing that the overwhelming detail of the book succeeds in demonstrating is the breadth of subject matter Kissinger dealt with, the unrelenting hard work it demanded, and the fierce schedule he maintained. Japanese textiles, Common Market, Ostpolitik, ABMs and MIRVs, Palestinian hijacking, Soviet submarines in Cuba, Soviet missiles in Egypt, channels to China, Nixon to Romania, Polish riots, crisis in Jordan, war in Pakistan, summit in Moscow, the Year of Europe, the death of Nasser, visit to the Shah, and through it all, secret and subsequently formal conferences in Paris with the North Vietnamese. It was no job for a self-doubter, which Kissinger is anything but. All this seemed to him to require his personal presence. He was continually in motion, talking, traveling, which may not have been the most creative use of his time. Once, in the years before prominence, when a colleague asked him what he thought of Secretary of State John Foster Dulles, he thought for a moment and replied, "He travels too much."

Kissinger did contribute creative policy to the Middle East in his rejection of that dream of never-never land, the "comprehensive" solution. He understood that disengagement between Israel and Egypt had no chance of success if it had to be negotiated as part of an overall settlement and, as he points out with admirable common sense, "if there was no chance of success I saw no reason for us to involve ourselves" in the attempt. He preferred to try for an interim agreement to break the impasse and open the way to further advances. Thus originated the step-by-step process, to be dramatized by the Kissinger shuttle in the next term, that eventually achieved progress where none had been registered for thirty years.

In the end, however, although Russia and the Middle East may be more important for the future, it is Vietnam that is the test of the man and the statesman, and of his mark on American history. The necessity of American withdrawal having already been acknowledged by both candidates in 1968, the effort to negotiate terms that would save our face occupied Kissinger from the day he took office. The difficulty was that the administration was bent on negotiating a withdrawal that would not look like deserting Saigon, that would not destroy the confidence of other peoples in America, that would "offer a fair and equitable settlement to all," in short, that would make America look good—all of which was a contradiction in terms with the fact of withdrawal. Under domestic protest, withdrawal had already begun while negotiations were under way, which amounted to a signal to Hanoi that it did not have to meet American terms. A belligerent does not have to negotiate "fair and equitable" terms with an enemy on his way out who has given up the goal of victory.

Throughout the interminable talks with the North Vietnamese in Paris, Kissinger kept rediscovering that Hanoi did not want a compromise settlement, that Hanoi "had no intention of withdrawing its own forces" from the South, that Hanoi "would be satisfied only with victory," that, in short, good terms from our point of view were unobtainable. The only bargaining lever left to us was to make continuation of the war a greater risk to Hanoi than a settlement would be. Hence the bombing and the offensive against North Vietnamese sanctuaries in Cambodia. Military action was not pursuit of a military solution but an argument by force that would bring Hanoi to an agreement to leave Saigon in place and allow the United States to depart looking strong.

The failure of creative policy was the failure to consider that confidence in America meanwhile was not being furthered by the spectacle of our military impotence in a guerrilla war in Asia. A great role in foreign affairs could have been played by an adviser who could have brought us to a withdrawal on the basis that we had done all we could or ought to do for Saigon and that its ultimate survival depended on itself, or otherwise would be valueless, as indeed it proved. Kissinger lacked the imagination and, doubtless, the influence for that solution. In the end, Christmas bombing and all, after four years' talk at a cost of nineteen thousand more American lives and untold more lives and destruction in Vietnam, the terms obtained were no better than might have been obtained at the start. The four years of additional death and devastation were a waste.

Kissinger acknowledges none of this. Even less does he understand the domestic dissent of the time, although it is a constant theme in the book and clearly the factor that most deeply disturbed him. He treats it as a perverse opposition that, by encouraging Hanoi to stall, frustrated his negotiations. He quotes the *Wall Street Journal* statement that "Americans want an acceptable exit from Indochina, not a deeper entrapment" and the *New York Times* statement that bitter experience had "exhausted the credulity of the American people and Congress" and the *Milwaukee Journal* statement that "if [the South Vietnamese] can't stand on their own feet now it is too late. The U.S. can no longer stand the internal frustrations and disruptions that the bloody, tragic and immoral war is costing," but he does not absorb the message. His comment is that the national debate was "engulfed in mass passion," not that it was telling him something he should have listened to. Apropos of the congressional vote to terminate action in Cambodia that finally blocked the Executive in 1973, he writes that Cambodia was the victim of "the breakdown of our democratic political process," when in fact what was taking place was the functioning, not the breakdown, of that process. It is unsafe to have high office filled by someone who does not know the difference.

Kissinger complains that "we faced a constant credibility gap at home" and that he could have succeeded "if the public had trusted our goals," but he never traces any connection between the public's lack of trust and the acts and policies of the administration he represented. He has no inkling of the concomitant damage: that the cost of playing tough may come too high; that a foreign policy that alienates one's countrymen and causes dislike and distrust of government is not worth what it might gain against the adversary; that a nation's strength lies ultimately in its self-esteem and confidence in what is right; and that whatever damages these damages the nation.

Mankind's Better Moments

For a change from prevailing pessimism, I should like to recall some of the positive and even admirable capacities of the human race. We hear very little of them lately. Ours is not a time of self-esteem or self-confidence—as was, for instance, the nineteenth century, when self-esteem may be seen oozing from its portraits. Victorians, especially the men, pictured themselves as erect, noble, and splendidly handsome. Our self-image looks more like Woody Allen or a character from Samuel Beckett. Amid a mass of worldwide troubles and a poor record for the twentieth century, we see our species—with cause—as functioning very badly, as blunderers when not knaves, as violent, ignoble, corrupt, inept, incapable of mastering the forces that threaten us, weakly subject to our worst instincts; in short, decadent.

The catalogue is familiar and valid, but it is growing tiresome. A study of history reminds one that mankind has its ups and downs and during the ups has accomplished many brave and beautiful things, exerted stupendous endeavors, explored and conquered oceans and wilderness, achieved marvels of beauty in the creative arts and marvels of science and social progress; has loved liberty with a passion that throughout history has led men to fight and die for it over and over again; has pursued knowledge, exercised reason, enjoyed laughter and pleasures, played games with zest, shown courage, heroism, altruism, honor, and decency; experienced love; known comfort, contentment, and occasionally happiness. All these qualities have been part of human experience, and if they have not had as important notice as the negatives nor exerted as wide and persistent an influence

Jefferson Lecture, Washington, D.C., April 1980. *American Scholar*, Autumn 1980.

as the evils we do, they nevertheless deserve attention, for they are currently all but forgotten.

Among the great endeavors, we have in our own time carried men to the moon and brought them back safely—surely one of the most remarkable achievements in history. Some may disapprove of the effort as unproductive, too costly, and a wrong choice of priorities in relation to greater needs, all of which may be true but does not, as I see it, diminish the achievement. If you look carefully, all positives have a negative underside—sometimes more, sometimes less—and not all admirable endeavors have admirable motives. Some have sad consequences. Although most signs presently point from bad to worse, human capacities are probably what they have always been. If primitive man could discover how to transform grain into bread, and reeds growing by the riverbank into baskets; if his successors could invent the wheel, harness the insubstantial air to turn a millstone, transform sheep's wool, flax, and worms' cocoons into fabric—we, I imagine, will find a way to manage the energy problem.

Consider how the Dutch accomplished the miracle of making land out of sea. By progressive enclosure of the Zuider Zee over the last sixty years, they have added half a million acres to their country, enlarging its area by eight percent and providing homes, farms, and towns for close to a quarter of a million people. The will to do the impossible, the spirit of can-do that overtakes our species now and then, was never more manifest than in this earth-altering act by the smallest of the major European nations.

A low-lying, windswept, waterlogged land, partly below sea level, pitted with marshes, rivers, lakes, and inlets, sliding all along its outer edge into the stormy North Sea with only fragile sand dunes as nature's barrier against the waves, Holland, in spite of physical disadvantages, has made itself into one of the most densely populated, orderly, prosperous, and, at one stage of its history, dominant nations of the West. For centuries, ever since the first inhabitants, fleeing enemy tribes, settled in the bogs where no one cared to bother them, the Dutch struggled against water and learned how to live with it: building on mounds, constructing and reconstructing seawalls of clay mixed with straw, carrying mud in an endless train of baskets, laying willow mattresses weighted with stones, repairing each spring the winter's damage, draining marshes, channeling streams, building ramps to their attics to save the cattle in times of flood, gaining dike-enclosed land from the waves in one place and losing as much to the revengeful ocean somewhere else, progressively developing methods to cope with their eternal antagonist.

The Zuider Zee was a tidal gulf penetrating eighty miles into the land over an area ten to thirty miles wide. The plan to close off the sea by a dam across the entire mouth of the gulf had long been contemplated but never adopted, for fear of the cost, until a massive flood in 1916, which left saltwater standing on all the farmlands north of Amsterdam, forced the issue. The act for enclosure was passed unanimously by both houses of Parliament in 1918. As large in ambition as the country was small, the plan called for a twenty-mile dike from shore to shore, rising twenty feet above sea level, wide enough at the top to carry an auto road and housing for the hydraulic works, and as much as six hundred feet wide on the sea bottom. The first cartload of gravel was dumped in 1920.

The dike was but part of the task. The inland sea it formed had to be drained of its saltwater and transformed from salt to fresh by the inflow from lower branches of the Rhine. Four polders, or areas rising from the shallows, would be lifted by the draining process from under water into the open air. Secondary dikes, pumping stations, sluices, drainage ditches to control the inflow, as well as locks and inland ports for navigation, had to be built, the polder lands restored to fertility, trees planted, roads, bridges, and rural and urban housing constructed, the whole scheduled for completion in sixty years.

The best-laid plans of engineers met errors and hazards. During construction, gravel that had been painstakingly dumped within sunken frameworks would be washed away in a night by heavy currents or a capricious storm. Means proved vulnerable, methods sometimes unworkable. Yet slowly the dike advanced from each shore toward the center. As the gap narrowed, the pressure of the tidal current rushing through increased daily in force, carrying away material at the base, undermining the structure, and threatening to prevent a final closing. In the last days a herd of floating derricks, dredges, barges, and every piece of available equipment was mustered at the spot, and fill was desperately poured in before the next return of the tide, due in twelve hours. At this point, gale winds were reported moving in. The check dam to protect the last gap showed signs of giving way; operations were hurriedly moved thirty yards inward. Suspense was now extreme. Roaring and foaming with sand, the tide threw itself upon the narrowing passage; the machines closed in, filled the last space in the dike, and it held. Men stood that day in 1932 where the North Sea's waves had held dominion for seven hundred years.

As the dry land appeared, the first comers to take possession were the birds. Gradually, decade by decade, crops, homes, and civilization followed, and unhappily, too, man's destructive intervention. In World War II the retreating Germans blew up a section of the dike, completely flooding the western polder, but by the end of the year the Dutch had pumped it dry, resowed the fields in the spring, and over the next seven years restored the polder's farms and villages. Weather, however, is never conquered. The disastrous floods of 1953 laid most of coastal Holland under water. The Dutch dried themselves out and, while the work at Zuider Zee continued, applied its lessons elsewhere and lent their hydraulic skills to other countries. Today the *Afsluitdijk*, or Zuider Zee road, is a normal thoroughfare. To drive across it between the sullen ocean on one side and new land on the other is for that moment to feel optimism for the human race.

Great endeavor requires vision and some kind of compelling impulse, not necessarily practical as in the case of the Dutch, but sometimes less definable, more exalted, as in the case of the Gothic cathedrals of the Middle Ages. The architectural explosion that produced this multitude of soaring vaults—arched, ribbed, pierced with jeweled light, studded with thousands of figures of the stone-carvers' art—represents in size, splendor, and numbers one of the great, permanent artistic achievements of human hands. What accounts for it? Not religious fervor alone but the zeal of a dynamic age, a desire to outdo, an ambition for the biggest and the best. Only the general will, shared by nobles, merchants, guilds, artisans, and commoners, could command the resources and labor to sustain so great an undertaking. Each group contributed donations, especially the magnates of commerce, who felt relieved thereby from the guilt of money-making. Voluntary work programs involved all classes. "Who has ever seen or heard tell in times past," wrote an observer, "that powerful princes of the world, that men brought up in honors and wealth, that nobles—men and women—have bent their haughty necks to the harness of carts and, like beasts of burden, have dragged to the abode of Christ these wagons loaded with wines, grains, oil, stones, timber and all that is necessary for the construction of the church?"

Abbot Suger, whose renovation of St.-Denis is considered the start of Gothic architecture, embodied the spirit of the builders. Determined to create the most splendid basilica in Christendom, he supervised every aspect of the work from fund-raising to decoration, and caused his name to be inscribed for immortality on keystones and capitals. He lay awake worrying, as he tells us, where to find trees large enough for the beams, and went personally with his carpenters to the forest to question the woodcutters under oath. When they swore that nothing of the kind he wanted could be found in the area, he insisted on searching for them himself and, after nine hours of scrambling through thorns and thickets, succeeded in locating and marking twelve trees of the necessary size.

Mainly the compelling impulse lay in the towns, where, in those years, economic and political strengths and wealth were accumulating. Amiens, the thriving capital of Picardy, decided to build the largest church in France, "higher than all the saints, higher than all the kings." For the necessary space, the hospital and bishop's palace had to be relocated and the city walls moved back. At the same time Beauvais, a neighbor town, raised a vault over the crossing of transept and nave to an unprecedented height of 158 feet, the apogee of architects' daring in its day. It proved too daring, for the height of the columns and spread of the supports caused the vault to collapse after twelve years. Repaired with undaunted purpose, it was defiantly topped by a spire rising 492 feet above ground, the tallest in France. Beauvais, having used up its resources, never built the nave, leaving a structure foreshortened but glorious. The interior is a fantasy of soaring space; to enter is to stand dazed in wonder, breathless in admiration.

The higher and lighter grew the buildings and the slenderer the columns, the more new expedients and techniques had to be devised to hold them up. Buttresses flew like angels' wings against the exteriors. This was a period of innovation and audacity, and a limitless spirit of excelsior. In a single century, from 1170 to 1270, six hundred cathedrals and major churches were built in France alone. In England in that period, the cathedral of Salisbury, with the tallest spire in the country, was completed in thirty-eight years. The spire of Freiburg in Germany was constructed entirely of filigree in stone as if spun by some supernatural spider. In the St.-Chapelle in Paris the fifteen miraculous windows swallow the walls; they have become the whole.

Embellishment was integral to the construction. Reims is populated by five thousand statues of saints, prophets, kings and cardinals, bishops, knights, ladies, craftsmen and commoners, devils, animals and birds. Every type of leaf known in northern France is said to appear in the decoration. In carving, stained glass, and sculpture the cathedrals displayed the art of medieval hands, and the marvel of these buildings is permanent even when they no longer play a central role in everyday life. Rodin said he could feel the beauty and presence of Reims even at night when he could not see it. "Its power," he wrote, "transcends the senses so that the eye sees what it sees not."

Explanations for the extraordinary burst that produced the cathedrals are several. Art historians will tell you that it was the inventon of the ribbed vault. Religious historians will say it was the product of an age of faith which believed that with God's favor anything was possible; in fact it was not a period of untroubled faith, but of heresies and Inquisition. Rather, one can only say that conditions were right. Social order under monarchy and the towns was replacing the anarchy of the barons, so that existence was no longer merely a struggle to stay alive but allowed a surplus of goods and energies and greater opportunity for mutual effort. Banking and commerce were producing capital, roads were making possible wheeled transport, universities nourishing ideas and communication. It was one of history's high tides, an age of vigor, confidence, and forces converging to quicken the blood.

Even when the historical tide is low, a particular group of doers may emerge in exploits that inspire awe. Shrouded in the mists of the eighth century, long before the cathedrals, Viking seamanship was a wonder of daring, stamina, and skill. Pushing relentlessly outward in open boats, the Vikings sailed south, around Spain to North Africa and Arabia, north to the top of the world, west across uncharted seas to American coasts. They hauled their boats overland from the Baltic to make their way down Russian rivers to the Black Sea. Why? We do not know what engine drove them, only that it was part of the human endowment.

What of the founding of our own country, America? We take the *Mayflower* for granted—yet think of the boldness, the enterprise, the determined independence, the sheer grit it took to leave the known and set out across the sea for the unknown where no houses or food, no stores, no cleared land, no crops or livestock, none of the equipment or settlement of organized living awaited.

Equally bold was the enterprise of the French in the northern forests of the American continent, who throughout the seventeenth century explored and opened the land from the St. Lawrence to the Mississippi, from the Great Lakes to the Gulf of Mexico. They came not for liberty like the Pilgrims, but for gain and dominion, whether in spiritual empire for the Jesuits or in land, glory, and riches for the agents of the King; and rarely in history have men willingly embraced such hardship, such daunting adventure, and persisted with such tenacity and endurance. They met hunger, exhaustion, frostbite, capture and torture by Indians, wounds and disease, dangerous rapids, swarms of insects, long portages, bitter weather, and hardly ever did those who suffered the experience fail to return, re-enter the menacing but bountiful forest, and pit themselves once more against danger, pain, and death.

Above all others, the perseverance of La Salle in his search for the mouth of the Mississippi was unsurpassed. While preparing in Quebec, he mastered eight Indian languages. From then on he suffered accidents, betrayals, desertions, losses of men and provisions, fever and snow blindness, the hostility and intrigues of rivals who incited the Indians against him and plotted to ambush or poison him. He was truly pursued, as Francis Parkman wrote, by "a demon of havoc." Paddling through heavy waves in a storm over Lake Ontario, he waded through freezing surf to beach the canoes each night, and lost guns and baggage when a canoe was swamped and sank. To lay the foundations of a fort above Niagara, frozen ground had to be thawed by boiling water. When the fort was at last built, La Salle christened it Crèvecoeur—that is, Heartbreak. It earned the name when in his absence it was plundered and deserted by its half-starved mutinous garrison. Farther on, a friendly Indian village, intended as a destination, was found laid waste by the Iroquois with only charred stakes stuck with skulls standing among the ashes, while wolves and buzzards prowled through the remains.

When at last, after four months' hazardous journey down the Great River, La Salle reached the sea, he formally took possession in the name of Louis XIV of all the country from the river's mouth to its source and of its tributaries—that is, of the vast basin of the Mississippi from the Rockies to the Appalachians—and named it Louisiana. The validity of the claim, which seems so hollow to us (though successful in its own time), is not the point. What counts is the conquest of fearful adversity by one man's extraordinary exertions and inflexible will.

Happily, man has a capacity for pleasure too, and in contriving ways to entertain and amuse himself has created brilliance and delight. Pageants, carnivals, festivals, fireworks, music, dancing and drama, parties and picnics, sports and games, the comic spirit and its gift of laughter—all the range of enjoyment from grand ceremonial to the quiet solitude of a day's fishing has helped to balance the world's infelicity.

The original Olympic Games held every fourth year in honor of Zeus was the most celebrated festival of classic times, of such significance to the Greeks that they dated their history from the first games in 776 B.C. as we date ours from the birth of Christ. The crown of olive awarded to the winner in each contest was considered the crown of happiness. While the Romans took this to be a sign of the essential frivolity of the Greek character, the ancient games endured for twelve centuries, a longer span than the supremacy of Rome.

Homo ludens, man at play, is surely as significant a figure as man at war or at work. In human activity the invention of the ball may be said to rank with the invention of the wheel. Imagine America without baseball, Europe without soccer, England without cricket, the Italians without bocci, China without Ping-Pong, and tennis for no one. Even stern John Calvin, the examplar of Puritan self-denial, was once discovered playing bowls on Sunday, and in 1611 an English supply ship arriving at Jamestown found the starving colonists suppressing their misery in the same game. Cornhuskings, logrollings, barn-raisings, horseraces, and wrestling and boxing matches have engaged America as, somewhat more passively, the armchair watching of football and basketball does today.

Play was invented for diversion, exertion, and escape from routine cares. In colonial New York, sleighing parties preceded by fiddlers on horseback drove out to country inns, where, according to a participant, "we danced, sang, romped, ate and drank and kicked away care from morning to night." John Audubon, present at a barbecue and dance on the Kentucky frontier, wrote, "Every countenance beamed with joy, every heart leaped with gladness . . . care and sorrow were flung to the winds."

Play has its underside, too, in the gladiatorial games, in cockfights and prizefights, which arouse one of the least agreeable of human characteristics, pleasure in blood and brutality, but in relation to play as a whole, this is minor.

Much of our pleasure derives from eating and sex, two components which have received an excess of attention in our time—allowing me to leave them aside as understood, except to note how closely they are allied. All those recipes, cuisines, exotic foods, and utensils of kitchen chic seem to proliferate in proportion to pornography, sex therapy, blue movies, and instructive tales for children on pederasty and incest. Whether this twin increase signifies decadence or liberation is disputable. Let us move on to other ground.

To the carnival, for instance. Mardi Gras in all its forms is an excuse for letting go; for uninhibited fun before the abstinence of Lent; for dressing up, play-acting, cavorting in costumes and masks, constructing imaginative floats; for noise, pranks, jokes, battles of flowers and confetti, balls and banquets, singing and dancing, and fireworks. In the Belgian carnival of Gilles-Binche, originating in the sixteenth century in honor of Charles V's conquest of Peru, the dancers are spectacular in superlatively tall feather headdresses representing the Incas, and brilliant costumes trimmed with gold lace and tinkling bells. They wear wooden shoes to stamp out the rhythm of their dance and carry baskets of oranges symbolizing the treasures of Peru with which they pelt the onlookers. In the celebrated Palio of Siena at harvest time, a horse and rider from each neighborhood race madly around a sloping cobblestoned course in the public square, while the citizens shriek in passionate rivalry. Walpurgis Night on the eve of May Day is an excuse for bacchanalia in the guise of witches' revels; winter's festival at Christmas is celebrated by gift-giving. Humanity has invented infinite ways to enjoy itself.

No people have invented more ways than have the Chinese, perhaps to balance floods, famine, warlords, and other ills of fate. The clang of gongs, clashing of cymbals, and beating of drums sound through their long history. No month is without fairs and theatricals when streets are hung with fantasies of painted lanterns and crowded with "carriages that flow like water, horses like roaming dragons." Night skies are illumined by firecrackers—a Chinese invention—bursting in the form of peonies, flowerpots, fiery devils. The ways of pleasure are myriad. Music plays in the air through bamboo whistles of different pitch tied to the wings of circling pigeons. To skim a frozen lake in an ice sleigh with a group of friends on a day when the sun is warm is rapture, like "moving in a cup of jade." What more delightful than the ancient festival called "Half an Immortal," when everyone from palace officials to the common man took a ride on a swing? When high in the air, one felt like an Immortal; when back to earth once again, human—no more than to be for an instant a god.

In Europe's age of grandeur, princes devised pageants of dazzling splendor to express their magnificence, none more spectacular than the extravaganza of 1660 celebrating the marriage of Leopold I of Austria to the Infanta of Spain. As the climax to festivities lasting three months, an equestrian contest of the Four Elements was performed in the grand plaza, each element represented by a company of a thousand, gorgeously costumed. Water's company were dressed in blue and silver covered with fish scales and shells; Air's in gold brocade shaded in the colors of the rainbow; Earth's decorated with flowers; Fire's with curling flames. Neptune, surrounded by marine monsters and winds, rode in a car drawn by a huge whale spouting water. Earth's car contained a garden with Pan and shepherds, drawn by elephants with castles on their backs; Air rode a dragon escorted by thirty griffins; Fire was accompanied by Vulcan, thirty Cyclopes, and a flame-spouting salamander. A rather irrelevant ship carrying the Argonauts to the Golden Fleece was added for extras. The contest was resolved when a star-studded globe, arched by an artificial rainbow representing Peace, rolled across the plaza and opened to display a Temple of Immortality from which emerged riders impersonating the fifteen previous Hapsburg emperors, ending with Leopold in person. Dressed as Glory, in silver lace and diamonds, and wearing his crown, he rode in a silver seashell drawn by eight white horses and carrying seven singers in jeweled robes, who serenaded the Infanta. Then followed the climactic equestrian ballet performed by four groups of eight cavaliers each, whose elaborate movements were marked by trumpet flourishes, kettledrums, and cannon salutes. In a grand finale a thousand rockets blazed from two artificial mountains named Parnassus and Aetna, and the sky was lit in triumph by the Hapsburg acrostic AEIOU standing for *Austria Est Imperare Omne Universo*, meaning, approximately, "Austria rules the world."

The motive may have been self-aggrandizement, but the results were sumptuous and exciting; viewers were enthralled, performers proud, and the designer of the pageant was made a baron. It was a case of men and women engaged in the art of enjoyment, a function common to all times, although one would hardly know it from today's image of ourselves as wretched creatures forever agonizing over petty squalors of sex and drink as if we had no other recourse or destiny.

The greatest recourse, and mankind's most enduring achievement, is art. At its best, it reveals the nobility that coexists in human nature along with flaws and evils, and the beauty and truth it can perceive. Whether in music or architecture, literature, painting or sculpture, art opens our eyes, ears, and feelings to something beyond ourselves, something we cannot experience without the artist's vision and the genius of his craft. The placing of Greek temples, like the Temple of

Poseidon on the promontory at Sunion, outlined against the piercing blue of the Aegean Sea, Poseidon's home; the majesty of Michelangelo's sculptured figures in stone; Shakespeare's command of language and knowledge of the human soul; the intricate order of Bach, the enchantment of Mozart; the purity of Chinese monochrome pottery with its lovely names—celadon, oxblood, peach blossom, clair de lune; the exuberance of Tiepolo's ceilings where, without picture frames to limit movement, a whole world in exquisitely beautiful colors lives and moves in the sky; the prose and poetry of all the writers from Homer to Cervantes to Jane Austen and John Keats to Dostoevski and Chekhov—who made all these things? We—our species—did. The range is too vast and various to do justice to it in this space, but the random samples I have mentioned, and all the rest they suggest, are sufficient reason to honor mankind.

If we have (as I think) lost beauty and elegance in the modern world, we have gained much, through science and technology and democratic pressures, in the material well-being of the masses. The change in the lives of, and society's attitude toward, the working class marks the great divide between the modern world and the old regime. From the French Revolution through the brutal labor wars of the nineteenth and twentieth centuries, the change was earned mainly by force against fierce and often vicious opposition. While this was a harsh process, it developed and activated a social conscience hardly operative before. Slavery, beggary, unaided misery, and want have, on the whole, been eliminated in the developed nations of the West. That much is a credit in the human record, even if the world is uglier as a result of adapting to mass values. History generally arranges these things so that gain is balanced by loss, perhaps in order not to make the gods jealous.

The material miracles wrought by science and technology—from the harnessing of steam and electricity to anesthesia, antisepsis, antibiotics, and woman's liberator, the washing machine, and all the labor-savers that go with it—are too well recognized in our culture to need my emphasis. Pasteur is as great a figure in the human record as Michelangelo or Mozart—probably, as far as the general welfare is concerned, greater. We are more aware of his kind of accomplishment than of those less tangible. Ask anyone to suggest the credits of mankind and the answer is likely to start with physical things. Yet the underside of scientific progress is prominent and dark. The weaponry of war in its ever-widening capacity to kill is the deadly example, and who is prepared to state with confidence that the over-all effect of the automobile, airplane, telephone, television, and computer has been, on balance, beneficent?

Pursuit of knowledge for its own sake has been a more certain good. There was a springtime in the eighteenth century when, through knowledge and reason, everything seemed possible; when reason was expected to break through religious dogma like the sun breaking through fog, and man, armed with knowledge and reason, would be able at last to control his own fate and construct a good society. The theory that because this world exists it is the best of all possible worlds spread outward from Leibniz; the word "optimism" was used for the first time in 1737.

What a burst of intellectual energies shook these decades! In twenty years, 1735–55, Linnaeus named and classified all of known botany, Buffon systematized natural history in thirty-six volumes, and an American, John Bartram, scoured the wilderness for plants to send to correspondents in Europe. Voltaire, Montesquieu, and Hume investigated the nature of man and the moral foundations of law and society. Benjamin Franklin demonstrated electricity from lightning. Dr. Johnson by himself compiled the first dictionary of the English language; Diderot and the Encyclopedists of France undertook to present the whole of knowledge in enlightened terms. The Chinese secret of making porcelain having been uncovered by Europeans, its manufacture flourished at Meissen and Dresden. Clearing for the Place de la Concorde, to be the most majestic in Europe, was begun in Paris. No less than 150 newspapers and journals circulated in England. The novel was exuberantly born in the work of Richardson and Fielding. Chardin, a supreme artist, portrayed humanity with a loving brush in his gentle domestic scenes. Hogarth, seeing another creature, exposed the underside in all its ribaldry and squalor. It was an age of enthusiasm; at the first London performance of Handel's *Messiah* in 1743, George II was so carried away by the "Hallelujah Chorus" that he rose to his feet, causing the whole audience to stand with him and thereby establishing a custom still sometimes followed by *Messiah* audiences. The man in whom the spirit of the age was to flower, Thomas Jefferson, was born.

If the twenty-year period is stretched by another ten, it includes the reverberating voice of Rousseau's *Social Contract*, Beccaria's ground-breaking study *Essay on Crimes and Punishment*, Gibbon's beginning of the *Decline and Fall*, and, despite the Lisbon earthquake and *Candide*, the admission of "optimism" into the dictionary of the Académie Française.

Although the Enlightenment may have overestimated the power of reason to guide human conduct, it nevertheless opened to men and women a more humane view of their fellow passengers. Slowly the harshest habits gave way to reform—in treatment of the insane, reduction of death penalties, mitigation of the fierce laws against debtors and poachers, and in the passionately fought cause for abolition of the slave trade.

The humanitarian movement was not charity, which always carries an overtone of being done in the donor's interest, but a more disinterested benevolence or altruism, motivated by conscience. It was personified in William Wilberforce, who in the later eighteenth century stirred the great rebellion of the English conscience against the trade in human beings. In America the immorality of slavery had long troubled the colonies. By 1789 slavery had been legally abolished by the New England states followed by New York, New Jersey, and Pennsylvania, but the southern states, as their price for joining the Union, insisted that the subject be excluded from the Constitution.

In England, where the home economy did not depend on slave labor, Wilberforce had more scope. His influence could have carried him to the Prime Minister's seat if personal power had been his goal, but he channeled his life instead toward a goal for mankind. He instigated, energized, inspired a movement whose members held meetings, organized petitions, collected information on the horrors of the middle passage, showered pamphlets on the public, gathered Nonconformist middle-class sentiment into a swelling tide that, in Trevelyan's phrase, "melted the hard prudence of statesmen." Abolition of the slave trade under the British flag was won in 1807. The British Navy was used to enforce the ban by searches on the high seas and regular patrols of the African coast. When Portugal and Spain were persuaded to join in the prohibition, they were paid a compensation of £300,000 and £400,000 respectively by the British taxpayer. Violations and smuggling continued, convincing the abolitionists that, in order to stop the trade, slavery itself had to be abolished. Agitation resumed. By degrees over the next quarter-century, compensation reduced the opposition of the West Indian slave-owners and their allies in England until emancipation of all slaves in the British Empire was enacted in 1833. The total cost to the British taxpayer was reckoned at £20 million.

Through recent unpleasant experiences we have learned to expect ambition, greed, or corruption to reveal itself behind every public act, but, as we have just seen, it is not invariably so. Human beings do possess better impulses, and occasionally act upon them, even in the twentieth century. Occupied Denmark, during World War II, outraged by Nazi orders for deportation of its Jewish fellow citizens, summoned the courage of defiance and transformed itself into a united underground railway to smuggle virtually all eight thousand Danish Jews out to Sweden, and Sweden gave them shelter. Far away and unconnected, a village in southern France, Le Chambon-sur-Lignon, devoted itself to rescuing Jews and other victims of the Nazis at the risk of the inhabitants' own lives and freedom. "Saving lives became a hobby of the people of Le Chambon," said one of them. The larger record of the time was admittedly collaboration, passive or active. We cannot reckon on the better impulses predominating in the world, only that they will always appear.

The strongest of these in history, summoner of the best in men, has been zeal for liberty. Time after time, in some spot somewhere on the globe, people have risen in what Swinburne called the "divine right of insurrection"—to overthrow despots, repel alien conquerors, achieve independence—and so it will be until the day power ceases to corrupt, which, I think, is not a near expectation.

The ancient Jews rose three times against alien rulers, beginning with the revolt of the Maccabees against the effort of Antiochus to outlaw observance of the Jewish faith. Mattathias the priest and his five sons, assembling loyal believers in the mountains, opened a guerrilla war which, after the father's death, was to find a leader of military genius in his son Judah, called Maccabee or the Hammer. Later honored in the Middle Ages as one of the Nine Worthies of the world, he defeated his enemies, rededicated the temple, and re-established the independence of Judea. In the next century the uprising of the Zealots against Roman rule was fanatically and hopelessly pursued through famines, sieges, the fall of Jerusalem and destruction of the temple until a last stand of fewer than a thousand on the rock of Masada ended in group suicide in preference to surrender. After sixty years as an occupied province, Judea rose yet again under Simon Bar Kochba, who regained Jerusalem for a brief moment of Jewish control but could not withstand the arms of Hadrian. The rebellion was crushed, but the zeal for selfhood, smoldering in exile through eighteen centuries, was to revive and regain its home in our time.

The phenomenon continues in our own day, in Algeria, in Vietnam, although, seen at close quarters and more often than not manipulated by outsiders, contemporary movements seem less pure and heroic than those polished by history's gloss—as, for instance, the Scots under William Wallace, the Swiss against the Hapsburgs, the American colonies against the mother country.

I have always cherished the spirited rejoinder of one of the great colonial landowners of New York who, on being advised not to risk his property by signing the Declaration of Independence, replied, "Damn the property; give me the pen!" On seeking confirmation for purposes of this essay, I am deeply chagrined to report that the saying appears to be apocryphal. Yet not its spirit, for the signers well knew they were risking their property, not to mention their heads, by putting their names to the Declaration.

Nor did they escape. Left vulnerable by Washington's defeat on Long Island, their estates were deliberately wrecked by the British, their homes ransacked and looted, books and papers burned, furniture smashed, livestock and stores destroyed, tenants and servants driven out, a thousand acres of Lewis Morris' timberland left in stumps. All were reduced to living by the charity of friends during the war. Philip Livingston died without ever seeing his home and lands again; the rich merchant William Floyd was permanently ruined. Other affluent men who signed had much to lose—Hancock of Massachusetts, who wrote his name large so that no one would mistake it, Lee of Virginia, Carroll of Baltimore. George Washington himself epitomized the spirit later in the war when he wrote to reproach his overseer at Mount Vernon for supplying provisions to a British landing party that had sailed up to the Potomac and threatened to burn the estate unless their demands were met. It would have been "less painful," he wrote, to have learned that, as a result of refusal, "they had burnt my House and laid my plantation in ruins." Economic self-interest, as this illustrates, is not always our guiding instinct.

So far I have considered qualities of the group rather than of the individual—except for art, which in most cases is a product of the single spirit. Happiness, too, is an individual matter. It springs up here or there, haphazard, random, without origin or explanation. It resists study, laughs at sociology, flourishes, vanishes, reappears somewhere else. Take Izaak Walton, author of *The Compleat Angler*, that guide to contentment as well as fishing, of which Charles Lamb said, "It would sweeten any man's temper at any time to read it." Though Walton lived in distracted times of revolution and regicide, though he adhered to the losing side in the English Civil War, though he lost in their infancy all seven children by his first wife and the eldest son of his second marriage, though he was twice a widower, his misfortunes could not sour an essentially buoyant nature. "He passed through turmoil," in the words of a biographer, "ever accompanied by content."

Walton's secret was friendship. Born to a yeoman family and apprenticed in youth as an ironmonger, he managed to gain an education and, through sweetness of disposition and a cheerful religious faith, became a friend on equal terms of various learned clergymen and poets whose lives he wrote and works he prefaced—among them John Donne, George Herbert, and Michael Drayton. Another companion, Charles Cotton, wrote of Izaak, "In him I have the happiness to know the worthiest man, and to enjoy the best and truest friend any man ever had."

The Compleat Angler, published when the author was sixty, glows in the sunshine of his character. In it are humor and piety, grave advice on the idiosyncrasies of fish and the niceties of landing them, delight in nature and in music. Walton saw five editions reprinted in his lifetime, while unnumerable later editions secured him immortality. The surviving son by his second wife became a clergyman; the surviving daughter married one and gave her father a home among grandchildren. He wrote his last work at eighty-five and died at ninety after being celebrated in verse by one of his circle as a "happy old man" whose life "showed how to compass true felicity." Let us think of him when we grumble.

Is anything to be learned from my survey? I raise the question only because most people want history to teach them lessons, which I believe it can do, although I am less sure we can use them when needed. I gathered these examples not to teach but merely to remind people in a despondent era that the good in mankind operates even if the bad secures more attention. I am aware that selecting out the better moments does not result in a realistic picture. Turn them over and there is likely to be a darker side, as when Project Apollo, our journey to the moon, was authorized because its glamour could obtain subsidies for rocket and missile development that otherwise might not have been forthcoming. That is the way things are.

Whole philosophies have evolved over the question whether the human species is predominately good or evil. I only know that it is mixed, that you cannot separate good from bad, that wisdom, courage, and benevolence exist alongside knavery, greed, and stupidity; heroism and fortitude alongside vainglory, cruelty, and corruption.

It is a paradox of our time in the West that never have so many people been so relatively well off and never has society been more troubled. Yet I suspect that humanity's virtues have not vanished, although the experiences of our century seem to suggest that they are in abeyance. A century that took shape in the disillusion which followed the enormous effort and hopes of World War I, that saw revolution in Russia congeal into the same tyranny it overthrew, saw a supposedly civilized nation revert under the Nazis into organized and unparalleled savagery, saw the craven appeasement by the democracies, is understandably marked by suspicion of human nature. A literary historian, Van Wyck Brooks, discussing the 1920s and '30s, spoke of "an eschatological despair of the world." Whereas Whitman and Emerson, he wrote, "had been impressed by the worth and good sense of the people, writers of the new time" were struck by their lusts, cupidity, and violence, and had come to dislike their fellow men. The same theme reappeared in a recent play in which a mother struggled against her two "pitilessly contemptuous" children. Her problem was that she wanted them to be happy and they did not want to be. They preferred to watch horrors on television. In essence this is our epoch. It insists upon the flaws and corruptions, without belief in valor or virtue or the possibility of happiness. It keeps turning to look back on Sodom and Gomorrah; it has no view of the Delectable Mountains.

We must keep a balance, and I know of no better prescription than a phrase from Condorcet's eulogy on the death of Benjamin Franklin: "He pardoned the present for the sake of the future."

III
LEARNING FROM HISTORY

Is History a Guide to the Future?

The commonest question asked of historians by laymen is whether history serves a purpose. Is it useful? Can we learn from the lessons of history?

When people want history to be utilitarian and teach us lessons, that means they also want to be sure that it meets scientific standards. This, in my opinion, it cannot do, for reasons which I will come to in a moment. To practice history as a science is sociology, an altogether different discipline which I personally find antipathetic—although I suppose the sociologists would consider that my deficiency rather than theirs. The sociologists plod along with their noses to the ground assembling masses of statistics in order to arrive at some obvious conclusion which a reasonably perceptive historian, not to mention a large part of the general public, knows anyway, simply from observation—that social mobility is increasing, for instance, or that women have different problems from men. One wishes they would just cut loose someday, lift up their heads, and look at the world around them.

If history were a science, we should be able to get a grip on her, learn her ways, establish her patterns, know what will happen tomorrow. Why is it that we cannot? The answer lies in what I call the Unknowable Variable—namely, man. Human beings are always and finally the subject of history. History is the record of human behavior,

Address, Chicago Historical Society, October 1966.

the most fascinating subject of all, but illogical and so crammed with an unlimited number of variables that it is not susceptible of the scientific method nor of systematizng.

I say this bravely, even in the midst of the electronic age when computers are already chewing at the skirts of history in the process called Quantification. Applied to history, quantification, I believe, has its limits. It depends on a method called "data manipulation," which means that the facts, or data, of the historical past—that is, of human behavior—are manipulated into named categories so that they can be programmed into computers. Out comes—hopefully—a pattern. I can only tell you that for history "data manipulation" is a built-in invalidator, because to the degree that you manipulate your data to suit some extraneous requirement, in this case the requirements of the machine, to that degree your results will be suspect—and run the risk of being invalid. Everything depends on the naming of the categories and the assigning of facts to them, and this depends on the quantifier's individual judgment at the very base of the process. The categories are not revealed doctrine nor are the results scientific truth.

The hope for quantification, presumably, is that by processing a vast quantity of material far beyond the capacity of the individual to encompass, it can bring to light and establish reliable patterns. That remains to be seen, but I am not optimistic. History has a way of escaping attempts to imprison it in patterns. Moreover, one of its basic data is the human soul. The conventional historian, at least the one concerned with truth, not propaganda, will try honestly to let his "data" speak for themselves, but data which are shut up in prearranged boxes are helpless. Their nuances have no voice. They must carry one fixed meaning or another and weight the result accordingly. For instance, in a quantification study of the origins of World War I which I have seen, the operators have divided all the diplomatic documents, messages, and utterances of the July crisis into categories labeled "hostility," "friendship," "frustration," "satisfaction," and so on, with each statement rated for intensity on a scale from one to nine, including fractions. But no pre-established categories could match all the private character traits and public pressures variously operating on the nervous monarchs and ministers who were involved. The massive effort that went into this study brought forth a mouse— the less than startling conclusion that the likelihood of war increased in proportion to the rise in hostility of the messages.

Quantification is really only a new approach to the old persistent effort to make history fit a pattern, but *reliable* patterns, or what are otherwise called the lessons of history, remain elusive.

For instance, suppose Woodrow Wilson had not been President of the United States in 1914 but instead Theodore Roosevelt, who had been his opponent in the election of 1912. Had that been the case, America might have entered the war much earlier, perhaps at the time of the *Lusitania* in 1915, with possible shortening of the war and incalculable effects on history. Well, it happens that among the Anarchists in my book *The Proud Tower* is an obscure Italian named Miguel Angiolillo, whom nobody remembers but who shot dead Premier Canovas of Spain in 1897. Canovas was a strong man who was just about to succeed in quelling the rebels in Cuba when he was assassinated. Had he lived, there might have been no extended Cuban insurrection for Americans to get excited about, no Spanish-American War, no San Juan Hill, no Rough Riders, no Vice-Presidency for Theodore Roosevelt to enable him to succeed when another accident, another Anarchist, another unpredictable human being, killed McKinley. If Theodore had never been President, there would have been no third party in 1912 to split the Republicans, and Woodrow Wilson would not have been elected. The speculations from that point on are limitless. To me it is comforting rather than otherwise to feel that history is determined by the illogical human record and not by large immutable scientific laws beyond our power to deflect.

I know very little (a euphemism for "nothing") about laboratory science, but I have the impression that conclusions are supposed to be logical; that is, from a given set of circumstances a predictable result should follow. The trouble is that in human behavior and history it is impossible to isolate or repeat a given set of circumstances. Complex human acts cannot be either reproduced or deliberately initiated—or counted upon like the phenomena of nature. The sun comes up every day. Tides are so obedient to schedule that a timetable for them can be printed like that for trains, though more reliable. In fact, tides and trains sharply illustrate my point: One depends on the moon and is certain; the other depends on man and is uncertain.

In the absence of dependable recurring circumstance, too much confidence cannot be placed on the lessons of history.

There *are* lessons, of course, and when people speak of learning from them, they have in mind, I think, two ways of applying past experience: One is to enable us to avoid past mistakes and to manage better in similar circumstances next time; the other is to enable us to anticipate a future course of events. (History could tell us something about Vietnam, I think, if we would only listen.) To manage better next time is within our means; to anticipate does not seem to be.

World War II, for example, with the experience of the previous war as an awful lesson, was certainly conducted, once we got into it, more intelligently than World War I. Getting into it was another matter. When it was important to anticipate the course of events, Americans somehow failed to apply the right lesson. Pearl Harbor is the classic example of failure to learn from history. From hindsight we now know that what we should have anticipated was a surprise attack by Japan in the midst of negotiations. Merely because this was dishonorable, did that make it unthinkable? Hardly. It was exactly the procedure Japan had adopted in 1904 when she opened the Russo-Japanese War by surprise attack on the Russian fleet at Port Arthur.

In addition we had every possible physical indication. We had broken the Japanese code, we had warnings on radar, we had a constant flow of accurate intelligence. What failed? Not information but *judgment*. We had all the evidence and refused to interpret it correctly, just as the Germans in 1944 refused to believe the evidence of a landing in Normandy. Men will not believe what does not fit in with their plans or suit their prearrangements. The flaw in all military intelligence, whether twenty or fifty or one hundred percent accurate, is that it is no better than the judgment of its interpreters, and this judgment is the product of a mass of individual, social, and political biases, prejudgments, and wishful thinkings; in short, it is human and therefore fallible. If man can break the Japanese code and yet not believe what it tells him, how can he be expected to learn from the lessons of history?

Would a computer do better? In the case of Pearl Harbor, probably yes. If one could have fed all the pieces of intelligence available in November 1941 into a computer, it could have hardly failed to reply promptly, "Air attack, Hawaii, Philippines" and probably even "December 7." But will this work every time? Can we trust the lessons of history to computers? I think not, because history will fool them. They may make the right deductions and draw the right conclusions, but a twist occurs, someone sneezes, history swerves and takes another path. Had Cleopatra's nose been shorter, said Pascal, the whole aspect of the world would have been changed. Can a computer account for Cleopatra?

Once long ago when the eternal verities seemed clear—that is, during the Spanish Civil War—I thought the lessons of history were unmistakable. It appeared obvious beyond dispute that if fascism under Franco won, Spain in the foreshadowed European war would become a base for Hitler and Mussolini, the Mediterranean would become an Italian lake, Britain would lose Gibraltar and be cut off from her empire east of Suez. The peril was plain, the logic of the thing implacable, every sensible person saw it, and I, just out of college, wrote a small book published in England to point it up, all drawn from the analogy of history. The book showed how, throughout the eighteenth and nineteenth centuries, Britain had consistently interposed herself against the gaining of undue influence over Spain by whatever power dominated the continent. The affair of the Spanish marriages, the campaigns of Wellington, the policies of Castlereagh, Canning, and Palmerston all were directed toward the same objective: The strongest continental power must be prevented from controlling Spain. My treatise was, I thought, very artful and very telling. It did not refer to the then current struggle, but let the past speak for itself and make the argument. It was an irrefutable one— until history refuted it. Franco, assisted by Hitler and Mussolini, *did* win, European war *did* follow, yet unaccountably Spain remained neutral—at least nominally. Gibraltar did not fall, the portals of the Mediterranean did *not* close. I, not to mention all the other "premature" anti-fascists, as we were called, while morally right about the general danger of fascism, had been wrong about a particular outcome. The lessons of history I had so carefully set forth simply did not operate. History misbehaved.

Pearl Harbor and Spain demonstrate two things: One, that man fails to profit from the lessons of history because his prejudgments prevent him from drawing the indicated conclusions; and, two, that history will often capriciously take a different direction from that in which her lessons point. Herein lies the flaw in systems of history.

When it comes to systems, history played her greatest betrayal on Karl Marx. Never was a prophet so sure of his premises, never were believers so absolutely convinced of a predicted outcome, never was there an interpretation of history that seemed so foolproof. Analyzing the effects of the Industrial Revolution, Marx exposed the terrible riddle of the nineteenth century: that the greater the material progress, the wider and deeper the resulting poverty, a process which could only end, he decided, in the violent collapse of the existing order brought on by revolution. From this he formulated the doctrine of *Verelendung* (progressive impoverishment) and *Zusammenbruch* (collapse) and decreed that since working-class self-consciousness increased in proportion to industrialization, revolution would come first in the most industrialized country.

Marx's analysis was so compelling that it seemed impossible history could follow any other course. His postulates were accepted by followers of his own and later generations as if they had been graven on the tablets of Sinai. Marxism as the revealed truth of history was probably the most convincing dogma ever enunciated. Its influence was tremendous, incalculable, continuing. The founder's facts were correct, his thinking logical and profound; he was right in everything but his conclusions. Developing events did not bear him out. The working class grew progressively better, not worse, off. Capitalism did not collapse. Revolution came in the least, not the most, industrialized country. Under collectivism the state did not wither but extended itself in power and function and in its grip on society. History, ignoring Marx, followed her own mysterious logic, and went her own way.

When it developed that Marx was wrong, men in search of determinism rushed off to submit history to a new authority—Freud. His hand is now upon us. The Unconscious is king. At least it was. There are new voices, I believe, claiming that the Unconscious is a fraud—iconoclasm has reached even Freud. Nevertheless, in his effect on the modern outlook, Freud, I believe, unquestionably was the greatest influence for change between the nineteenth and twentieth centuries. It may well be that our time may one day be named for him and the Freudian Era be said to have succeeded the Victorian Era. Our understanding of human motivation has taken on a whole new dimension since his ideas took hold. Yet it does not seem to me that unconscious sexual and psychological drives are as relevant in all circumstances as they are said to be by the Freudians, who have become as fixed in their system as were the orthodox Marxists. They can supply historians with insights but not with guidance to the future because man *en masse* cannot be relied upon to behave according to pattern. All salmon swim back to spawn in the headwaters of their birth; that is universal for salmon. But man lives in a more complicated world than a fish. Too many influences are at work on him to make it applicable that every man is driven by an unconscious desire to swim back to the womb.

It has always seemed to me unfortunate, for instance, that Freud chose the experiences of two royal families to exemplify his concept of the Oedipus and Elektra complexes. Royalty lives under special circumstances, particularly as regards the issue of power between the sovereign and his heir, which are not valid as universal experience. The legend of Oedipus killing his father may have derived from the observed phenomenon that every royal heir has always hated his father, not because he wants to sleep with his mother but because he wants to ascend the throne. If the parental sovereign happens to be his mother, he hates her just as much. She will dislike him equally from birth because she knows he is destined to take her place, as in the case of Queen Victoria and her eldest son, who became Edward VII. That is not Freudian, it is simply dynastic.

As for Elektra, it is hard to know what to make of that tale. The House of Atreus was a very odd family indeed. More was going on there than just Elektra being in love with her father. How about Orestes, who helped her to kill their mother, or killed her himself, according to another version? Was not that the wrong parent? How come he did not kill his father? How about Iphigenia, the sister, whom Agememnon killed as a sacrifice? What is the Freudian explanation for that? They do not say, which is not being historical. A historian cannot pick and choose his facts; he must deal with all the evidence.

Or take Martin Luther. As you know, Professor Erik Erikson of Harvard has discovered that Luther was constipated from childhood and upon this interesting physiological item he has erected a system which explains everything about his man. This is definitely the most camp thing that has happened to history in years. It even made Broadway. Nevertheless I do not think Luther pinned the 95 Theses on the church door at Wittenberg solely or even mainly because of the activity, or inactivity rather, of his anal muscle. His personal motive for protest may have had an anal basis for all I know, but what is important historically is the form the protest took, and this had to do with old and deep social grievances concerned with the worldliness of the church, the sale of indulgences, corruption of the clergy, and so on. If it had not been Luther who protested, it would have been someone else; Protestantism would have come with or without him, and its causes had nothing whatever to do with his private physiological impediment. Professor Erikson, I am sure, was attempting to explain Luther, not Protestantism, but his book has started a fad for psycho-history among those without the adequate knowledge or training to use it.

Following Freud there flourished briefly a minor prophet, Oswald Spengler, who proclaimed the Decline of the West, based on an elaborate study of the lessons of history. Off and on since then people have been returning to his theme, especially since World War II and the end of colonialism. The rise of China and the rash of independence movements in Asia and Africa have inspired many nervous second looks at Spengler. Europe is finished, say the knowing ones; the future belongs to the colored races and all that.

People have been burying Europe for quite some time. I remember a political thinker for whom I had great respect telling me in the thirties that Europe's reign was over; the future belonged to America, Russia, and China. It was a new and awful thought to me then and I was immensely impressed. As I see it now, his grouping has not been justified. I do not think Russia and America can be dissociated from Europe; rather, we are extensions of Europe. I hesitate to be dogmatic about Russia, but I am certain about the United States. American culture stems from Europe, our fortunes are linked with hers, in the long run we are aligned. My impression is that Europe, and by extension the white race, is far from finished. Europe's vitality keeps reviving; as a source of ideas she is inexhaustible. Nuclear fission, the most recent, if unwanted, advance, came from the work of a whole series of Europeans: Max Planck, the Curies, Einstein, Rutherford, Fermi, Nils Bohr, Szilard. Previously the three great makers of the modern mind, Darwin, Marx, and Freud, were Europeans. I do not know of an original idea to have importantly affected the *modern* world which has come from Asia or Africa (except perhaps for Gandhi's concept of non-violent resistance or civil disobedience, and, after all, Thoreau had the same idea earlier).

It does not seem to me a passing phenomenon or an accident that the West, in ideas and temporal power, has been dominant for so long. Far from falling behind, it seems to be extending its lead, except in the fearful matter of mere numbers and I like to think the inventiveness of the West will somehow eventually cope with that. What is called the emergence of the peoples of Asia and Africa is taking place in Western terms and is measured by the degree to which they take on Western forms, political, industrial, and otherwise. That they are losing their own cultures is sad, I think, but I suppose it cannot be helped. The new realm is space, and that too is being explored by the West. So much for Spengler.

Theories of history go in vogues which, as is the nature of vogues, soon fade and give place to new ones. Yet this fails to discourage the systematizers. They believe as firmly in this year's as last year's, for, as Isaiah Berlin says, the "obstinate craving for unity and symmetry at the expense of experience" is always with us. When I grew up, the economic interpretation of history, as formulated with stunning impact by Charles Beard, was the new gospel—as incontrovertible as if it had been revealed to Beard in a burning bush. Even to question that financial interests motivated our Founding Fathers in the separation from Britain, or that equally mercenary considerations decided our entrance into the First World War, was to convict oneself of the utmost naïveté. Yet lately the fashionable—indeed, what appears to be the required—exercise among historians has been jumping on Beard with both feet. He and the considerable body of his followers who added to his system and built it up into a dogma capable of covering any historical situation have been knocked about, analyzed, dissected, and thoroughly disposed of. Presently the historical establishment has moved on to dispose of Frederick Jackson Turner and his theory of the Frontier. I do not know what the new explanation is, but I am sure there must be some thesis, for, as one academic historian recently ruled, the writing of history requires a "large organizing idea."

I visualize the "large organizing idea" as one of those iron chain mats pulled behind by a tractor to smooth over a plowed field. I see the professor climbing up on the tractor seat and away he goes, pulling behind his large organizing idea over the bumps and furrows of history until he has smoothed it out to a nice, neat, organized surface —in other words, into a system.

The human being—you, I, or Napoleon—is unreliable as a scientific factor. In combination of personality, circumstance, and historical moment, each man is a package of variables impossible to duplicate. His birth, his parents, his siblings, his food, his home, his school, his economic and social status, his first job, his first girl, and the variables inherent in all of these, make up that mysterious compendium, personality—which then combines with another set of variables: country, climate, time, and historical circumstance. Is it likely, then, that all these elements will meet again in their exact proportions to reproduce a Moses, or Hitler, or De Gaulle, or for that matter Lee Harvey Oswald, the man who killed Kennedy?

So long as man remains the Unknowable Variable—and I see no immediate prospect of his ever being pinned down in every facet of his infinite variety—I do not see how his actions can be usefully programmed and quantified. The eager electronic optimists will go on chopping up man's past behavior into the thousands of little definable segments which they call Input, and the machine will whirr and buzz and flash its lights and in no time at all give back Output. But will Output be dependable? I would lay ten to one that history will pay no more attention to Output than it did to Karl Marx. It will still need historians. Electronics will have its uses, but it will not, I am confident, transform historians into button-pushers or history into a system.

Vietnam

WHEN, WHY, AND HOW TO GET OUT

I should like to offer a number of propositions. One, we are fighting a war in Asia for an objective no one can define. If it is to make the world safe from aggression, that is a slogan, not a possibility. If it is to contain communism, that is not to be accomplished by destroying the society where the containment is being tried out. If it is to keep Asia open to our access and enterprise, that is an aim which, as formulated by John Hay in the "Open Door" principle, is one of the basic doctrines of American foreign policy; but it always had a twin, "Do not get involved in a land war in Asia." We are trying to maintain the one by violating the other.

Further propositions: The situation in South Vietnam, as regards "freedom from aggression" and democratic institutions, not to mention the general welfare of the people, is worse off than it was before the U.S. moved in. The affairs and reputation of the U.S. itself have steadily deteriorated since our military involvement began. Control of the war and of the policy perpetuating it is in the hands of a President who has locked himself on course and, whether from personal pride or failure to comprehend what is happening, is unwilling to deviate, adjust, or alter direction. One keeps waiting for signs that this is not so—that Mr. Johnson may after all have an ear open to the sounds of history—but no signs appear. By now it seems an absolute that the President is unable to alter course; ergo that the war will not be terminated nor will we get out of it without a change of administration.

Why not termination by victory? Because militarily it is axiomatic

Newsday, March 8, 1968.

that a belligerent cannot win a war without gaining the initiative and taking the offensive, thereby either destroying the enemy's armed forces or cutting them off definitively from their source of supply. For reasons with which everyone is familiar we cannot engage in an all-out offensive. Nor, without virtually forcing Russia or China or both to retaliate, thus precipitating a world war, can we get around the back of North Vietnam to cut its line of communications. Commendably enough, the President has recognized this and has resisted, up to now at least, whatever pressure may be exerted on him either by soldiers understandably frustrated in their profession or by narrow-brained hawks of the "let's-finish-them-off" school.

Precluded from the all-out offensive, we are fighting the most costly and cruelly destructive of all conflicts—a war of attrition. No one has wanted to resurrect that phrase of evil memory from World War I, but it might as well be made explicit. The strategy is futile, in the first place, because the North Vietnamese and Viet Cong are fighting for their country and for a cause and therefore have a stronger motive for enduring than we have, besides resting on the material support of Russia and China. It is indefensible in the second place because it is destroying the land and welfare and lives of the people we are supposed to be fighting for.

Yet we persist, with escalation our only answer, as the generals of 1914–18 persisted in the progressive slaughter of the Western front, where the commanders stumbled forward in the old ruts, not questioning whether to assault the front again but only where along its wall to bang their heads. Johnson is General Sir Douglas Haig—with a significant difference: that whereas Haig's limitless capacity for throwing away lives was ultimately restrained by civilian control, Johnson *is* the civilian control. His is the last word—except for the electorate.

In 1914–18 the Allies won the war of attrition in the end only because of the accretion of a new belligerent, the U.S. In the present case it is plain from the evidence that we are not winning—even if we knew what, in this war, constitutes winning, which is not clear to anyone. On February 23 the *Wall Street Journal*, which is not committed to any position except one of hardheaded realism, acknowledged that "the logic of the battlefield" suggests that the U.S. could be "forced out of an untenable position" and that this country should "be prepared for the bitter taste of a defeat beyond America's power to prevent."

I doubt if that suggestion has ever before been made in our history, but now that someone has been bold enough to say it, the prospect need not be—outside the closed mind of the White House circle—unthinkable. The integrity of neither our territory nor our political system would be affected. It would mean humiliation (which might conceivably be good for us) but not disaster. It would encourage communism, which is the penalty we would have to pay. Although bad business, this is not the fatal catastrophe that some pretend. The theory that if Vietnam goes "they all go" is not impressive. North Vietnam has certainly exhibited a fierce enough spirit of independence to warrant the expectation that it will not be sucked into the Chinese orbit. If China has not become the tool of Russia, why should North Vietnam become the tool of China? To be swallowed by China is a shared fear of the nations of Asia. It is more probable that a strong, independent Vietnam, communist or not, would be a buffer against China rather than an avenue of Chinese expansion.

Failing military victory, can the war be terminated by negotiation? It seems unlikely. With the various Vietnamese parties to the struggle bitterly irreconcilable and the problem compounded by U.S. prestige being bound up in it, the chance of useful negotiation is poor, if not nil. Quarrels over which nations go to war are rarely settled by negotiation. Korea was a rare exception, and though Mr. Truman was a more flexible and more reasonable man than Mr. Johnson, even that case required a new occupant of the White House. In the present case, as long as it is Russia's interest to keep us bleeding and bogged down in Asia, which is to say to keep North Vietnam fighting, and as long as the prospect of gaining control of the whole country remains open to Hanoi, there seems small reason our opponents should be ready to negotiate a settlement that would be acceptable to us—unless it were some face-saving arrangement enabling us to remove ourselves, leaving the field, after an interval, ultimately to them. If they negotiated on that basis, in order to stop the bombing and slaughter and gain a breathing spell, what is to stop a movement of "national liberation" from rising again?

The answer is "nothing"—and that is the crux. Where will and motive and energy and ability to resist aggression are not present it cannot be synthetically induced, nor substituted for, nor can the country in question be propped up from outside. Our support of South Vietnam is like Russia's in Egypt: endless and limitless because without us they have no strength. Nor will it ever develop as long as a massive foreign presence is maintained in their midst, willing to undertake their task for them.

We must continue to exert our effort at the pressure points of communism but only where it can be operative in support of clients able, ready, and motivated to defend their own way of life. It should not be spent on quicksands. Our attempt, under a "Let George (or Uncle Sam) do it" policy, to control the destinies of Asia is self-defeating—and doomed. It is neo-colonialism. It is against history.

What then can be done? One way of stopping wars, so far only imposed on small nations, is by the cease-fire order of the international community. If enough nations were interested in bringing about peace, there is no valid reason why the U.N. should not energize itself to issue a cease-fire order addressed to both Vietnams as well as to the U.S. This would give Mr. Johnson an out which he might be wise enough (though it is not a good bet) to accept, if arranged before election day.

Failing that, another course is open. The U.S. could say with dignity and honesty that we had fulfilled our commitment to South Vietnam by giving all the support at our command in money, arms, and the lives of our citizens; that from here on we plan to withdraw our men at a given rate, say fifty thousand a month, with the parting suggestion that their places be filled by those nations with more immediate interest in the area—for instance, Japan, Australia, the Philippines, Indonesia, and whoever else is sufficiently concerned. If the capacity in them is lacking, then the effort in which we are now engaged is purposeless anyway and should, if we can summon the necessary courage and common sense, be closed down.

COALITION IN VIETNAM—NOT WORTH ONE MORE LIFE

If the goal of coalition government still lies behind the conditions on which the Nixon administration is prepared to make its exit from Vietnam, there can be no foreseeable exit. We have been pursuing this goal (whether from conviction or for public consumption one cannot say) for four years. As recently as Mr. Kissinger's last visit to

New York Times, May 26, 1972.

Paris he carried with him, as he told the press, "a plan for coalition." On what basis of reasonable expectation? Between erstwhile enemies in a civil conflict, the only form of coalition that can occur is that which results when a snake swallows a rabbit. One side or another must be eventually engorged.

How can there be compromise over a division so fundamental that it requires recourse to war? Could the South and North have agreed to stop fighting after Gettysburg and form a joint government? Or Robespierre share power with Louis XVI? Or Generalissimo Franco settle into coalition with Loyalists after the Spanish Civil War? Our own experience in Asia is a nearer guide.

We pursued coalition doggedly and deludedly between the Nationalists and Communists in China in the years 1944–7 only to end in failure, in the defeat of our war aims in Asia, and in the final collapse of America's client.

The argument for coalition at that time seemed compelling, if not to professional observers in the field, at least to policy-makers in the capital who, following the law of their kind, evolve policy to fit a picture in their heads rather than to fit the situation. The basic premise and stated war aim of our effort in the Far East in World War II was a strong, stable, united China on our side after the war, to fill the vacuum that would be left by the defeat of Japan and maintain the peace and stability of Asia in the post-war world. The long-threatened outbreak of civil war in China would nullify that objective. To avert such an outcome, as well as for other short-term military reasons, coalition between the two fiercely inimical parties in China was, as we saw it, imperative. It seemed obtainable because both sides professed to want it and agreed to negotiate.

The Communists' desire was genuine because they intended to use coalition as a base from which to expand and were confident they could make it a stage on the way to national power, and also because as a participant in legal government they could receive American arms. For exactly these reasons Chiang Kai-shek had no intention whatever of opening his government to the camel's nose, but under American pressure he had to play the game of negotiations because his already failing regime was dependent on American arms and other aid. Like any bargainer determined to avoid a fulfillment without overtly taking the negative, Chiang proposed terms unacceptable to the other side, in this case his control of the Communist armed forces. Equally unprepared to commit suicide, the Communists in their turn proposed terms and safeguards unacceptable to Chiang.

With the U.S. as anxious broker, demands and concessions, deadlocks and renewals continued for two and a half years, past the end of World War II, with the dispatch by President Truman of the outstanding American figure of the war, General George Marshall, as mediator. He persisted for a year, but as mediator the U.S. was in the end unavailing, having restricted its options in advance all to one side. Although in one moment of transitory agreement Chiang and Mao were photographed across a table raising their glasses to each other with cordial smiles of an old hate, there never was a real possibility of the two camps reaching mutually acceptable terms, since the survival of one necessarily meant the demise of the other.

As General Stilwell observed, wryly watching the progress of the Marshall mission, "George can't walk on water." If George could not, can we expect more of Le Duc Tho, President Nixon, or Henry Kissinger?

Coalition, despite its support by a variety of doves, has never been more than a fragile front to permit us to withdraw with what the Nixon administration calls "honor," a word used to fill the absence of any other rationale. As such it is not worth the spending of one more life. To walk out of Vietnam might still be done with dignity. Let us forgo for a little while further talk of honor.

THE CITIZEN VERSUS THE MILITARY

The relation of the civilian citizen to the military is a subject usually productive of instant emotion and very little rational thinking.

Peace-minded people seem to disapprove study of the soldier, on the theory that if starved of attention he will eventually vanish. That is unlikely. Militarism is simply the organized form of natural aggression. The same people who march to protest in the afternoon will stand in line that evening to see the latest in sadistic movies and thoroughly enjoy themselves watching blood and pain, murder, torture, and rape.

Commencement Address, Williams College, June 1972.

To register one's dissent from the war in Vietnam by expressing disgust for the military and turning one's back on whatever shape the military wears is a natural impulse. But the error of that war, together with two other developments—the newly acquired permanence of the military role in our society and the shift to an all-volunteer force—are powerful, urgent reasons why more enlightened and better-educated citizens should *not* turn their backs and not abdicate their responsibility for controlling military policies.

Earlier in this century the French writer Julien Benda elaborated his thesis of "the treason of the intellectuals." He accused them of betraying the life of the mind and the realm of reason by descending into the arena of political, social, and national passions. Now we have a treason of the intellectuals in reverse. While military-industrial and military-political interests penetrate all policy-making and add their weight to every political decision, the enlightened citizen refuses his participation, climbs out of the arena, and leaves control to the professionals of war.

Let us look at the facts of the case.

Contrary to the general impression, nuclear firepower, because it is too lethal to use, has reduced, not enlarged, the scope of war, with the secondary and rather sinister result that while unlimited war is out, limited war is in, not as a last resort in the old-fashioned way, but as the regular, on-going support of policy.

This development means that the military arm will be used more for political and ideological ends than in the past, and that because of chronic commitment and the self-multiplying business of deterrence and a global strategy of preparedness for two and a half wars—or whatever is this week's figure—the technological, industrial, and governmental foundations for this enterprise have become so gigantic, extended, and pervasive that they affect every act of government and consequently all our lives.

We now maintain two thousand military bases in thirty-three countries and have Military Assistance Advisory groups functioning in fifty countries and disbursing arms and aid amounting to nearly $4 billion a year. To furnish these programs in addition to the war in Vietnam and the regular armed forces of the United States, there are defense plants or installations in 363 out of the 435 congressional districts in this country—in five-sixths of the total.

Who benefits? Who profits? Who lobbies in Congress to keep them in operation or to attract new plants where there are none? If you say it is the Pentagon, do not forget the local merchants and manufacturers, the local labor unions and employers, and the local

Congressman whom we put there and whom we can recall. Who pays for our present military budget of $84 billion? The taxpayers—who also have the vote.

Traditionally, the American Army has considered itself the neutral instrument of state policy. It exists to carry out the government's orders and when ordered into action does not ask "Why?" or "What for?" But the more it is used for political ends and the more deeply its influence pervades government, the less it can retain the stance of innocent instrument. The same holds true of the citizen. Our innocence too is flawed.

The fundamental American premise has always been civilian control of the military. The Vietnam war is a product of civilian policy shaped by three successive civilian Presidents and their academic and other civilian advisers. The failure to end the war is also, in the last resort, civilian, since it is a failure by Congress to cut off appropriations.

And where does that failure trace back to? To where the vote is. I feel bewildered when I hear that easy, empty slogan "Power to the People!" Is there any country in the world whose people have more than ours?

To blame the military for this shameful war and renounce with disgust any share in their profession is a form of escapism. It allows the anti-war civilian to feel virtuous and uninvolved in the shame. It allows someone else to do the soldier's job, which is essential to an organized state and which in the long run protects the security of the high-minded civilian while he claims it is a job too dirty for him.

Certainly the conduct of this war, perhaps *because* it is purposeless and inane, has led to abominations and inhumanities by the military which cannot be forgiven and for which the West Pointer with his motto of "Duty, Honor, Country" is as much responsible as the semi-educated Lieutenant Calleys commissioned through OCS. But as one officer said, "We have the Calleys because those Harvard bastards won't fight"—"Harvard" being shorthand for *all* deferred college students.

Perhaps if there had been more college bastards instead of Calleys, there might have been mutinies or sitdowns instead of My Lais—certainly a preferable alternative. As for the Regular Army, it is likely that with morale so near ruin, there is nothing the professional officers want more than to get the ground forces out of Vietnam as quickly as possible, which is perhaps one reason why President Nixon is doing it.

The liberal's sneer at the military man does himself no honor, nor does it mark him as the better man. Military men are people. There are good ones and bad ones, some thoughtful and intelligent, some dimwits and dodos, some men of courage and integrity, some slick operators and sharp practicers, some scholars and fighters, some braggarts and synthetic heroes. The profession contains perhaps an over-supply of routinized thinking, servility to rank, and right-wing super-patriots, but every group has undesirable qualities that are occupationally induced.

It is not the nature of the military man that accounts for war, but the nature of man. The soldier is merely one shape that nature takes. Aggression is part of us, as innate as eating or copulating. As a student of the human record, I can say with confidence that peace is *not* the norm. Historians have calculated that up until the Industrial Revolution belligerent action occupied more man hours than any other activity except agriculture.

Human society started with the tribe—with a sense of "We" as opposed to "They." Tribe A can have no sense of identity unless it is conscious of the otherness of Tribe B. All life and thought and action, according to the anthropologist Lévi-Strauss, is based on this state of binary opposites: heaven and earth, earth and water, dark and light, right and left, north and south, male and female. These poles are not necessarily hostile, but hostility *is* inherent between the poles of We and They. When the tribes become conscious of otherness, they fight—for food or territory or dominance. This is inescapable and probably eternal. Students around the country and sympathetic faculty will not make it go away by chasing ROTC off campus, no matter how understandable the motive.

Freud called it the death wish, meaning self-destruction. It could just as well be called the life wish because it is an active instinct, a desire to fight, to conquer, and if also to kill, then to kill not self but others. The instinct says, "I shall conquer, I shall live." It is also a male instinct. Women, being child-bearers, have a primary instinct to preserve life. Probably if we had a woman in the White House and a majority of females in Congress, we could be out of Vietnam yesterday.

"Our permanent enemy," said William James in 1904, "is the rooted bellicosity of human nature. A millennium of peace would not breed the fighting instinct out of our bone and marrow." Has anything occurred in our century to suggest that James was wrong?

What this suggests is that we should face the military element rather than turn our backs on it, learn about it, even participate in it through ROTC. If the college-educated youths become the reserve officers upon whom the Army depends, then they are in a position to exert influence. *That* is the place to pull a strike. If all reserve officers walked out, the Army could not move.

Recently a retired Army colonel suggested that all Army career officers, not only reserve officers, "should be obtained through civilian college scholarship programs and direct entry from college ROTC." Now if that could be arranged, the educated civilian would really be at the controls. If the young want to make a revolution, that is the way to do it. Oliver Cromwell did not spend his time trying to close down Oxford. He built the New Model Army.

Our form of democracy—the political system which is the matrix of our liberties—rests upon the citizen's participation, not excluding —indeed, especially including—participation in the armed forces. That was the great principle of the French Revolution: the nation in arms, meaning the people in arms as distinct from a professional standing army. The nation in arms was considered the safeguard of the Republic, the guarantor against tyranny and military *coups d'état*.

The same idea underlies the fundamental American principle of the right to bear arms as guaranteed by our Bill of Rights for the specific purpose of maintaining "a well-regulated Militia" to protect "the security of a free state." To serve the state is what the Constitution meant, not, as the Gun Lobby pretends, the right to keep a pistol under your pillow and shoot at whomever you want to. To serve under arms in this sense is not only a right but a criterion of citizenship.

To abdicate the right because our armed forces are being used in a wrong war is natural. Nobody wants to share in or get killed in an operation that is both wicked and stupid. But we must realize that this rejection abdicates a responsibility of citizenship and contributes to an already dangerous development—the reappearance of the standing army. That is what is happening as a consequence of the changeover to an all-volunteer force. We will have an army even more separate, more isolated and possibly alienated from civilian society than ever. Military men have always cherished a sense of separateness from the civilian sector, a sense of special calling deriving from their choice of a profession involving the risk of life. They feel this separateness confers a distinction that compensates them to some extent for the risk of the profession, just as the glitter and pomp and brilliant uniforms and social prestige for the officers used to compensate the armies of Europe.

For the United States the draft was the great corrective—or would have been if it had worked properly. The draft has an evil name because it would have dragged young people into an evil war. Yet it remains the only way, if administered justly, to preserve the principle of the nation in arms. The college deferrals made it a mockery. The deferral system was as anti-democratic and elitist (to use the favorite word of those who consider themselves equalizers) as anything that has ever happened in the United States. I may be happy that it kept my kin and the sons of some of my friends out of Vietnam, but I am nonetheless ashamed of it.

We need to re-admit some common sense into conventional liberal thinking—or feeling—about the military. It seems to me urgent that we understand our relationship to the soldier's task free of emotion.

I know of no problem so subject as this one to what the late historian Richard Hofstadter called "the imbecile catchwords of our era like 'repression' and 'imperialism' which have had all the meaning washed out of them." Those who yell these words, he wrote, "simply have no idea what they are talking about."

The role of the military in our lives has become too serious a matter to be treated to this kind of slogan thinking, or non-thinking.

Historical Clues to Present Discontents

I suppose no one will dispute the fact that the world in mid-twentieth century is in serious, possibly desperate, trouble. You, the students, are heading into it while I am more fortunate in being on the way out, but we share the disadvantage of having been born into a disoriented age, a period of extreme disturbance and small encouragement. The last volume of the *Cambridge Modern History* covering 1898 to the present is entitled *The Age of Violence*—which, considering the not inconsiderable violence of previous eras, is quite a distinction.

The physical aspects of our troubles—pollution, war, overpopulation—you know all about, and equally the intangible aspects—that is, the general discontent and uneasiness, dissatisfaction of the young, bewilderment of the old, crime and tension, collapse of standards both aesthetic and ethical, the sexual wilderness and obsession with sadism, and so forth. The catalogue is long and very familiar and I need not run it down to the bitter end. My purpose is not to discuss the condition but to try, as a historian, to locate the cause.

Doubtless some of you will think this a meaningless endeavor, on the theory that the past is unimportant and that what counts is today. I gather from occasional excursions to the campuses that the young are passionately concerned with the present and inclined to shrug off the past as irrelevant. They want to know all about Kafka but not Plato, Sartre but not Shakespeare, Black Power but not the French

Address, Pomona College, February 1969.

Revolution, and they believe American history began with John F. Kennedy. Each student wants instant relevance from every subject, and he wants every subject to "hook in," as I heard it expressed at another university, to his own personal problem, whatever that may be. Narcissism and now-ism—the self and the present—are the two governing concerns of the campus at the moment. The advantage of history is knowing that there is as much relevance to be found in the Peloponnesian War as in yesterday's newspaper; more relevance in the Socratic dialogues than in some hastily concocted course in social psychology. What is relevant, after all, is human experience, and this has been accumulating for quite some time. Any person who considers himself, and intends to remain, a member of Western society inherits the Western past from Athens and Jerusalem to Runnymede and Valley Forge, as well as to Watts and Chicago of August 1968. He may ignore it or deny it, but that does not alter the fact. The past sits back and smiles and knows it owns him anyway. It seems to me perfectly obvious that we can no more escape the past than we can escape our own genes. "Others fear what the morrow may bring," said a Moslem sage, "but I am afraid of what happened yesterday."

History, which is my discipline, has been defined as the means by which society seeks to understand its past. Toward that understanding, I would like to offer the following proposition: that as a result of the historical experience of the twentieth century so far, man has lost faith in himself, as well as lost the guidelines he was once sure of, and that this loss is primarily responsible for our current distress.

To be specific: We have suffered the loss of two fundamental beliefs—in God and in Progress; two major disillusionments—in socialism and nationalism; one painful revelation—the Freudian uncovering of the subconscious; and one unhappy discovery—that the fairy godmother Science turns out to have brought as much harm as good. With the exception of the loss of religious faith, which began its modern decline about a hundred years ago—let us say for the sake of convenience, with Darwin—all the rest has occurred within the twentieth century. That makes for quite a load of discouragement in seventy years or approximately one lifetime.

As long as man thought himself the son of God, containing the divine spark and created by the finger of God as in that wonderful gesture pictured by Michelangelo on the Sistine ceiling, he had respect and even a little awe for himself; he could feel there was a purpose in his being here and even a concealed purpose in the evil that befell him or in the evil that he wrought; that, come what may, he was a part of the divine plan. Without wishing to offend individual beliefs, I would say that as a historical factor determining man's image of himself, this view no longer holds. We are on our own now, "a poor bare forked animal," in King Lear's words, and it is very uncomfortable.

Until the twentieth century opened, the idea of progress was the most firmly held conviction of the nineteenth century. Man believed himself both improvable and improving. He had acquired the enormous help of science—especially medical science—and of the machine, doubling or, rather, infinitely multiplying his work capacity, his health, comfort, and freedom of movement. Household plumbing and running water, the steam engine, electric light, refrigeration, sanitation, anesthesia and antisepsis, typewriters and lawnmowers, telegraph and telephone—the world was running over with new benefits. Material betterment was expected to bring moral progress. Living in better conditions, man was expected to become a better person. This was the credo of that energetic, optimistic age.

The terrible gulf between that expectation and current reality is at the bottom, I believe, of the malaise of today. Since the new century began, humans have been living better and behaving worse—see the welfare state and the Third Reich—than ever before in history. Subconsciously, or even consciously in some cases, we have become frightened by our own record. Let us look at the record.

The new century was born brawling with three wars under way at once in 1900: British fighting Boers in South Africa, Americans fighting Filipinos, and a mixed bag of foreigners fighting Chinese in the Boxer Rebellion. These were all small affairs on the periphery, but still not a happy omen.

At about the same time, we acquired a new way of looking at ourselves that stripped off the protection of Victorian draperies. In 1900 Freud published *The Interpretation of Dreams*, beginning the process called the Freudian revolution that over the next decades was to display before man the dark dimensions of his soul. As Macbeth was shown his murderous instincts in the witches' caldron, modern man has been shown what his unconscious holds—and this too has not been reassuring. Actions he had allowed himself to think were noble and generous turned out to be ignoble or selfish. Devotion to his mother was not admirable but Oedipal. If the unconscious could lead us into all these perverse and wicked ways independently of will, then man was not the captain of his soul that he thought he was. Confidence in our capacity to control our own destiny has been consequently undermined. Further, we have lost that convenient scapegoat, the Devil, as we have lost God. Formerly, when a person behaved badly or oddly he was said to be possessed by the Devil. Not any more. That divestment of responsibility is now denied us; the source is inside ourselves.

Applied to political behavior—that is, to man in the mass—the new knowledge of human nature destroyed confidence in a favorite concept of democracy: the ultimate common sense of the common people. Nineteenth-century liberalism had assumed that man was a rational being who operated naturally according to his own best interests, so that in the end, what was reasonable would prevail. On this principle liberals defended extension of the suffrage toward the goal of one man, one vote. But a rise in literacy and in the right to vote, as the event proved, did nothing to increase common sense in politics. The mob that is moved by waving the bloody shirt, that decides elections in response to slogans—Free Silver, Hang the Kaiser, Two Cars in Every Garage—is not exhibiting any greater political sense than Marie Antoinette, who said, "Let them eat cake," or Caligula, who made his horse a consul. The common man proved no wiser than the decadent aristocrat. He has not shown in public affairs the innate wisdom which democracy presumed he possessed.

Even before 1914 a whole school of English political philosophers and social psychologists, including Graham Wallas, author of the phrase "The Great Society," was overtaken by pessimism as a result of their studies of mass political behavior. One of them, William Trotter, in his book *Instincts of the Herd in Peace and War*, published in 1908, found the mob or herd instinct springing from the same dark and sinister well of the unconscious uncovered by Freud. Describing the herd instinct as an irrational force, "imitative, cowardly, cruel . . . and suggestible," Trotter concluded his famous essay with one of the most somber sentences ever written: "The probability is very great that, after all, man will prove but one more of Nature's failures."

In 1914 came the Great War, the event that begins our time, which was, so to speak, its womb. Summarizing its causes, an English historian, F. P. Chambers, in 1939 wrote, "The universal expression of belligerent will at this time is perhaps a phenomenon whose uniqueness history has not yet taken sufficiently into account. It was as if expanding wealth and multiplying population, as if the unconscious boredom of peace over nearly fifty unbroken years, had stored up a terrific potential which only waited for an accident to touch it off. Far from being innocents led to the slaughter, the peoples of Europe more truly led their leaders."

In that war men performed prodigies of valor and endurance, suffered and sacrificed and killed each other, moved by two convictions: that their country was right and that they were fighting to bring about a better order of things. If I may be forgiven for quoting myself, "When at last it was over, the war had many diverse results and one dominant one transcending all others: disillusion."

The fourteen points that looked so brave in the abstract melted as soon as they touched the hard reality of national interests among the victors. The Treaty of Versailles did not establish a peace of reason or even stability. The League of Nations, despite genuine and valiant effort, proved a failure (as has its successor, the United Nations). After four years, as Graham Wallas wrote, "of the most intense and heroic effort the human race has ever made," the hopes and beliefs possible before 1914 slowly shriveled.

No betrayal of hope was more profound than that in socialism. It is hard to convey to this generation how ardent, how dedicated, how convinced were the anarchists, socialists, Marxists, working-class and labor-union leaders, and all the advocates of whatever class or kind who believed in and struggled for the goal of social revolution—that great overturn which would wipe out the wickedness and oppression vested, as they thought, in property, and build a new order based on social justice. They believed that the brotherhood of the working class transcended national boundaries, that war would be stopped when the workers of the world would refuse to shoulder a rifle to fire on their comrades of another country. They believed that when they should succeed in their task—the overthrow of capitalism—social inequities and want would be eliminated, leaving man free to fulfill his nature to be good as God intended him. This idealism was a powerful engine of social progress, a real political force, the motive power and faith of men like Kropotkin, Jean Jaurès, Keir Hardie, Eugene Debs. Much of it was directed toward practical material ends and class gain—higher wages, shorter hours, better working conditions—but what fueled the movement was the fire of idealism of its leaders who believed themselves acting not merely for class or group but for all mankind.

I do not suppose I need to discuss the change represented by the labor movement—or rather labor establishment, for it is no longer a movement—of today. Labor has won the rights and the gains it was fighting for, and now virtually controls the employer instead of vice versa, but added comfort and welfare does not seem to have added to the wisdom or happiness of the human species. The illusion broke in 1914 when socialism fell a victim to nationalism and the working class went to war with no less enthusiasm than anyone else. Shortly afterward the longed-for goal, Revolution, was incredibly and actually achieved in one country. What excitement, what enthusiasm, what soaring hope! "I have seen the future and it works," proclaimed Lincoln Steffens. But if that was the future, it only proved history's most melancholy truth: that every revolution, as the French anarchist Sebastien Faure said, "ends in the reappearance of a new ruling class." Or in the case of Russia, as gradually became clear, in a new tyranny.

Not unnaturally, cynicism took hold in the 1920s and '30s. Compared to the pre-war period when the future seemed full of promise, these decades seemed a time when, in the phrase of Gertrude Stein, "there was no future any more."

At the same time, on the political scene the best international efforts for collective security—the Covenant of the League of Nations, the Washington Treaties for Naval Limitation, the Kellogg-Briand Pact by which fifteen nations renounced war as an instrument of national policy—were proved hollow in the face of determined aggression. Japan swallowed Manchuria and moved in on China, Germany rearmed and reoccupied the Rhineland unopposed, Italy annexed Ethiopia and a feeble attempt at sanctions was called off, and in Spain, where resistance to fascism at last took shape, it was smothered in the name of non-intervention.

What allowed these events to happen, I believe, was the reverse of belligerent will, or rather a sharply divided will as between aggressors and appeasers. The victors of the last war, with no motive like Germany's to resume battle, feared any disturbance in the *status quo*, especially the threat to property represented by communism. No one has so many fears as the property-owner; it is the householder who trembles, not the prowler outside. Greater than fear, the true enfeebler of the democracies was a kind of moral defeatism arising from the corpse of the last war. It sapped the will to resist aggression.

And so, barely twenty years after the most terrible experience mankind as a whole ever suffered, after the wounds and gangrene, the deaths, disease, destruction, the ravaged ground and leafless trees, the months and years in trenches, the mud and blood, shelling and gas, the smell of rotting corpses, the lice and typhus, the loss of homes, uprooting of populations, burning of villages, the starvation, misery, brutality, and suffering of all kinds—we went at it all over again.

How could it happen? Who would have imagined in 1919 that twenty years would be all the grace the world would allow itself? This is a terrible question and the most damaging testimony against man that the recording angel will have to bring—or at least it was until the 1960s, when the over-use of soil, air, and water is causing ruin of our environment that may earn a blacker mark.

Along with the Second World War occurred an episode of man's inhumanity to man which for sheer size, deliberate intent, and organized pursuit, was unprecedented. Its historical significance is not yet, I believe, fully appreciated. The German nation's attempt to exterminate the Jews and achieve what they neatly called a "final solution" was an act not easily reconcilable with our idea of human progress. The Germans, who conceived and carried it out nearly to completion, were considered one of the most, and by themselves *the* most, civilized of nations. Yet they plunged into an orgy of savagery conducted as a matter of approved national policy, on a level which humanity was supposed to have outgrown. What is no less significant is that the other nations—excepting Denmark but not excepting the United States, which had the least to fear—watched, let it happen, offered no extra asylum or rescue, and generally avoided interfering to a point that suggests they would not have been unhappy to see the final solution succeed.

Indeed, I believe we are witnessing something of the same phenomenon now in the treatment of Israel at the U.N. compared with its tolerance of Arab attacks. Anti-Semitism is very old, very convenient, latent in states as well as people, and evidently impossible to exorcise. I suspect the Jews will survive if only because the world needs them as the scapegoat of guilt of one kind or another. If they disappeared, the world would feel obliged to re-invent them.

A historian needs, I think, a perspective of at least twenty-five years, and preferably fifty, to form an opinion of any value, so I shall go no further into the present. Except for a quick look at science, or rather applied science—that is to say, technology, which is what the layman mainly sees. The four chief technological agents of change in the last twenty-five years or so have been the bomb, the tube, the computer, and the pill—that is, nuclear power, television, electronics, and contraception. As regards the revolution in sexual morality that is partly a result of the pill (although it is also a cyclical phenomenon that recurs in history), the aspect that is genuinely shocking is the careless breeding of unwanted children in increasing numbers. High-school adolescents often seem to regard pregnancy as a condition affecting only themselves, with no thought of it as a condition that brings to life another human being. Damaged and resentful as they grow up, these children will be a mounting charge upon society. Under the circumstances, it hardly seems rational to impose restrictions on contraception and abortion. When there are already too many people, no unwanted child should be born into the world.

The computer and the tube are beyond my scope for today, and even more so the bomb. Being quite properly scared of what we have wrought, we have not used it again since its first employment, but its strategy has reached the extremity of deterrence known as Mutual Assured Destruction, which carries the blunt acronym M-A-D, Mad. We seem to have pinned a label on ourselves in case some future historian should need a hint.

Meanwhile we use incessantly that equally lethal weapon, the automobile, which kills fifty thousand annually in the United States, not counting the thousands maimed—a self-inflicted Hiroshima every year. If one adds to the human casualties the land the automobile has destroyed by highways and parking lots, the pollution of air by its fumes, the horrors perpetrated upon the countryside by its gas stations, the choking of cities by its traffic, it can be reckoned easily the most destructive instrument ever devised by man. Yet at its inception it was a wonderful instrument of freedom that whirled people at exhilarating speeds and opened up new realms of movement and travel. Now it has become a monster of which every person needs one or more, usually twice the size and horsepower necessary for utility. The proliferation and evil effects could be controlled, but are not. Everyone suffers, but no one calls a halt.

The same unstoppable momentum seems to characterize other products of technology. What of a society that uses expensive and dwindling fuel to heat buildings in winter to eighty degrees because sixty is too cold, and then cools them in summer to sixty degrees because eighty is too hot? There is a craziness about all this, a sense of forces getting out of control, of the machine running away with man, which is another source of the general uneasiness of this age.

I recognize that I have not given a fair share so far to good and encouraging and pleasant things, but since my object has been to look for the origins of our discontent, the emphasis has necessarily been on trouble. Probably this is not unjustified because, on balance, I think the twentieth century so far has contained more bad than good, though it may look different from the future looking back. Perspective changes every view. The world is old and history long—some four thousand years of recorded history, of which the 1960s represent a quarter of one percent. In that perspective now-ism dwindles.

Does it serve any purpose to have unrolled this gloomy catalogue? I am not sure, but possibly the confusion of our time may seem less senseless and absurd when it can be shown to spring from real and demonstrable causes. It generally helps to know the reason for things.

Generalship

My subject tonight was suggested by your Commandant with no accompanying explanation; just the word "Generalship," unadorned. No doubt he could safely assume that the subject in itself would automatically interest this audience in the same way that motherhood would interest an audience of pregnant ladies. I do not know whether General Davis thought the subject would be appropriate for me because I am the biographer of a general who vividly illustrated certain qualities of generalship, both in their presence and their absence, or whether he had something of larger scope in mind.

In any event, as I considered the subject I became intrigued for several reasons: because it is important, because it is elusive, and because it is undergoing, I think, as a result of developments of the past twenty-five years, a radical transformation which may make irrelevant much of what we now know about it. I will come to that aspect later.

I should begin by saying that I have no greater qualification in this matter than if you had asked Tennyson to lecture on generalship because he wrote "The Charge of the Light Brigade." I did not write the biography of Stilwell in his capacity as soldier, but rather in his capacity as a focal figure and extraordinarily apt representative of the American relation to China. I did not write *The Guns of August* as a study of how war plans go wrong—at least I did not know I was doing that until it was all over. I am not primarily a military historian, and to the degree that I am one at all, it is more or less by accident. However, since life is only fun when you attempt something a little beyond your reach, I will proceed with the assignment.

In Colonel Heinl's *Dictionary of Military Quotations*, the subject

Address, U.S. Army War College, April 1972. *Parameters*, Spring 1972.

headings "Generals" and "Generalship" together take up more space than any other entry. If the closely related headings "Command" and "Leadership" are added, the subject as a whole takes up twice as many pages as any other. Why is it so important? The answer is, I suppose, because the qualities that enter into the exercise of generalship in action have the power, in a very condensed period of time, to determine the life or death of thousands, and sometimes the fate of nations. The general's qualities become, then, of absorbing interest not only to the military but to citizens at large, and it is obviously vital to the state to determine what the qualities are, to locate them in the candidates for generalship, and to ensure that the possessors and the positions meet.

I have also seen it said that senior command in battle is the only total human activity because it requires equal exercise of the physical, intellectual, and moral faculties at the same time. I tried to take this dictum apart (being by nature, or perhaps by profession, given to challenging all generalizations) and to think of rivals for the claim, but in fact no others will do. Generalship in combat does uniquely possess that distinction.

The qualities it requires divide themselves into two categories as I see it: those of character, that is, personal leadership, and those of professional capacity. When it comes to command in the field, the first category is probably more important than the second, although it is useless, of course, if separated from the second, and vice versa. The most brilliant master of tactics cannot win a battle if, like General Boulanger, he has the soul of a subaltern. Neither can the most magnetic and dashing soldier carry the day if, like General Custer, he is a nincompoop in deployment.

Courage, according to the Maréchal de Saxe, is the first of all qualities. "Without it," as he says undeniably, "the others are of little value since they cannot be used." I think "courage" is too simple a word. The concept must include both physical and moral courage, for there are some people who have the former without the latter, and that is not enough for generalship. Indeed, physical courage must also be joined by intelligence, for, as a Chinese proverb puts it, "A general who is courageous and stupid is a calamity." Physical, combined with moral, courage makes the possessor resolute, and I would take issue with De Saxe and say that the primary quality is resolution. That is what enables a man to prevail—over circumstances, over subordinates, over allies, and eventually over the enemy. It is the determination to win through, whether in the worst circumstance merely to survive or in a limited situation to complete the mission, but, whatever the circumstance, to prevail. It is this will to prevail, I think, that is the *sine qua non* of military action. If a man has it, he will also have, or he will summon from somewhere, the courage to support it. But he could be brave as a lion and still fail if he lacks the necessary will.

Will was what Stilwell had, the absolute, unbreakable, unbendable determination to fulfill the mission no matter what the obstacles, the antagonists, or the frustrations. When the road that he fought to cut through Burma at last reached China, after his recall, a message from his successor recognized that the first convoy to make the overland passage, though Stilwell wasn't there to see it, was the product of "your indomitable will."

Sensible men will say that will must be schooled by judgment lest it lead to greater investment of effort or greater sacrifice than the object is worth, or to blind persistence in an objective whose very difficulties suggest it was a mistake from the start. That is true enough; good judgment is certainly one among the essentials of generalship, perhaps the most essential, according to the naval historian Raymond O'Connor. He quotes C. P. Snow's definition of judgment as "the ability to think of many matters at once, in their interdependence, their related importance, and their consequences." Judgment may not always be that rational, but more intuitive, based on a feel of the situation combined with experience.

Sometimes judgment will counsel boldness, as when Admiral Nimitz, against the advice of every admiral and general in his command, insisted on assaulting Kwajalein, site of the Japanese Headquarters at the very heart of the Marshall archipelago, although this meant leaving the enemy-held outer islands on the American line of communications. In the event, American planes were able to keep the outer islands pounded down, while Kwajalein proved relatively undefended because the Japanese, thinking along the same lines as Nimitz' subordinates, had convinced themselves the Americans would not attempt to assault it.

More often than not, however, judgment counsels "Cannot" while will says "Can." In extremity the great results are gained when will overrides judgment. Will alone carried Washington through the winter of Valley Forge, that nadir of misery and neglect, and only his extraordinary will kept the freezing, half-starved, shoeless army, unpaid and unprovisioned by the Continental Congress, from deserting. Judgment would have said, "Go home." I suppose it was will that dragged Hannibal over the Alps although judgment might have asked what would happen after he gained his goal, just as judgment might have advised Stilwell that his mission—the mobilizing of an effective Chinese army under the regime of Chiang Kai-shek—was unachievable. Hannibal too failed in his objective: He never took Rome, but he has been called the greatest soldier of all time.

Sometimes the situation calls for will that simply says, "I will not be beaten"—and here too, in extremity, it must override judgment. After the awful debacle of four battles lost one after the other on the French frontiers in August 1914, and with the French Army streaming back in chaotic retreat and the enemy invading, judgment might have raised the question whether France was not beaten. That never occurred to the commander-in-chief, General Joffre, who possessed in unsurpassed degree a quality of great importance for generals: He was unflappable. Steadiness of temperament in a general is an asset at any time, and the crown of steadiness is the calm that can be maintained amid disaster. It may be that Joffre's immunity to panic was lack of imagination, or he may have suffered all the time from what Stilwell called "that sinking feeling" and concealed it. We do not know because he kept no diary. Whatever the source of his imperturbability, France was fortunate to have it in the right man at the right time. Certainly it was Gallieni who saw and seized the opportunity to retrieve disaster, and Foch and Franchet d'Esperey who supplied the *élan* to carry it through, but it was Joffre's ponderous, pink-cheeked, immovable assurance that held the army in being. Without him there might have been no army to make a stand at the Marne.

High on the list of a general's essentials is what I call the "Do this" factor. It is taken from the statement which Shakespeare put in the mouth of Mark Antony: "When Caesar says, 'Do this,' it is performed." This quality of command rests not only on the general's knowledge of tactics and terrain and resources and enemy deployment in a specific situation, but on the degree of faith that his subordinates have in his knowledge. "When Stilwell told you what to do in Burma," said an officer, "you had confidence that was the right thing to do. That is what a soldier wants to know." If officers and men believe a general knows what he is talking about and that what he orders is the right thing to do in the circumstances, they will do it, because most people are relieved to find a superior on whose judgment they can rest. That, indeed, is the difference between most people and generals.

I come now to the second category: that is, professional ability. This encompasses the capacity to decide the objective, to plan, to organize, to direct, to draw on experience, and to deploy all the knowledge and techniques in which the professional has been trained. For me to go further into this aspect and enter on a discussion of the professional principles of generalship does not, I think, make much sense; first, because if you do not know more about them than I do, you oughtn't to be here, and, second, because it seems to me very difficult to select absolutes. The principles depend to a great extent on time, place, and history, and the nature of the belligerents. I will only say that the bridge that joins the two categories—that connects personal leadership to professional ability—is intelligence, which is the quality De Saxe put second on his list after courage.

The kind of intelligence varies, I suppose, according to occupation: In a doctor it must be sympathetic; in a lawyer it is invariably pessimistic; in a historian it should be accurate, investigative, and synthesizing. In a military man, according to De Saxe's fine phrase, it should be "strong and fertile in devices." I like that; it is a requirement which you can tell has been drawn from a soldier's experience. It closely fits, I think, the most nearly perfect, or at any rate the least-snafued, professional military performance of our time, that of the Israelis in the Six-Day War of 1967.

In that microcosm, caught for us within the visible limits of six days, the qualities of resolution and nerve, the "Do this" factor, the deployment of expert skills, and a governing intelligence "strong and fertile in devices" all meshed and functioned together like the oiled parts of an engine. I need not go into the circumstances that made this happen, of which the chief one perhaps was that no retreat or defeat was possible—either would have meant annihilation in that sliver of a country the size of the state of Massachusetts. The Israelis' concept of generalship, however, does contain principles that can apply beyond their borders. To anticipate is one. To be skeptical, critical, flexible, and, finally, obstinate—obstinate in the execution of the mission—is another. This quality, which I have already mentioned in connection with Stilwell, seemed to be the requirement which the Israelis most emphasized in an officer.

The principle I found especially stressed, although more on the planning level than in the field, was knowledge of the enemy—of his capabilities, his training, his psychology—as complete and precise as prolonged study, familiarity, and every means of intelligence-gathering could make it. In this realm the Israelis have the advantage of knowing in advance the identity of the enemy: He lives next door. Yet it seems to me that Americans could learn from this lesson.

If we paid more attention to the nature, motivation, and capabilities, especially in Asia, of the opponent whom we undertake so confidently to smash—not to mention of the allies whom we support—we would not have made such a mess, such an *unexpected* mess, in Vietnam. We would not have found ourselves, to our confusion and dismay, investing more and more unavailing effort against a continually baffling capacity for resistance, and not only resistance but initiative. In the arrogance of our size, wealth, and superior technology, we tend to overlook the need to examine what may be different sources of strength in others. If in 1917 Edith Cavell could say, "Patriotism is not enough," we now need another voice of wisdom to tell us, "Technology is not enough." War is not one big engineering project. There are *people* on the other side—with strengths and will that we never bothered to measure. As a result of that omission we have been drawn into a greater, and certainly more ruinous, belligerent action than we intended. To fight without understanding the opponent ultimately serves neither the repute of the military nor the repute of the nation.

Having brought myself down to the present with a rush, I would like to examine generalship from here on in terms of the present. I know that military subjects are generally studied and taught by examples from the past, and I could go on with an agreeable talk about the qualities of the Great Captains with suitable maxims from Napoleon, and references to General Grant, and anecdotes about how King George, when told that General Wolfe was mad, replied, "I wish he would bite some other of my generals"—all of which you already know. Besides, it might well be an exercise in the obsolete, for with the change in war that has occurred since mid-twentieth century there must necessarily follow a change in generalship.

The concept of total war that came in with our century has already, I think, had its day. It has been backed off the stage by the advent of the total weapon, nuclear explosion, with its uncritical capacity for overkill. Since, regardless of first strike, there is enough nuclear power around to be mutually devastating to both sides, it becomes the weapon that cannot be used, thus creating a new situation. If war, as we have all been taught, is the pursuit of policy by means of force, we are now faced by the fact that there can be no policy or political object which can be secured with benefit by opening a nuclear war that wrecks all parties. Consequently, limited wars with limited objectives must henceforth be the only resort when policy requires support by military means. Upon investigation I find that this was perceived by some alert minds almost as soon as it happened, by former Ambassador George Kennan for one, who wrote in 1954, when everyone else was bemused by the Bomb, that nuclear weapons had not enlarged the scope of war but exactly the opposite, that "the day of total wars has passed, and that from now on limited military operations are the only ones that could conceivably serve any coherent purpose."

The significance of this development for the military man is bound to be disturbing because, as the British General Sir John Winthrop Hackett recently said in a talk to our Air Force Academy, "Limited wars for political ends are far more likely to be productive of moral strains . . . than the great wars of the past." The United States, it is hardly necessary to remark, is already suffering from the truth of that principle.

The change has been taking place over the past twenty years while we lived through it without really noticing—at least I as a civilian didn't notice. One needs to step outside a phenomenon in order to see its shape, and one needs perspective to be able to look back and say, "*There* was the turning point." As you can now see, Korea was our first political war. The train of events since then indicates that the role of the military is coming to be, as exhibited by the Russians in Egypt and ourselves in Southeast Asia, one of intervention in underdeveloped countries on a so-called "advisory" or "assistance" level with the object of molding the affairs of the client country to suit the adviser's purpose. The role has already developed its task force and training program in the Military Assistance Officers Program at Fort Bragg. According to its formulation, the task is to "assist foreign countries with internal security problems"—a nice euphemism for counter-insurgency—"and perform functions having sociopolitical impact on military operations."

In short, the mission of the military in this sociopolitical era is to be counter-revolution, otherwise the thwarting of communism or, if euphemism is preferred, nation-building, Vietnamizing, or perhaps Pakistanizing or Africanizing some willing or unwilling client. This is quite a change from defense of the continental United States which the founders intended should be our military function.

What does the change imply for generalship? "Has the Army seen the last of its great combat leaders of senior rank?" I quote that question from the recent book *Military Men* by Ward Just, correspondent of the *Washington Post*. Will there still be scope for those qualities of personal leadership that once made the difference? In the past it was the man who counted: Clive, who conquered India with eleven hundred men; Cortez, who took Mexico with fewer; Charles Martel, who turned back the Moslems at Tours; Nelson, who turned back Napoleon at Trafalgar (and incidentally evaluated one source of his prowess when he said, "If there were more Lady Hamiltons, there would be more Nelsons." Though that might be thought to please the Women's Lib people, who are down on me already, I am afraid it won't because from their point of view it's the wrong kind of influence. Anyway, that factor too may vanish, for I doubt if love or amorous triumph will play much role in inspiring generals to greater feats on the advisory or Vietnamizing level).

Above all, among the men of character who as individuals made a historic difference, there was Washington. When on his white horse he plunged into the midst of panicked men and with the "terrific eloquence of unprintable scorn" stopped the retreat from Monmouth, he evoked from Lafayette the tribute, "Never have I seen so superb a man."

Is he needed in the new army of today whose most desired postgraduate course, after this one, it has been said, is a term at the Harvard Business School? To fill today's needs the general must be part diplomat, part personnel manager, part weapons analyst, part sales and purchasing agent. Already General Creighton Abrams has been described by a reporter as *two* generals: one a "hell-for-leather, jut-jawed battlefield commander and the other a subtle and infinitely patient diplomat." For his successors the second role is likely soon to outweigh the first.

Out of that total human activity, physical, intellectual, and moral, how much will be left for the general to do? Given chemical detectors and people-sniffers, defoliators and biological weapons, infrared radar and electronic communication by satellite, not to mention, as once conceived by our planners, an invisible electric fence to keep out the enemy, the scope for decision-making in the field must inevitably be reduced. Artillery and even infantry fire, I understand, will be targeted by computers, extending from pocket-size models in the soldier's pack all the way to the console at headquarters. This is supposed to raise the dazzling prospect of eliminating human error, like Professor Skinner's vision of eliminating human evil by the teaching machine. The realization of either of those prospects, I can guarantee you as a historian, has about the same degree of probability as the return of the dinosaur.

The change that could be the most momentous would be a change in the relation of the military to the state. This is sensitive territory with potential for trouble, and I am entering here into an area of speculation which you may find refutable, and certainly arguable.

So that it may carry out the orders of government without hesitation or question, the officer corps has traditionally maintained, on the whole, a habit of non-partisanship, at least skin-deep, whatever individual ideological passions may rumble beneath the surface. Can this attitude last when the military find themselves being sent to fight for purposes so speculative or so blurred that they cannot support a legal state of war? You may say that it is a matter of semantics, but semantics make a good test. As a writer I can tell you that trouble in writing clearly invariably reflects troubled thinking, usually an incomplete grasp of the facts or of their meaning.

One wonders what proportion of officers in Southeast Asia today get through a tour of duty without asking themselves "Why?" or "What for?" As they make their sociopolitical rounds in the future, will that number uncomfortably grow? That is why the defunct principle that a nation should go to war only in self-defense or for vital and immediate national interest was a sound one. The nation that abides by it will have a better case with its own citizens and certainly with history. No one could misunderstand Pearl Harbor or have difficulty explaining or defining the need for a response. War which spends lives is too serious a business to do without definition. It *requires* definition—and declaration. No citizen, I believe, whether military or civilian, should be required to stake his life for what some uncertain men in Washington think is a good idea in gamesmanship or deterrence or containment or whatever is the governing idea of the moment.

If the military is to be used for political ends, can it continue to be the innocent automaton? Will the time come when this position is abandoned, and the Army or members of it will question and judge the purpose of what they are called upon to do? Not that they will necessarily be out of sympathy with government policy. Generally speaking, American policy since the onset of the cold war has been the containment of communism, with which, one may presume, the Army agrees. But the questions grow complex. What about Russia *vis-à-vis* China? What about India *vis-à-vis* Pakistan, where recently we skirted the consequences of folly by a hair? What about the Middle East? Suppose we decide that unless we rescue Syria from Russian influence, Iraq will fall? or suppose we transpose that principle to South America? You can play dominoes on any continent. What happens if we blunder again into a war on the wrong side of history?

That is not the military's fault, the military will reply. It is a civilian decision. The military arm remains under civilian control. Did not Truman fire MacArthur?

It is true that in America the military has never seriously challenged civilian rule, but in late years it hardly needs to. With a third of the national budget absorbed by military spending, with the cost of producing nuclear and other modern weapons having evidently no limits, with 22,000 defense contractors and 100,000 subcontractors operating in the United States, the interlocking of military-industrial interests grips the economy and pervades every agency of government.

The new budget of $83.4 billion for defense represents five times the amount allotted to education and nearly forty times the amount for control of pollution (our government having failed to notice that pollution by now is a graver threat to us than the Russians). It costs an annual average of about $10,000 to maintain each man in uniform compared to a national expenditure of $1,172.86 for each person in the United States; in other words, the man in uniform absorbs ten times as much. The Pentagon, where lies the pulse of all this energy and activity, spends annually $140 million on public relations *alone*, nearly twice as much as the entire budget of the National Endowment for Arts and Humanities. When military and military-connected interests penetrate government to that extent, the government becomes more or less the prisoner of the Pentagon.

In this situation, the location of ultimate responsibility for policy-making is no longer clearly discernible. What *is* clear is that while the military exerts that much influence in government, it cannot at the same time retain the stance of innocence.

It used to be that any difficulty of assignment could be taken care of under the sheltering umbrella of Duty, Honor, Country. As long as you had a *casus belli* like the *Maine* or the Alamo you could get through any dubious expedition without agony. The West Point formula may no longer suffice. Country is clear enough, but what is Duty in a wrong war? What is Honor when fighting is reduced to "wasting" the living space—not to mention the lives—of a people that never did us any harm? The simple West Point answer is that Duty and Honor consist in carrying out the orders of the government. That is what the Nazis said in their defense, and we tried them for war crimes nevertheless. We undercut our own claim at Nuremberg and Tokyo.

When fighting reaches the classic formula recently voiced by a soldier in the act of setting fire to a hamlet in Vietnam, "We must destroy it in order to save it," one must go further than duty and honor and ask, "Where is common sense?" I am aware that common sense does not figure in the West Point motto; nevertheless soldiers are no less subject to Descartes' law, "I think, therefore I am," than other mortals. Thinking will keep breaking in. That is the penalty of abandoning the purity of self-defense as *casus belli*. When a soldier starts thinking, according to the good soldier Schweik, "he is no longer a soldier but a lousy civilian." I do not know if it will come to that, but it serves to bring in the civilian point of view.

Does civilian society really want the Army to start thinking for itself? Does this not raise all sorts of dread potentials for right-wing coups or left-wing mutinies? While the military normally tends to the right, there *have* been other cases: Cromwell's New Model Army overturned the King, the naval mutiny at Kronstadt and desertions from the front brought on the Russian Revolution. Already we have a dangerously undisciplined enlisted force in Vietnam, which admittedly does not come so much from thinking as from general disgust. While this development is not political, from what one can tell, it is certainly not healthy.

I know that I have wandered far from my assignment, but I raise these questions because it seems to me that generalship will have to cope with them from now on. The trouble with this talk, as I imagine will now have become visible, is that I have none of the answers. That will take another breed of thinker. I can only say that it has always been a challenge to be a general; his role, like that of the citizen, is growing no easier.

Why Policy-Makers Do Not Listen

We have gathered to honor a group of Foreign Service officers —represented in the person of Jack Service—whom history has recognized as having been right; and not only history, but even, by act if not by acknowledgment, the present administration. Can there be anyone among that group who reported from China during World War II who, watching an American President journey in person to Communist China in 1971, was not conscious of an irony so acute as to make him shiver? Could anyone, remembering past attitudes, look at that picture of President Nixon and Chairman Mao in twin armchairs, with slightly queasy smiles bravely worn to conceal their mutual discomfort, and not feel a stunned sense that truth is indeed weirder than fiction? When I was young, the magazine *Vanity Fair* used to publish a series called "Impossible Interviews" by the artist-cartoonist Covarrubias in which he confronted Calvin Coolidge with Greta Garbo and John D. Rockefeller, Sr., with Stalin, but last year's meeting in Peking outdid Covarrubias.

Yet it could have happened twenty-five years earlier, sparing us and Asia immeasurable, and to some degree irreparable, harm, if American policy had been guided by the information and recommendations of the staff of the Chungking Embassy, then acknowledged to be the best-informed service group in China. It included the Ambassador, Clarence Gauss, the Counselor, George Atcheson, both deceased, and among the secretaries and consuls stationed all over China, besides Mr. Service, such men as John Paton Davies, Edward

Address, Foreign Service Association, January 1973. *Foreign Service Bulletin*, March 1973.

Rice, Arthur Ringwalt, Philip Sprouse, and alternately in the field and on the China Desk, Edmund Clubb and the late John Carter Vincent. Several had been born in China, many were Chinese-speaking, and some are happily here with us today.

For having been right, many of them were persecuted, dismissed, or slowed or blocked in their careers, with whatever damage done to them personally outweighed by damage done to the Foreign Service of the United States. No spectacle, Macaulay said, was so ridiculous as the British public in one of its periodic fits of morality—and none, one might add, so mean as the American public in one of its periodic witch-hunts. Your colleagues and predecessors were hounded because able and honest performance of their profession collided with the hysterics of the cold war manipulated by a man so absolutely without principles as to be abnormal, like the man without a shadow. I shall not pursue that story now, however important it is to you and to every citizen, because what I want to get at is a problem perhaps more abiding, and that is: why these men were not listened to even before they were persecuted.

The burden of their reports taken as a whole was that Chiang Kai-shek was on the way out and the Communists on the way in, and that American policy, rather than cling in paralyzed attachment to the former, might be well advised to take this trend into account. This was implicit in reports from officers who had no contact with the Communists but were united in describing the deterioration of the Kuomintang. It was made explicit by those who saw the Communists at first hand, like Service in his remarkable reports from Yenan, and Ludden, who journeyed into the interior to observe the functioning of Communist rule, and Davies, whose ear was everywhere. They were unequivocal in judging the Communists to be the dynamic party in the country; in Davies' words in 1944, "China's destiny was not Chiang's but theirs." This was not subversion, as our Red-hunters were to claim, but merely observation.

Any government that does not want to walk open-eyed into a quagmire, leading its country with it, would presumably re-examine its choices at such a point. That, after all, is what we employ Foreign Service officers *for*: to advise policy-makers of actual conditions on which to base a realistic program. The agonizing question is: Why are their reports ignored, why is there a persistent gap between observers in the field and policy-makers in the capital? While I cannot speak from experience, I would like to try to offer some answers as an out-side assessor.

In the first place, policy is formed by preconceptions, by long-implanted biases. When information is relayed to policy-makers, they respond in terms of what is already inside their heads and consequently make policy less to fit the facts than to fit the notions and intentions formed out of the mental baggage that has accumulated in their minds since childhood. When President McKinley had to decide whether to annex the Philippines in 1898, he went down on his knees at midnight, according to his own account, and "prayed to Almighty God for light and guidance." He was accordingly guided to conclude "that there was nothing left for us to do but to take them all, and to educate the Filipinos, and uplift and civilize and Christianize them, and by God's grace to do the very best we could by them, as our fellowmen for whom Christ died."

Actually, the main impulse at work was the pressure of the "manifest destiny" school for a steppingstone across the Pacific, but the mental baggage of a President in the 1890s required him to act in terms of Almighty God and the White Man's Burden, just as the mental fix of his successors in our time has required them to react in terms of anti-communism. Closer observers than Almighty God could have informed McKinley that the Filipinos had no strong desire to be Christianized or civilized or exchange Spanish rule for American, but rather to gain their independence. This being overlooked, we soon found ourselves engaged not in civilizing but in a cruel and bloody war of repression, much to our embarrassment. Failure to take into account the nature of the other party often has an awkward result.

The same failure afflicted President Wilson, who had a mental fix opposite from McKinley's, in favor of progressivism, reform, and the New Freedom. So fixed was his mind that when the reactionary General Huerta carried out a coup in Mexico in 1913, Wilson became obsessed by the idea that it devolved upon him to tear the usurper off the backs of the Mexican people so that Mexico might be ruled by the consent of the governed. "My passion is for the submerged eighty-five percent who are struggling to be free," he said, but the reality was that the submerged eighty-five percent were cowering in their huts unable to distinguish a difference between Huerta and his rival Carranza. Wilson, however, sent in the Marines to seize Vera Cruz, an intervention that not only appalled him by costing American lives, but succeeded only in deepening the turmoil in Mexico and drawing the United States into further intervention two years later against that man of the people, Pancho Villa. Political passion is a good thing but even better if it is an *informed* passion.

Roosevelt's bias too was in favor of the progressive. George Kennan has told how, when the Embassy staff in Moscow began reporting the facts of the Stalinist purges of the 1930s, revealing a tyranny as terrible as the Czars', the President discounted the reports as the product of what he considered typical State Department striped-pants mentality. It was not only inconvenient but disturbing to be in receipt of reports that would have required a change of attitude toward the Soviet Union (foreign policy obeys Newton's law of inertia: It keeps on doing what it is doing unless acted on by an irresistible force). Rather than be discomfited by these disclosures, which Roosevelt's own bias caused him to believe were biased, the Russian Division was closed down, its library scattered, and its chief reassigned. This desire not to listen to unhappy truths—"Don't confuse me with facts"—is only human and widely shared by chiefs of state. Was not the bearer of bad news often killed by ancient kings? Chiang Kai-shek's vindictive reaction to unpleasant news was such that his ministers gradually ceased to bring him any, with the result that he lived in a fantasy.

Your reports must also pass through a screen of psychological factors at the receiving end: temperament, or private ambitions, or the fear of not appearing masterful, or a ruler's inner sense that his manhood is at stake. (This is a male problem that fortunately does not trouble women—which might be one advantage of having a woman in high office. Whatever inner inadequacy may gnaw at a woman's vitals, it does not compel her to compensate by showing how tough she is. You might cite Golda Meir in objection, but one gets the impression that her toughness is natural rather than neurotic, besides required by the circumstances.)

Proving his manhood was, I imagine, a factor pushing President Nasser of Egypt into provoking war with Israel in 1967 so that he could not be accused of weakness or appear less militant than the Syrians. One senses it as a factor in the personalities of Johnson and Nixon in regard to withdrawing from Vietnam; there was that horrid doubt, "Shall I look soft?" It was clearly present in Kennedy too; on the other hand, it does not seem to have bothered Eisenhower, Truman, or FDR.

A classic case of man's temperament obscuring the evidence is brought out by John Davies in his recent book, *Dragon by the Tail*. Stalin's greatest error, he points out, was to underestimate Chinese Communism. "He was deceived by his own cynicism. He did not think Mao could make it because, astonishingly enough, of his own too little faith in the power of a people's war."

Of all the barriers that reports from the field must beat against, the most impenetrable is the disbelief of policy-makers in what they do not want to believe. All the evidence of a German right-wing thrust obtained by the French General Staff in the years immediately preceding 1914, including authentic documents sold to them by a German officer, could not divert them from their own fatal plan of attack through the center or persuade them to prepare a defense on their left. In 1941 when the double agent Richard Sorge in Tokyo reported to Moscow the exact dates of the coming German invasion, his warning was ignored because the Russians' very fear of this event caused them not to believe it. It was filed under "doubtful and misleading information." The same principle dominated Washington's reception of the reports from China in the 1940s. No matter how much evidence was reported indicating that the collapse of the Kuomintang was only a matter of time, nothing could induce Washington to loosen the connection tying us to Chiang Kai-shek nor rouse the policy-makers from what John Service then called an "indolent short-term expediency."

National myths are another obstacle in the way of realism. The American instinct of activism, the "can do" myth, has lately led us into evil that was not necessary and has blotted the American record beyond the power of time to whiten. Stewart Alsop made the interesting point Sunday [January 28] in the *New York Times Book Review* that American Presidents since Roosevelt have disliked the State Department and leaned heavily on the military because the military tend to be brisk, can-do problem-solvers while senior Foreign Service officers tend to be "skeptical examiners of the difficulties"; and worried uncertain Presidents will prefer positive to negative advice. You will notice that this reliance on military advice coincides with the era of air power and has much to do, I think, with the enormous attraction of the easy solution—the idea that a horrid problem can be solved by fiat from the air, without contact, without getting mixed up in a long dirty business on the ground. The influence of air power on foreign policy would make an interesting study.

Activism in the past, the impulse to improve a bad situation, to seek a better land, to move on to a new frontier, has been a great force, *the* great force, in our history, with positive results when it operates in a sphere we can control. In Asia that is not the case, and the result has been disaster. Disregarding local realities and depth of motivation, disregarding such a lesson as Dien Bien Phu, we feel impelled to take action rather than stay out of trouble. It would help if we could learn occasionally to let things seek an indigenous solution.

The costliest myth of our time has been the myth of the Communist monolith. We now discover happily if belatedly that the supposed Sino-Soviet unity is in fact a bitter antagonism of two rivals wrapped in hate, fear, and mutual suspicion. Our original judgment never had much to do with facts, but was rather a reflection of fears and prejudices. Knee-jerk reactions of this kind are not the best guide to a useful foreign policy, which I would define as the conduct of relations and exercise of influence so as best to serve an enlightened self-interest.

The question remains, what can be done to narrow the gap between information from the field and policy-making at home? First, it remains essential to maintain the integrity of Foreign Service reporting, not only for the sake of what may get through, but to provide the basis for a change of policy when the demand becomes imperative. Second, some means must be found to require that preconceived notions and emotional fixations be periodically tested against the evidence. Perhaps legislation could be enacted to enforce a regular pause for rethinking, for questioning the wisdom of an accepted course of action, for cutting one's losses if necessary.

By a circuitous route I come to Jack Service, the focus of this meeting.

Mr. Service was born in China in the province of Szechuan, the son of missionary parents serving with the YMCA. His youth was spent in China until he returned to the United States to attend Oberlin College, from which he graduated in 1932. He also acquired a classmate as wife and anyone who knows Caroline Service will recognize this as an early example of Jack's good judgment. After passing the Foreign Service exams, he returned to China because no openings were available during the Depression, and entered the profession by way of a clerk's job in Kunming. Commissioned as a Foreign Service officer in 1935, he served in Peking and Shanghai, and joined the Embassy in Chungking in 1941. During the war years he served half his time in the field, seeing realities outside the miasma of the capital. This opportunity culminated when after being attached to Stilwell's staff, he served as political officer with the American Military Observers Mission to Yenan, the first official American contact with the Communists. His series of conversations with Mao, Chou En-lai, Chu Teh, Lin Piao, and other leaders, embodied in vivid almost verbatim reports with perceptive comments, are a historical source of prime and unique importance. Equally impressive are the examples that show Service passionately trying to persuade and convince the policy-makers, as in the brief prepared for Vice-President Wallace in June 1944 and the famous group telegram to the Department, largely drafted by Service—a desperate effort by the Embassy staff to halt the Hurley drift down the rapids with Chiang Kai-shek. If there was passion in this, it was at least informed passion.

Following arrest in the Amerasia affair in 1945, Service was exonerated and cleared, and promoted in 1948 to Class 2 officer—only to be plunged back under all the old charges in 1949 when the Communist victory in China set off our national hysteria and put Senator McCarthy, in strange alliance with the China Lobby, in charge of the American soul. If Chiang Kai-shek were to keep American support, it was imperative that the "loss" of China, so-called, should be seen as no failure from inside but the work of some outside subversive conspiracy. That specter exactly fitted certain native American needs. Along with others, Service suffered the consequences. Despite a series of acquittals, he was pinned with a doubt of loyalty and dismissed from the Foreign Service by Secretary Dean Acheson in 1951, as Davies and Vincent were subsequently dismissed by Secretary Dulles. Six years of pursuing redress through the courts finally brought a unanimous verdict in his favor by the Supreme Court of the United States in 1957. He rejoined the Foreign Service, but was kept out of any assignment that would use his knowledge and experience of China. When it was clear that the Kennedy administration would offer no better, Service resigned in 1962 and has since served with the Center for Chinese Studies at the University of California in Berkeley.

Fortunately for the record and the reputation of the Foreign Service, the reports of Service and his colleagues from China in the 1940s are now where anyone can consult them—in the published volumes of *U.S. Foreign Relations, China Series*. Under the inflexible verdict of history, they stand up.

Watergate and the Presidency

SHOULD WE ABOLISH THE PRESIDENCY?

Owing to the steady accretion of power in the executive over the last forty years, the institution of the Presidency is not now functioning as the Constitution intended, and this malfunction has become perilous to the state. What needs to be absolished, or fundamentally modified, I believe, is not the executive power as such but the executive power as exercised by a single individual.

We could substitute true Cabinet government by a directorate of six, to be nominated as a slate by each party and elected as a slate for a single six-year term with a rotating chairman, each to serve for a year as in the Swiss system. The Chairman's vote would carry the weight of two to avoid a tie. (Although a five-man Cabinet originally seemed preferable when I first proposed the plan in 1968, I find that the main departments of government, one for each member of the Cabinet to administer, cannot be rationally arranged under fewer than six headings—see below.)

Expansion of the Presidency in the twentieth century has dangerously altered the careful tripartite balance of governing powers established by the Constitution. The office has become too complex and its reach too extended to be trusted to the fallible judgment of any one individual. In today's world no one man is adequate for the reliable disposal of power that can affect the lives of millions—which may be one reason lately for the notable non-emergence of great men. Russia

New York Times, February 13, 1973.

no longer entrusts policy-making to one man. In China governing power resides, technically at least, in the party's central executive committee, and when Mao goes the inheritors are likely to be more collective than otherwise.

In the United States the problem of one-man rule has become acute for two reasons. First, Congress has failed to perform its envisioned role as safeguard against the natural tendency of an executive to become dictatorial, and equally failed to maintain or even exercise its own rights through the power of the purse.

It is clear, moreover, that we have not succeeded in developing in this country an organ of representative democracy that can match the Presidency in positive action or prestige. A Congress that can abdicate its right to ratify the act of war, that can obediently pass an enabling resolution on false information and remain helpless to remedy the situation afterward, is likewise not functioning as the Constitution intended. Since the failure traces to the lower house—the body most directly representing the citizenry and holding the power of the purse—responsibility must be put where it belongs: in the voter. The failure of Congress is a failure of the people.

The second reason, stemming perhaps from the age of television, is the growing tendency of the Chief Executive to form policy as a reflection of his personality and ego needs. Because his image can be projected before fifty or sixty or a hundred million people, the image takes over; it becomes an obsession. He must appear firm, he must appear dominant, he must never on any account appear "soft," and by some magic transformation which he has come to believe in, he *must* make history's list of "great" Presidents.

While I have no pretensions to being a psychohistorian, even an ordinary citizen can see the symptoms of this disease in the White House since 1960, and its latest example in the Christmas bombing of North Vietnam. That disproportionate use of lethal force becomes less puzzling if it is seen as a gesture to exhibit the Commander-in-Chief ending the war with a bang, not a whimper.

Personal government can get beyond control in the U.S. because the President is subject to no advisers who hold office independently of him. Cabinet ministers and agency chiefs and national-security advisers can be and are—as we have lately seen—hired and fired at whim, which means that they are without constitutional power. The result is that too much power and therefore too much risk has become subject to the idiosyncrasies of a single individual at the top, whoever he may be.

Spreading the executive power among six eliminates dangerous challenges to the ego. Each of the six would be designated from the time of noination as secretary of a specific department of government affairs, viz:

1. Foreign, including military and CIA. (Military affairs should not, as at present, have a Cabinet-level office because the military ought to be solely an instrument of policy, never a policy-making body.)
2. Financial, including Treasury, taxes, budget, and tariffs.
3. Judicial, covering much the same as at present.
4. Business (or Production and Trade), including Commerce, Transportation, and Agriculture.
5. Physical Resources, including Interior, Parks, Forests, Conservation, and Environment Protection.
6. Human Affairs, including HEW, Labor, and the cultural endowments.

It is imperative that the various executive agencies be incorporated under the authority of one or another of these departments.

Cabinet government is a perfectly feasible operation. While this column was being written, the Australian Cabinet, which governs like the British by collective responsibility, overrode its Prime Minister on the issue of exporting sheep to China, and the West German Cabinet took emergency action on foreign-exchange control.

The usual objection one hears in this country that a war emergency requires quick decision by one man seems to me invalid. Even in that case, no President acts without consultation. If he can summon the Joint Chiefs, so can a Chairman summon his Cabinet. Nor need the final decision be unilateral. Any belligerent action not clearly enough in the national interest to evoke unanimous or strong majority decision by the Cabinet ought not to be undertaken.

How the slate would be chosen in the primaries is a complication yet to be resolved. And there is the drawback that Cabinet government could not satisfy the American craving for a father-image or hero or superstar. The only solution I can see to that problem would be to install a dynastic family in the White House for ceremonial purposes, or focus the craving entirely upon the entertainment world, or else to grow up.

A FEAR
OF THE REMEDY

The Democratic party, fearing the advantage that incumbency would give Mr. Agnew in 1976, shrinks from the idea of impeachment. So do the Republicans, fearing the blow to their party. All of us shrink from the tensions and antagonisms that a trial of the President would generate. Yet this is the only means of terminating a misconducted Presidency that our system provides.

If it is the sole means, then we should be prepared to undertake it, no matter how uncomfortable or inexpedient. Political expediency should not take precedence over decency in government.

Fear of the remedy can be more dangerous in ultimate consequences than if we were to show ourselves capable of the nerve and the will to use a constitutional process when circumstances demand it. The show itself, if realistic, could well bring about the best solution: a voluntary termination of Mr. Nixon's Presidency. This would be a boon to the country because the Nixon administration is already Humpty-Dumpty; it cannot be put together again credibly enough to govern effectively.

The present crisis in government will not be resolved on the basis of whether or not Mr. Nixon can be legally proved to have personally shared in obstructing justice in the Watergate case. His administration has been shown to be pervaded by so much other malfeasance that the Watergate break-in is no more than an incident. To confine the issue to that narrow ground seems a serious error. Forget the tapes. What we are dealing with here is fundamental immorality.

The Nixon administration, like any other, is an entity, a whole, for which he is responsible and from which he is indivisible. Its personnel, including those now under indictment, were selected and appointed by him, its conduct determined by him, its principles—or lack of them—derived from him. Enough illegal, unconstitutional,

New York Times, August 7, 1973.

and immoral acts have already been revealed and even acknowledged to constitute impeachable grounds. The Domestic Intelligence Program of 1970, authorized by the President, and startling in its violation of the citizen's rights, would alone be sufficient to disqualify him from office. Indeed, this item is the core of the problem, for it indicates not only the administration's disregard for, but what almost seems its ignorance of, the Bill of Rights.

The Dirty Tricks Department with its forgeries and frame-ups, burglaries and proposed firebombings, operated right out of the White House under the supervision of the President's personal appointees. Is he separable from them? Key members of the Committee to Re-Elect the President, who have already pleaded guilty to perjury and conspiracy to obstruct justice, were lent by or transferred from the White House. Is Mr. Nixon separable from them? Two of his former Cabinet officers are now awaiting judicial trial. Is he separable from them? His two closest advisers, his director of the FBI, his second nominee as Attorney General have all resigned under the pressure of mounting disclosures. Is he separable from them? Corrupt practice in the form of selling government favor to big business as in the case of ITT and the milk lobby have been his administration's normal habit. Is he separable from that—or from the use of the taxpayer's money to improve his private homes?

Finally, under his authorization, the Pentagon carried on a secret and falsified bombing of Cambodia and lied about it to Congress, while the President himself lied to this country about respecting Cambodia's neutrality. There will be no end to the revelations of misconduct because misconduct was standard operating procedure.

In the light of this record, the question whether Mr. Nixon did or did not verbally implicate himself in the cover-up of Watergate is not of the essence. The acts that needed covering and the process of covering were performed by members of his administration.

The lesson being taught to the country by Senator Ervin and his colleagues is an education itself. Next to letting the people know, the prosecution and legal punishment of individuals is secondary. Yet I wish the Senate select committee would enlarge its focus because the emphasis on documentary or tape-recorded proof contains perils. If, as is conceivable, the proof fails, we will be left with a government too compromised ever to be trusted and too damaged to recover authority. In such case an impotent or paralyzed government will, like Chiang Kai-shek's, harden its monarchial or dictatorial tendencies, already well developed in the Nixon regime. Worse, we will have demonstrated for the benefit of Mr. Nixon's successors what measure of cynicism and what deprivation of their liberties the American people are ready to tolerate. From there the slide into dictatorship is easy.

At this time in world history when totalitarian government is in command of the two other largest powers, it is imperative for the United States to preserve and restore to original principles our constitutional structure. The necessary step is for Congress and the American public to grasp the nettle of impeachment if we must.

A LETTER TO THE HOUSE OF REPRESENTATIVES

"Those who expect to reap the blessings of freedom," wrote Tom Paine, "must undergo like men the fatigue of supporting it." In the affairs of a nation founded on the premise that its citizens possess certain "inalienable" rights, there comes a time when those rights must be defended against creeping authoritarianism. Liberty and authority exist in eternal stress, like the seashore and the sea. Executive authority is forever hungry; it is its nature to expand and usurp.

To protect against that tendency, which is as old as history, the framers of our Constitution established three co-equal branches of government. In October 1973 we have come to the hour when that arrangement must be called upon to perform its function. Unless the Executive is brought into balance, the other two branches will dwindle into useless appendages. The judiciary has done its part; by defying it the President brought on the crisis. The fact that he reversed himself does not alter the fact that he tried, just as the fact that he reneged on the domestic-surveillance plan of 1970—a fundamental invasion of the Bill of Rights—does not cancel the fact that he earlier

Washington Post, October 28, 1973.

authorized it, nor does withdrawing from Cambodia cancel the fact of lying to the public about American intervention.

The cause for impeachment remains, because President Nixon cannot change—and the American people cannot afford—the habit of illegality and abuse of executive power which has been normal to him. Responsibility for the outcome now rests upon the House of Representatives, which the framers entrusted with the duty of initiating the corrective process. If it does not bring the abuse of executive power to account, it will have laid a precedent of acquiescence—what the lawyers call constructive condonement—that will end by destroying the political system whose two-hundredth birthday we are about to celebrate.

No group ever faced a more difficult task at a more delicate moment. We are in the midst of international crisis; we have no Vice-President; his nominated successor is suddenly seen, in the shadow of an empty Presidency, as hardly qualified to move up; the administration is beleaguered by scandal and criminal charges; public confidence is at low tide; partisan politics for 1976 are in everyone's mind; and the impeachment process is feared as likely to be long and divisive and possibly paralyzing. Under the circumstances, hesitancy and ambivalence are natural.

Yet the House must not evade the issue, for now as never before it is the hinge of our political fate. The combined forces of Congress and the judiciary are needed to curb the Executive because the Executive has the advantage of controlling all the agencies of government—including the military. The last should not be an unthinkable thought. The habit of authoritarianism, which the President has found so suitable, will slowly but surely draw a ruler, if cornered, to final dependence on the Army. That instinct already moved Mr. Nixon to call out the FBI to impound the evidence.

I do not believe the dangers and difficulties of the situation should keep Congress from the test. Certainly the situation in the Middle East is full of perils, including some probably unforeseen. But I doubt if the Russians would seize the opportunity to jump us, should we become embroiled in impeachment. Not that I have much faith in nations learning from history; what they do learn is the lesson of the last war. To a would-be aggressor, the lesson of both world wars is not to count on the theory held by the Germans and Japanese that the United States, as a great lumbering mush-minded degenerate democracy, would be unable to mobilize itself in time to prevent their victory. I am sure this lesson is studiously taught in Russian General Staff courses.

Nor should we be paralyzed by fear of exacerbating divisions within this country. We are divided anyway and always have been, as any independently minded people should be. Talk of unity is a pious fraud and a politician's cliché. No people worth its salt is politically united. A nation in consensus is a nation ready for the grave.

Moreover, I think we can forgo a long and malignant trial by the Senate. Once the House votes to impeach, that will be enough. Mr. Nixon, I believe, will resign rather than face an investigation and trial that he cannot stop. If the House can accomplish this, it will have vindicated the trust of the founders and made plain to every potential President that there are limits he may not exceed.

DEFUSING
THE PRESIDENCY

The American Presidency has become a greater risk than it is worth. The time has come to consider seriously the substitution of Cabinet government or some form of shared executive power.

There is no use continually repeating that the form arranged by the Framers of the Constitution must serve forever unchanged. Monarchy too was once considered immutable and even divinely established, but it had to give way under changed conditions. The conditions of American executive power today, commanding agencies, techniques, and instruments unimaginable in the eighteenth century, no more resemble the conditions familiar to Jefferson and Madison than they do those under Hammurabi.

The Framers may have been the most intelligent and far-seeing political men ever to operate at one time in our history, but they could not foretell the decline of the Congress. In too willing subservience it confirmed as Vice-President an appointee of an already discredited President and will doubtless do so again in the case of Nelson A. Rockefeller. The executive will then consist of an appointee

New York Times, September 20, 1974.

and his appointee, which is not what the Framers designed. The checks and balances they devised are out of balance.

For one brief euphoric moment when the House Judiciary Committee functioned, it seemed the system might have revived, but when the House failed to carry through a vote on impeachment and the Senate said nothing, the self-emasculation was completed. If lost virginity cannot be restored, neither can lost virility. I do not think the trend is toward righting the balance.

The Presidency has gained too great a lead; it has bewitched the occupant, the press, and the public. While this process has been apparent from John F. Kennedy on, it took the strange transformation of good old open-Presidency Gerald R. Ford to make it clear that the villain is not the man but the office.

Hardly had he settled in the ambiance of the White House than he began to talk like Louis XIV and behave like Richard M. Nixon. If there was one lesson to be learned from Watergate, it was the danger in overuse of the executive power and in interference with the judicial system. Within a month of taking office Mr. Ford has violated both at once. The swelling sense of personal absolutism shows in those disquieting remarks: "The ethical tone will be what I make it . . . ," "In this situation I am the final authority . . . ," and, in deciding to block the unfolding of legal procedure, "My conscience says it is my duty. . . ." Our judicial system can operate well enough without the dictate of Mr. Ford's conscience. To be President is not to be czar.

But Mr. Ford is not alone responsible. The press overplayed him as it overplayed John Kennedy and the absurd pretensions of Camelot. The *New York Times* published Mr. Ford's picture twelve times on the front page in the first fourteen days of his tenure. Why? We all know what he looks like. But if it can be said that the press gives the public what it wants, then all of us are responsible. By packing our craving for father-worship into the same person who makes and executes policy—a system no other country uses—we have given too much greatness to the Presidency. It seizes hold of the occupant as we have seen it do with Mr. Kennedy, Lyndon B. Johnson, and Mr. Nixon. It has led Mr. Ford into an entirely unnecessary breach of our last rampart, the judicial process, an act that can only be explained as being either crooked—that is, by some undercover deal with his predecessor—or stupid. We cannot at this date afford either at the head of the American government.

Nor is the Presidency getting first-rate men. The choice between candidates in the last three elections has been dismal. Things now happen too fast to allow us time to wait until the system readjusts itself. The only way to defuse the Presidency and minimize the risk of a knave, a simpleton, or a despot exercising supreme authority without check or consultation is to divide the power and spread the responsibility. Constitutional change is not beyond our capacity.

On Our Birthday— America as Idea

The United States is a nation consciously conceived, not one that evolved slowly out of an ancient past. It was a planned idea of democracy, of liberty of conscience and pursuit of happiness. It was the promise of equality of opportunity and individual freedom within a just social order, as opposed to the restrictions and repressions of the Old World. In contrast to the militarism of Europe, it would renounce standing armies and "sheathe the desolating sword of war." It was an experiment in Utopia to test the thesis that, given freedom, independence, and local self-government, people, in Kossuth's words, "will in due time ripen into all the excellence and all the dignity of humanity." It was a new life for the oppressed, it was enlightenment, it was optimism.

Regardless of hypocrisy and corruption, of greed, chicanery, brutality, and all the other bad habits man carries with him whether in the New World or Old, the founding idea of the United States remained, on the whole, dominant through the first hundred years. With reservations, it was believed in by Americans, by visitors who came to aid our Revolution or later to observe our progress, by immigrants who came by the hundreds of thousands to escape an intolerable situation in their native lands.

The idea shaped our politics, our institutions, and to some extent

Newsweek, July 12, 1976.

our national character, but it was never the only influence at work. Material circumstances exerted an opposing force. The open frontier, the hardships of homesteading from scratch, the wealth of natural resources, the whole vast challenge of a continent waiting to be exploited, combined to produce a prevailing materialism and an American drive bent as much, if not more, on money, property, and power than was true of the Old World from which we had fled. The human resources we drew upon were significant: Every wave of immigration brought here those people who had the extra energy, gumption, or restlessness to uproot themselves and cross an unknown ocean to seek a better life. Two other factors entered the shaping process—the shadow of slavery and the destruction of the native Indian.

At its Centennial the United States was a material success. Through its second century the idea and the success have struggled in continuing conflict. The Statue of Liberty, erected in 1886, still symbolized the promise to those "yearning to breathe free." Hope, to them, as seen by a foreign visitor, was "domiciled in America as the Pope is in Rome." But slowly in the struggle the idea lost ground, and at a turning point around 1900, with American acceptance of a rather half-hearted imperialism, it lost dominance. Increasingly invaded since then by self-doubt and disillusion, it survives in the disenchantment of today, battered and crippled but not vanquished.

What has happened to the United States in the twentieth century is not a peculiarly American phenomenon but a part of the experience of the West. In the Middle Ages plague, wars, and social violence were seen as God's punishment upon man for his sins. If the concept of God can be taken as man's conscience, the same explanation may be applicable today. Our sins in the twentieth century—greed, violence, inhumanity—have been profound, with the result that the pride and self-confidence of the nineteenth century have turned to dismay and self-disgust.

In the United States we have a society pervaded from top to bottom by contempt for the law. Government—including the agencies of law enforcement—business, labor, students, the military, the poor no less than the rich, outdo each other in breaking the rules and violating the ethics that society has established for its protection. The average citizen, trying to hold a footing in standards of morality and conduct he once believed in, is daily knocked over by incoming waves of venality, vulgarity, irresponsibility, ignorance, ugliness, and trash in all senses of the word. Our government collaborates abroad with the worst enemies of humanity and liberty. It wastes our substance on useless proliferation of military hardware that can never buy security no matter how high the pile. It learns no lessons, employs no wisdom, and corrupts all who succumb to Potomac fever.

Yet the idea does not die. Americans are not passive under their faults. We expose them and combat them. Somewhere every day some group is fighting a public abuse—openly and, on the whole, notwithstanding the FBI, with confidence in the First Amendment. The U.S. has slid a long way from the original idea. Nevertheless, somewhere between Gulag Archipelago and the featherbed of cradle-to-the-grave welfare, it still offers a greater opportunity for social happiness—that is to say, for well-being combined with individual freedom and initiative—than is likely elsewhere. The ideal society for which mankind has been striving through the ages will remain forever beyond our grasp. But if the great question, whether it is still possible to reconcile democracy with social order and individual liberty, is to find a positive answer, it will be here.

A NOTE ON THE TYPE

The text of this book was set on the Linotype in Janson, a
recutting made direct from type cast from matrices long
thought to have been made by the Dutchman Anton Janson,
who was a practicing type founder in Leipzig during the
years 1668–87. However, it has been conclusively demonstrated that these types are actually the work of Nicholas Kis
(1650–1702), a Hungarian, who most probably learned his
trade from the master Dutch type founder Dirk Voskens.
The type is an excellent example of the influential and sturdy
Dutch types that prevailed in England up to the time
William Caslon developed his own incomparable designs
from them.

This book was composed by The Maryland Linotype
Composition Company, Inc., Baltimore, Maryland. It was
printed and bound by American Book–Stratford Press, Inc.,
Saddle Brook, New Jersey.

Designed by Judith Henry